P.S. Look out for snakes

P.S. Look out for snakes

THE LOVE LETTERS OF
BRIAN FARRELL AND MARIE-THÉRÈSE DILLON
(1954-55)

EDITED BY
MIRIAM FARRELL-SHTAIERMAN

KATOUNIA PRESS

P.S. Look out for Snakes
First edition published by
Katounia Press, Dublin, 2022
www.KatouniaPress.com

ISBN 978-1-8383454-2-6

Set in Freight Text Pro and Freight Sans Pro 11.5/15.5
Cover and book design by Alba Esteban
Front cover picture: Brian and Marie-Thérèse, BA conferring ceremony, UCD, 1953.
Back cover picture: Newlyweds, Brian and Marie-Thérèse, Cambridge, 1955.

University College Dublin
Ireland's Global University

For my mama, Marie-Thérèse

Education begins a gentleman, but reading, good
company and reflection must finish him.
JOHN LOCKE

CONTENTS

FOREWORD

I am writing this at my desk in RTÉ, and a wonderful photograph of Brian and Marie-Thérèse Farrell is looking right at me. I keep it beside my laptop as I love it. It reminds me of such happy times. Taken casually when Brian was retiring, also in the photo are Noel Curran, RTÉ's former DG, Ed Mulhall, former Head of News and Current Affairs, and myself. It's a joyous picture.

Brian was joyous.

I felt very privileged to work alongside Brian and to call him a friend. When I began to work on *Prime Time*, he was one of the most respected broadcasters in Ireland. He also had an important national role and presence at significant state occasions. It was his face and voice that oversaw all major events – including general elections, the big leaders' debates and funerals of taoisigh and other prominent figures in Irish public life. He was known by everyone in the country, and respected. His was the voice of calm authority.

Brian was kind to me from the beginning. He always carried his position and knowledge lightly. Taking me under his wing, he gently gave me advice and direction, like a caring father. One top tip he gave me I still abide by to this day. 'Always, always write down the name of the person you are interviewing, Miriam,' he told me one afternoon, 'because in the heat of live television, it's so easy to forget.' I have never forgotten that, and the other night, when I was interviewing Leo Varadkar, whom I know so well, I thought of Brian and wrote down at the top of my cards, in block capitals, Leo Varadkar.

I am convinced that Brian's innate decency and all-round good guy persona, was partly because of his marriage to Marie-Thérèse. He was a happy man, content in his life. He had a great home life, which he often spoke about. His work was really the icing on the cake, far from the most important part of his life. Marie-Thérèse and his seven children always took precedence over everything else.

Brian also always took his wife's advice and good counsel. He would often come in to work and tell me what Marie-Thérèse had thought about the previous night's show and her critique was always spot on. His image - especially his sartorial choices - was also always overseen by her. They were an incredibly close couple.

That is why these letters between them both from the earliest days of their courtship are so wonderful to have and to read. It was a great idea of their daughter Miriam to gather them and put them in book form. It is a beautiful memoir and tribute to them both. I know Brian would be so pleased and proud.

Miriam O'Callaghan
Current affairs presenter with RTÉ

PREFACE

In 1954, Brian Farrell and Marie-Thérèse Dillon were engaged but, like many young people at the time, they had no money. Jobs in the academic world, to which Brian aspired, were very scarce. Brian won a scholarship to Harvard, the first step on what became a successful academic career but it also meant a long separation from Marie-Thérèse. This book, based on recently discovered letters, is the story of that separation.

It is a love story.

The letters, written almost daily testify to a love that endured, despite the stresses and strains of separation. They cover a host of subjects; interactions with family and friends, worries about money or the absence of it, and Dublin life, especially the academic world of UCD – then in Earlsfort Terrace – and the politics of the Dillon family, with Marie-Thérèse's uncle James Dillon[1] - with whom she rarely agreed - a major figure in Fine Gael.

But it is much more than a love story. Brian was a fine writer, a sharp-eyed observer of the American scene, vividly describing the new world in which he found himself, especially the academic scene, but also ranging into politics; - attending McCarthy and anti-McCarthy rallies, following the elections, hitch-hiking over large areas of the country – always with an eye for the telling detail, even to his comments on American girls (almost certainly to reassure Marie-Thérèse): 'by and large they seem incapable of conversation. They say 'yes', 'no,' wonderful', 'gosh' but never say anything'.

He also keeps a close eye on the Irish scene. Many, who later became prominent, make appearances; Ronan Keane, later

---

1   James Matthew Dillon (1902–1986), one of Theo Dillon's younger brothers, was a Fine Gael politician who served as leader of the opposition and leader of Fine Gael (1959–65) and Minister for Agriculture (1948–51 and 1954–57). He was a TD from 1932–69.

Chief Justice, Attorney General Declan Costello, even the Irish-American actor Carol O'Connor – while the world of UCD is ever present. His big fear was that the President Michael Tierney would 'move the university to Stillorgan, turn it into a Catholic University with attendant clerical control over appointments'.

Marie-Thérèse, for her part, has her own colourful and direct style, worrying about saving enough for their wedding and her fare to the States, giving him instructions from afar about his clothes, describing the ins-and-outs of managing a clothing factory, and keeping him up to date on all the gossip about their friends and the latest political rumours.

This is a warm, charming and very readable book which captures the mood of the 1950s, and allows us look into a love that was deep and enduring.

Maurice Manning
Chancellor of the National University of Ireland

ACKNOWLEDGEMENTS

Before acknowledging my thanks to friends and family who have made this book possible, I'd like to express my heartfelt gratitude to those who are no longer with us: my dear Pops, Brian Farrell, who gave the best bear-hugs in the world, my grandmother, Marie Dillon, who I never knew and now mourn, Myles Dillon for being a father to my orphaned mother, his wife, Bessie Dillon for being a grandmother to us all, Mary Murphy for keeping a watchful eye over my mother, ; George Roach, who I supposedly cursed at the age of three, to whom I also owe an apology as well as an acknowledgement; he was a true friend to my parents, and, finally, to whoever was responsible for teaching my parents good handwriting.

My biggest thanks goes to my childhood friend and soul sister, Fiona Biggs, for her advice, professional help and for always being there when I need her. Thanks to my siblings – Naomi, Bernard, David, Rachel, Theo and Brian – for their encouragement and approval. A special thanks to Naomi, her husband Kieran, and David for helping me with practical details. To my own children – Tamar, Alon, Neta and Oren – who let me go on and on about their grandparents' letters, with a special note of gratitude to Alon for helping me write endless book proposals. Thanks to their father, my beloved Koby, who makes me feel like I can do anything and gives me room to do it.

My sincere thanks to UCD for their generous contribution and help in promoting this book, with special thanks to Eilis O'Brien and Noelle Moran for their time and patience.

Finally, thanks to my godfather and cousin, John Dillon for being my mentor and providing a home for this book.

INTRODUCTION

'Out of the darkness this elegant, splendidly dressed young woman appeared. She sprang up on the stage, wielding a large and dangerous looking pair of outsize shears. Grabbing the flimsy hem of my rough hessian tunic she proclaimed, "That's far too long!" and sliced off about a foot of material. I decided this was a lady to be kept at arm's length.'

Brian Farrell describing his first encounter with Marie-Thérèse Dillon at a rehearsal of *Deirdre of the Sorrows* in UCD's DramSoc in 1951.

My strongest childhood memory is the sound of my parents' chatter; over supper, in front of the TV and when they were getting ready for bed, chatter sprinkled with great guffaws of laughter from my father, for my mother was, and remains to this day, a great wit. She is also half-Swiss and renowned for dumping what she considers 'clutter' and 'useless', without an ounce of regret. Brian, on the other hand, was a sentimentalist, and his office in the politics department in UCD became a cache for the items he saved from Marie-Thérèse's blitzes over the years. On retirement from UCD, he was allowed to bring home his most-valued books and one grey metal cabinet, and it was here, in its bottom drawer, that Brian kept their letters.

On a balmy Sunday evening, in mid-July 1954, Marie-Thérèse

and Brian took the bus from town to Killiney,[2] for one last walk together before Brian set off on his travels. Marie-Thérèse wrote in one of her letters, 'I was sitting beside you on the bus pretending to be interested in who was going into and leaving the toilets at College Street, and crying quietly to myself, wondering how I would endure the months to follow.' But she didn't let her feelings spoil her last weekend with Brian. They walked up Killiney Hill and settled down on a grassy spot; Brian cracked jokes and Marie-Thérèse hid her sadness, laughing gaily. She wanted him to remember her happy, smiling face in the months to come. 'No one likes the company of a sad person', she was known to remark in later years. So they chatted and made plans for their future; then, linking arms, they walked to Killiney station and took the train back to Booterstown for supper followed by coffee cake, one of Brian's favourites.

The following day, Brian set off for America, to complete his Master's at Harvard. He had won the prestigious Fulbright Scholarship, an opportunity that he couldn't turn down, even though it meant leaving his fiancé for nearly eight months. Marie-Thérèse supported his decision to go, since a wedding didn't seem likely until Brian had established some sort of a career, and in the atmosphere of 'doom and gloom'[3] that prevailed in Ireland at the time, there wasn't much hope of that happening any time soon. So, with her blessing, off he went.

And this is where their letters begin.

---

2   Killiney was where MT lived with her parents until her father (Theo (TWT) Dillon) died. It was always her favourite place to visit.

3   1950s Ireland is referred to as the 'worst decade' since the Great Famine. Dublin still housed the poorest slums in Europe; many families occupied a single room with inappropriate toilet facilities and no access to hot water. When the small rural farming community went into irreversible decline, the Irish state made little effort to develop new industries. With no hope of employment, many of the young emigrated.

The Letters

Chapter 1

LATE JULY–AUGUST 1954

'Getting engaged so young was seen as a very adventurous thing to do in UCD in the early 1950s, and I remember my history tutor, Hugh Kearney, telling me that there were three things a serious undergraduate did not do – he looked deep into my red eyes and said: 'He does not drink, he does not engage in amateur dramatics (I was running DramSoc at the time), and he does not form honourable attachments'.

Brian Farrell, talking to Brenda Power of the Sunday Tribune, May 1994.

[MARIE-THÉRÈSE TO BRIAN]

5, Trimleston Gardens, Booterstown,[1]
Saturday, 22 July

Darling,

I'm so excited, as if I were going too! Maybe in a way I am! Everything you feel, I feel, and I know I'll see some of the wonderful things through your eyes. Take great care of yourself. Don't trust many – they aren't all as honest as yourself! (that I feel is a weak argument!)

Most Important, Don't stop loving me or stop praying for 'us'. Sleep well tonight – all my love, Marie-Thérèse

* * *

The above letter came in an envelope which is covered on both sides with the following lists:[2]

- **In Wardrobe Trunk:** Dinner Jacket and pants, Grey suit, Linen jacket and pants, all shirts (& collars), all ties, all hankies, T-shirts, 1 pair Underpants,[3] 2 pairs Braces, clean pyjamas, 2 towels, X-ray, BA and bathing togs, photos (BA), 3 scarves, 2 pairs wool socks.
- **Soft case:** jumpers, books, long comb, my photo!!!
- **Carry-All:** shoes, old pants
- **Don't Forget:** Alarm clock, brushes (hair), shaving kit, wash bag (+contents), pyjamas (in use), dirty shirt and linen! Extra coats, nylon shirt and socks.

1 MT writes all her letters from this address, where she lived with her widowed mother. They moved there from Thorncroft, Killiney after her father died.

2 An example of MT's well-organised personality and her habit of making lists, which continued throughout her married life.

3 Meant to last for seven and a half months?!

P.S. LOOK OUT FOR SNAKES

2

My Darling,

Shannon is a hive of activity with the most well-equipped[4] 'Mens' I have ever seen. Laid out is a Remington (I used my own) and a collection of about six safety razors, a dozen or so after-shave lotions, creams and scents and a couple of hair oils. The tweed shop, post office, café etc. ... remain open all night. So do the Customs, but, thank God, they didn't look at your beautiful packing (oh my grey hairs from your packing!). Strangely enough, while there is a small newsagents, there are no books (not even 'Penguins',[5] as you would call them) on sale here.

If you get a chance to send on my papers etc. ... pet, will you address them to: c/o Bapt. Keppler, Counsellor for Foreign Students, 24, Quinay St., Cambridge, Mass.

And now goodnight.

God bless your sleep and keep you safe for your loving, Brian.

 3

I'm having my first contact with Nth. America. This is a very bleak sort of Airport – with a 'typically American' gag – automatic shoe machines. The flight across left on time and was very comfortable. Most of the time, we caught faraway glimpses of the sea through the thick clouds, but we were above in the clear air with a great red sun looking over our tail.

---

4   Clearly to cater for American tourists.
5   Once MT designed a jacket for Brian with 'pockets large enough for a penguin', which her seamstress took to mean the bird!

They served breakfast – French fritters with a little carton of syrup and coffee with carton of cream and little packets of sugar. The fritters were crowned with fried apple.[6]

On the flight I met Barbara Claire Jenks, just back from the Summer School, who sends her regards to Mrs Murphy,[7] and I was also introduced to Connie[8] 'The Wild Colonial Boy' Foley – purveyor of Irish ballads (God bless the mark) to the American market.

The weather so far down on earth is close, rather than fine (58 degrees here) and our next hop is Boston, and then New York.

As you can see, I'm now really excited, but you know, my darling, that my thoughts are still and always with you. Do look after yourself and remember me – toothless[9]-and-all as I am. Give my love to your Mother and enjoy that holiday.

P.S. TRAGEDY – get out your war-paint. I've been holding hands with the girl in the seat in front for some time. She is a pretty little blonde and catches the eye of all the men. One of them even took her bottle of milk into the 'Toilet' to cool it down for her. She is now crawling over a settee on the other side.

---

6   And this was coach travel, not first class.

7   Mary was the wife of Gerard Murphy, Celtic scholar and close friend of TWT (Theo) Dillon, MT's father. Gerard was in the same Swiss sanatorium as Theo and he and his wife Mary were witnesses at Theo and Marie's wedding. Mary watched over MT and filled in as a 'parent' when both MT's parents died.

8   Connie Foley was a world-famous artist and tenor, born in Tralee in 1925. He died at Leeds, England, in 1975. His music lives on through the 500 songs he recorded.

9   All his life, Brian wore a plate with three false top teeth. Once, many years later, he appeared on TV without his teeth and MT phoned RTÉ and told them to tell him to 'stop smiling'. The Farrell family and friends were glued to the screen for the moment when his earpiece told him 'not to smile'!

I made it! We stopped down at Boston for 15 minutes and, after a further hour's flying, arrived in New York. Between Gander and Boston we were served lunch: tomato juice and then (hot) chicken and mushroom sauce with rice and peas, rolls, mince pie and coffee. At both Boston and N.Y. temperature 81–82 degrees[11].

On arrival at Idlewild[12] we were held up slightly by health and immigration but they were very pleasant, as, indeed, were the Customs.

John[13] (Kelly) sent me a cable, so I phoned him and I expect him to visit Bard[14] at the weekend. He wants me to spend a couple of weeks in Virginia in September, but I don't know yet if I'll go.

So, to continue the saga, pet. We were met by two pleasant fussy Americans and, since I had missed the last train to Bard, they arranged for me to stay here. This is a fourteen-storey YMCA hostel, I'm on the 9th floor in room 955, so you can tell the size of the place. It is very pleasant and has the enormous asset of showers, and do you need them! The room costs $1.85 (say 16/6-) and is very comfortable. They have a lovely snack bar where a double egg, rashers and coffee plus hot buttered (yes butter!) toast and an ice cream cost me about 5/6.[15]

---

10   William Sloane House YMCA, at 356 West 34th Street in Manhattan was the largest residential YMCA building in the nation.

11   Fahrenheit.

12   Idlewild airport was named after the golf course it displaced and later renamed JFK.

13   Brian met an American, John Kelly, in a pub in Dublin and they got talking; John invited Brian to visit when he came over to America

14   Bard College is a private liberal arts college in Annandale-on-Hudson, New York. The campus overlooks the Hudson River and Catskill Mountains. This is where the Fulbright scholars did their orientation course before starting the academic year at Harvard.

15   $1.48 – in today's money $35 (€29.67).

New York has been uniformly hot … even now, with the night quite dark, most of the men are in shirt sleeves. The customs, as I said, the travellers' guides and all sorts of people have been very kind. On the bus from Long Island I met a very pleasant young doctor from Boston who gave me his card and wants me to have dinner with his folks some weekend – name inevitably Irish – Brock Lynch.

Tonight I walked down town pretty slowly, taking it in. Coming in from the airport I had seen the remains of an accident, and also a scrap between two carloads of people (actually fighting) at a busy cross-section. Despite the late hour, many of the skyscraper windows were lit – as were all the marvellous neon signs. Most of the shops seemed to be having sales (shades of Dublin), and I was really amazed to see places open selling clothes and shoes.

Tomorrow I am to leave from Grand Central Station – a huge interior like Liverpool Cathedral in size, but with a very dingy exterior. Hanging in the hallway is an enormous American flag (about 20 by 35 feet), and the whole thing is very impressive in a peculiar sort of way.

Outside in the street the taxicabs (in bright yellows, checks, reds and blues) literally crawl along each curve in an apparently unending queue, and so do my tired thoughts crawl out to you, my dearest.

 5

[MARIE-THÉRÈSE TO BRIAN]
Wednesday morning, 28 July

Your 2 letters arrived, cheering me up, despite the wind – we've been having a terrible gale for the last two days – and I do hate it with you floating somewhere off the Coast of America.

Dearest, however readable my letters may be, my love letters (a fine distinction) are nothing near as good as yours.

P.S. LOOK OUT FOR SNAKES

By now you are safely 'there' – with a strange 'twang' ringing in your ears (American accents!) and probably full of coffee and cookies – were you tired? And is it terribly hot? (if so, how I envy you!)

By this morning's post I also got a letter from Miss Bennett,[16] she says: ' Mrs Manning[17] will write to her daughter Mrs Howe,[18] who lives in Cambridge with her husband[19] who belongs to the Faculty of Law – both he and his family are well known in Boston's literary circles – he was editor of Justice Holmes' correspondence. Anyway I'm to send her your college address when you are settled.

I hope to get down to the Garret[20] tonight to collect papers etc. and will post them tomorrow. They should take about 6 weeks, which means you can expect them mid-September.

My ring[21] arrived this morning – Oh! It's lovely and fits perfectly. It's locked away safely, and no one will see it till I reach America.

The dress[22] was finished last night and was fitted amid cries of approval – I almost expected 'Mother' to clap!! The daughter was thrilled! Anyway, I'm to have supper with them tomorrow evening. On Friday Sheila Coakley[23] and Con are coming for the eve-

....

16 Louie Bennett (1870–1956) was an Irish suffragette, trade unionist, journalist and writer. She lived in a cottage near Theo and Marie Dillon's home 'Thorncroft' in Killiney and would babysit MT whenever they needed. She never married, but lived beside her lifelong companion Helen Chenevix.

17 Louie Bennett's married sister.

18 Mary Manning Howe Adams (1905–1999), known as Molly, was Louie Bennett's niece. She was a novelist, playwright and film critic. Born and raised in Dublin, Manning was active in the Dublin theatrical world until 1935, when she moved to Boston and married Mark De Wolfe Howe, a Harvard law professor. When her husband died in 1967, Manning returned to live in Monkstown, Dublin, and wrote for various publications such as *Hibernia* and *The Irish Times*. She later returned to Cambridge, where she married Faneuil Adams in 1980.

19 Mark DeWolf Howe was a Harvard law professor.

20 The nickname for 13 Little Mary Street, which Brian and Neil Porter shared as students.

21 MT's engagement ring had been sent off to be sized.

22 MT designed and made wedding dresses on the side to generate extra income.

23 Sheila Coakley was in Mount Anville school with MT and later worked in administration in UCD. She was a lifelong friend of Brian and MT and was godmother to their second son, David.

ning, and I'm looking forward to Aunt Agnes's[24] visit tonight and will write to you all about it tomorrow.

P.S. Look out for snakes!

 6

[BRIAN TO MARIE-THÉRÈSE]
Bard College, N.Y. State, Thursday, 29 July

This is a really delightful spot. We travelled from N.Y. yesterday, about 90 miles by train, extremely comfortable, and were met and driven about four miles up to the College.

Bard College overlooks the Hudson and is surrounded by trees and green fields. Squirrels run all over and the birds are almost exotic in colouring. The food is excellent and three of us share a three-roomed apartment.

Today I had my first swim in the college swimming pool[25] and attended my first class. The course is very general but interesting, and I have already started to work on American diplomacy. The staff is very pleasant and everything is informal. Tea today was organised as a picnic, but it rained heavily immediately after (and since). Yesterday in N.Y. it was overcast, with a temperature of 100 degrees, but here we had magnificent sunshine until about seven. This evening we went down to the Nathansons – he[26] lectures here – and had a very nice time. We were three Japs, a Brazilian, a Dutchman and myself, discussing jurisprudence and

24 Agnes Stokes was Brian's aunt and godmother. He was sent from Manchester at the age of ten to live with Agnes and Nick Stokes at 13 Little Mary Street when the Second World War broke out. He never returned to England except for visits. Agnes and Nick had no children of their own and Brian came from a family of five children, so he essentially became an only child – something he shared with MT, who was also an only child.

25 Brian always loved swimming and as a student frequented the Iveagh Baths in Dublin, where he used to wash his clothes in the bathwater, and take them home wet in his briefcase. MT's comment on that was, 'You can take the man out of the slum, but you can't take the slum out of the man!'

26 Nathaniel L. Nathanson (1908 – 83) was a law lecturer on the Fulbright Programme.

legal philosophy with Professor Cohn of New York. There are students (about 40) from Germany, Finland, Sth Africa, Spain, India, South America etc. ...

I phoned John[27] yesterday and he may be calling here to pick me up some weekend. Either way, I'll probably go down to Virginia in September.

Although, the library here is very good on history, I still plan to visit the Roosevelt Memorial Library, where I believe they have documents on the U.S. attitude to Irish neutrality.[28]

 7

[MARIE-THÉRÈSE TO BRIAN]
Thursday, 29 July

Well, I've collected the notes; don't worry – just a small bundle. They were feather light![29] Gr ... r ...r, there I was walking up Henry St, weak in body, dragging this ton weight along, an easy prey for any husky soldier,[30] well lucky it was early, so none were drunk enough to approach me!!

Actually yesterday was quite an eventful evening, Myles[31] called in about 7.00 with 15 lbs of raspberries. When Mama weakly offered to pay, he won her affection by refusing! He enquired after you most particularly. We then went on to speak of other things but, as he was leaving Mama stated most emphatically that she 'missed Brian Farrell very much because he treated her much better than anyone else' ... Myles crept out (they understand each other very well, I hope) and then gave me a lift to Little Mary Street. I was home plus notes when Aunt Peg[32] rang to say that

27 John Kelly, Virginia.
28 A subject Brian is considering for his thesis.
29 Dripping sarcasm.
30 Irish Free State soldiers.
31 Myles Dillon, Celtic scholar and younger brother of Theo, whom he adored. Myles watched over Theo's widow and daughter and played the role of mentor to Brian.
32 Another aunt of Brian's, sister of his mother.

she was very late arriving in, so they were only coming then. Both Aunty Peg and Aunt Agnes are in very good form.

The weather is now really cold. I'm sleeping under an eiderdown and am wearing my heavy pullover all day. Aunt Agnes's little black jumper is a work of art![33] I'm taking it on my holidays. I'm not showing the ring to anyone, except Mama, who thinks it's very beautiful.

By the way, when I was in the flat[34] I saw that Aunt Agnes had done a super job of cleaning up. She's thinking of moving back in September. I'll send the notes before I go away, that is if the parcel post office in the GPO is open in the evenings, and I can get in on time!

P.S. Judge Mathew mentioned in 'Marshall Hall'[35] is my great-grandfather, Myles says.

 8

[**BRIAN TO MARIE-THÉRÈSE**]
Bard College, Friday, 30 July

Everything here including the weather is really fine. Last night we had an open-air concert with a co-operative group doing a course here, and it was magnificent to sit out and watch fireflies flitting all over.

We have started work and our day is fairly full. I shall be helping our two semantics people – Alice Hermes[36] (don't worry, she is in her forties) and Mike Rado – with English speech training. They are lovely people and I have spent quite a lot of time with them. They both train Broadway actors – specialising in giving people accents and dialect speech – and they really are very good.

33 Aunt Agnes was a wonderful knitter, and knitted Aran sweaters for the whole Farrell clan over the years.
34 13 Little Mary Street. Aunt Agnes redecorated and moved back in once Brian and Neil Porter had left.
35 A reference to the great defender Edward Marshall Hall (1858–1927), who, when he appeared before Judge James Charles Mathew, was rude, and that was the start of bad feeling between the two men. Judge Mathew was TWT Dillon's maternal grandfather.
36 Alice Hermes went on to become a renowned speech therapist at HB Studio, a performing and acting school in New York.

The other members of the staff are also very kind, especially the Frauenfelders[37] (he is Swiss, by the way). They are going out of their way to make Bard College a special experience. Tomorrow, we're going to a drive-in movie and today, a few of us were driven into Red Hook, the local town. In effect it is only a cross-road of shops, but it really is lovely. All the houses are white, timber buildings and the countryside round about is lovely. The food here is wonderful and I find much less need of constant cold water (although I take a shower twice a day). The weather is hot and sunny and the College itself, lying well back from the road in its own grounds, is a fine building.

And now, my dear, what about you? I do hope you enjoy this short holiday in Achill and that you look after yourself for me: so don't get sunstroke or drown or anything. Do remember me to all in Dublin when you get back, and hope for the best in my exam (!) tomorrow. Actually, it is a simple sort of English proficiency test (run on American lines) and should be quite an interesting experience.

 9

[BRIAN TO MARIE-THÉRÈSE]
Bard College, 31 July–1 August

These two will have to go together because I couldn't get stamps earlier. Today about five of us were driven by Bill Asip[38] down to Barrytown for Mass. Afterwards I spent about an hour trying to play tennis. Yesterday we had this test in English proficiency, and I was marking the papers for a couple of hours. Incidentally, I headed the list with 74 – of course, there are only two other English speakers here (Marion Dixon from England and Schumann from South Africa). In the evening we were driven in about six cars to Hyde Park for the drive-in movie. The charge per skull was 70

---

37   William Frauenfelder, a Swiss émigré, was a language professor at Bard.
38   Bill Asip was director of physical education at Bard.

cents, but for that we were given three full-length films. We got back here at about 2.30 a.m.

I have just come back from Asips. Each of the staff had about six of us to their home for supper. The Asips, who have four little girls, are Catholics. We had a lovely evening, especially when Mrs Asip, talking about the cream for coffee, said it was only the 'top of the bottle'.[39] It brought me right back home to you, my darling, and to all the wonderful weekends we have spent together. But don't worry, dearest, there will soon be so much time we can spend together.

How are you and the girls getting on in Achill? Is there any news about a maid, and how is your mother? It's beginning to sound like a question time, isn't it, pet? At present I'm drafting a chart for Mike Rado's speech analysis and also trying to write a paper for our first seminar on Tuesday, so as you can see I'm getting somewhat into my stride. At the same time I'm enjoying my free time, playing table-tennis and swimming. I now find that if I can work off some of my sweat and then have a shower, I feel much cooler for the rest of the day.

The group here is quite mature and I was amazed to find that the other five guests, mostly foreign students, were all married. Gotto from Japan gave us all a shock. He had said that he'd like to stay for about three years in the US as he had no father or mother. Someone then asked, if he had any brothers or sisters and he replied, 'No ... only a wife.' Moreover, apparently he didn't very much care what happened to her!

....

39   In the past when milk was delivered in glass bottles on Dublin doorsteps the 'top of the bottle' was the cream that rose to the top.

P.S. LOOK OUT FOR SNAKES

10

As you will know by now, I spent the weekend in N.Y. (more later) and arrived back on a three-and-a-half-hour milk train with two earnest Germans in tow to a hushed Bard – everyone was listening to some Chief Sitting Horse or Something talking about Red Indians. Feeling tired and hungry, I was thrilled to find THREE letters and a postcard from you waiting to be devoured. 'Thank you' seems such a trivial saying, but anyway thank you, my darling (incidentally thank your mother for hers – I'll try to write very soon).

Well, last week as I told you the campus was infested by these silly Americans for Democratic Action[40] who are pseudo-intellectuals, half-baked political hacks (their support of Stevenson[41] definitely lost him votes), and are constantly talking about Israel. Amongst them was a little monster called Lilian, who was the original pain-in-the-neck: she was giving me a marked persecution complex (would you believe it?), but fortunately the staff ganged up to save me from it all. Then on Saturday I overawed and shocked her (you must remember that she is 'beyond socialism', whatever that means) when John[42] arrived in a gleaming new Cadillac.

As I told you in my letter from the Yale Club, we had a lovely drive down. On Sunday we went to Mass in St Patrick's, a very impressive and almost Dublin-like church, and then after a leisurely

---

40   Though strongly anti-communist, the ADA was still subject to significant McCarthyist scrutiny. The plight of the ADA during that period prompted former First Lady Eleanor Roosevelt to accept a position as honorary chair of the organisation in 1953, and in doing so, put Senator McCarthy in a position in which he would have had to 'call her a communist as well' to continue his inquiries into the activities of the group. Because of her actions, many ADA leaders credited her with 'saving' the organisation.

41   Adlai Ewing Stevenson II (1900– 65) was an American, lawyer, politician and diplomat. He was the thirty-first governor of Illinois from 1949–53, and he won the Democratic Party's nomination for president in the 1952 and 1956 elections. In both elections, Stevenson suffered landslide defeats to the Republican Dwight D. Eisenhower.

42   John Kelly, Virginia.

breakfast we had lunch in the Plaza (a rather old-fashioned but very good hotel on Central Park). The food was excellent, but – a simple soup, egg-dish, ice-cream, coffee lunch, for both of us – cost about £4!! By the way, I should mention that once we reached the club on Saturday John had the car garaged and we went everywhere by taxi.

We then went to meet some of John's friends. There was a man who looks like a Cuban Charlie Chaplin and is about 50, and Katy, a woman who is a tough old lady of 70 or so. Also present were a marine helicopter instructor and a miniature French poodle. They have a beautiful apartment in an old apartment house on Riverside, and Katy spent her time telling me they had just bought a house in California – the photographs of it were magnificent – John told me later that she has the controlling interest in Coca-Cola!

We then visited John's publisher friend, a very pleasant Irish-American called Bob something. He has a tiny but really civilised apartment practically covered in books. For a while we played some really lovely opera recordings and then we went out to dinner. This we had in 'Chandlers' on East 46th Street (that doesn't really mean anything to me either, darling). I had an enormous steak – about 14 inches by 5 by 3: very juicy and tender, but really not as tasty as your weekend mixed grill. The spectacular thing here was that one could pick one's own lobster (there was a tankful), and John had one, and autographed it before it was prepared. Dinner was very pleasant and the talk was good. Later we went back to the Yale Club.

This is a big club and rather old-fashioned, but extremely comfortable and the service beyond reproach. This morning, after a light breakfast I went to look at some bookshops[43] (didn't buy anything), while John went to his brokers. We had lunch – one of these great American double-decker sandwiches[44] – and then I said goodbye and crossed over the street to Grand Central Station and so back to Bard. I hope to go down to Virginia about the 8th September for a fortnight.

....

43   All his life, Brian loved to browse through bookshops.
44   Double-decker sandwiches became one of Brian's favourite snacks.

11
Achill Head Hotel, Wednesday, 4 August

Have just today received your letter from Bard College and I am delighted by the sound of it all. You'll be oh-so-brown and I hope quite a bit fatter[45] in a few weeks!! But I hope the women are dreadful.

We must visit Achill some time together, it's an island of contrasts and all pleasant! The hotel is still packed, people who only booked for the weekend are sleeping (what little sleep they need) in the play room, but the bar seems to be open 24 hours of the day, and some men are bringing their 'fire-water' into breakfast. How they remain pleasant, I do not know, but everyone is friendly and polite! Of your existence everyone knows and I've refused to drink with or go dancing with nearly every man in the hotel. Cat that I am, I've refused more than the others have been offered!! The girls, I think, are being very foolish: on Sunday 3 country boys (friends of Eva's) took them dancing and promised to take them to another dance tonight. They didn't turn up by 10.30 so a (very respectable married) man from the hotel offered to drive them down and they were just leaving with him when one of the boys turned up at 11.30 and, instead of ignoring him, they fell into his arms and forgave him all!! I'm still swimming at their stupidity.

Today was a pet day,[46] so after lunch we all went to the sea (and took photos) then some farmers asked us to 'cock' hay, so from 4–6 I was raking hay, and great fun it is! Con has decided she'll not marry a farmer.

Have you ever heard of a Frank Dwyer from Trinity? Remember we were discussing 'pink' people[47] in Dublin? Well, we were involved in an argument on Monday evening, he's madly pro-Stalin and a most unpleasant type. I was so rude that we've cut each other since then.

---

45 Brian had a fast metabolism and was very skinny as a young man.
46 A beautiful day.
47 Someone sympathetic to Communism without being a member of the Communist Party.

Tomorrow I'm having an early swim, and then going amethyst hunting[48] about 7 miles from here. The girls are too, if they are in a fit state after the dance they've gone to tonight. There's no doubt you've had to put up with a lot from me and that I'm terribly spoilt!! But that's your fault and I love you for it.

 12

[BRIAN TO MARIE-THÉRÈSE]
Bard College Thursday, 6 August

Dearest, I'm sorry I couldn't write yesterday, but we spent most of the day in Poughkeepsie[49] (a city about 20/30 miles away). We first went to Vassar[50] – a big girls' college which was very pleasant – the girls were away on vacation. And then drove to the city to see the town manager, who gave us a short talk on the city government.

My paper went down well, and on Tuesday evening I went with one of the Spaniards to have an informal dinner with the Gomerys, which was very enjoyable. There were a few regular Bard students there, and we got together with a guitar and folk songs.

John (Kelly) phoned me and hopes to run me up to N.Y. for the weekend. Our weather remains beautifully dry and sunny and we are planning a campfire sing-song for tonight. Next week, when the ADA people have left campus, I hope we shall be better able to get down to work. I'm hoping to go to the Roosevelt Library soon, where I may be able to see some stuff on American and Irish neutrality.[51]

---

48 Amethysts can be found on Achill Island.
49 Poughkeepsie is a city in New York State's Hudson Valley.
50 Vassar College is a private, co-educational, liberal arts college in Poughkeepsie, New York. Founded in 1861 by Matthew Vassar, it was the second degree-granting institution of higher education for women in the US, closely following Elmira College.
51 Brian was considering America's attitude towards Irish neutrality in the Second World War as a topic for his MA thesis.

13

My Dearest, yesterday we had the first meeting of students to form a union and I was, unfortunately, elected secretary. Later we went to a reception at which we met more of the Bard faculty and local people. Tonight our union meeting was given details of next week's activities, which include two 'field-trips' (i.e. days out) and a visit – it is hoped – to Tanglewood Musical Festival[52] in Massachusetts. This latter is apparently as well known over here as, say, Glyndebourne[53] and Edinburgh Festival with us. At present, however, we can merely await the event.

Today was a more-or-less typical orientation day programme. At 10.30 we had a seminar. These are held twice weekly instead of the usual lecture (1 hour), followed by a discussion (¼ hour). At the seminar a student reads or gives a paper for ½ hour or so, followed by a discussion, and about 11.20 another student gives a second paper. This takes us up to lunchtime at 12.15–12.30. Today being Friday, we had tomato salad, salmon with very nice 'gay chips' (potato crisps) and a glass of milk, followed by a sort of cake dessert and tea/coffee. Then at 1.10, with the two other members of the executive – the President, Schumann from Sth Africa and Mrs Mongia from India (who has a really wonderful collection of saris and Indian dresses, but is deadly serious) – we met Mr Frauenfelder to discuss union matters.

---

52   Tanglewood is a music venue in the towns of Lenox and Stockbridge in the Berkshire Hills of western Massachusetts. It has been the summer home of the Boston Symphony Orchestra since 1937.

53   Glyndebourne is an English country house near the town of Lewes, East Sussex, believed to be 600 years old. Since 1934 it has been the venue for the annual Glyndebourne Music Festival.

1.30 to about 3.45 I worked in the library (which is very good), and then I went down to the pool, where the sun was beautiful and the water cool and refreshing. Those ADA (Americans for Democratic Action) are still here, so it was a bit crowded. I lay in the sun for a while and then worked on a chart for Mike Rado. He has analysed the speech defects of the students under about half a dozen general headings and under 52 different sounds. He is an interesting person, having worked on the 'Voice of America' and counter-intelligence in Eastern Europe. After tea, which starts 6.15–6.30 and consisted of vegetable soup (very nice – I had two bowls – but not up to your mother's standard), fish, fried potatoes, spinach, milk, tea/coffee – we held a union meeting until 8.15. I then wrote up my minutes: spent an hour or so chatting to Alice Hermes, Mike, Charlie Muller (Frauenfelder's assistant) and Marc Frauenfelder, and then had a game of ping-pong, glanced in at a dance in the gym (last night – Thursday – we had square dancing with a really wonderful caller), had a cup of coffee, worked here for an hour or so, and then settled down to write.

 14

[MARIE-THÉRÈSE TO BRIAN]
Booterstown, Sunday, 8 August

Arrived home last night, after a 9 hour journey, and found your letters of the 30th and 1st waiting – also Mama in great form. I am now using her pen, as mine was borrowed on my holidays and never returned!

This English test sounds most amusing – have you still got a test paper? I'd love to see one, maybe you could send it on! Now I've a little disappointment for you ... I can't send you your notes as they are now on their way to Harvard ... anyway, they take 6 weeks, so they won't arrive till mid-September.

Your letters give me more pleasure than you can imagine. I'm with you under those great leafy trees – in those nice people's homes, and on those hot evenings ... but you'll always play tennis alone! I'll watch!

I'm as brown as a nut, Mama says. Achill was a wonderful holiday. But despite good food, I didn't put on an ounce ... but Mama says my eyes are the palest blue ... all the early nights.

Father John Lavery[54] called up this morning and asked after you – Father Brian[55] is also expected any day. Mary Murphy[56] called while I was away and entertained Mama.

My engagement ring was much admired and very useful too!! Really I had the happiest holiday possible, despite your absence. We took a few photos too, and I hope to send you one of me, near the end of the week. Are you being snapped? I'd love one!

Heard a story about Desmond Williams,[57] dating from a few months back: an Englishman was staying with him, and one evening they abandoned a petrol-less car in Sandycove and walked home to Glenageary. The next morning they caught the train from Glenageary and got out at Sandycove. Desmond limped up to the engine driver and asked him to wait a few minutes, as he had some business to transact there. At Desmond's pace they limped off up to the garage, got the car seen to, and came back to the station 15 minutes later, where the train was patiently waiting to take them to town! No wonder he never bothers to get a car if he can use a train as a taxi! I also heard that that trip to Germany (a month

54   John Lavery went to school with Theo Dillon at Mount Saint Benedict (Gorey). He is remembered as being a tall, fine man. His brother Frank Lavery was an eye specialist who lived in a house between Dalkey and Glenageary. After Theo died, MT worked for a few months as his secretary, and that's when she knew she could never be a secretary.

55   Brian Dillon (1905–79) (also known as Fr Mathew) was the youngest son of John Dillon and was a qualified barrister who became a priest and entered the Benedictine order at Glenstal Abbey. He was MT's godfather.

56   Wife of Gerard (Henry) Murphy (1901 – 1959), Celtic scholar.

57   Thomas Desmond Williams (1921–87) was Professor of Modern History at UCD from 1949 to 1983.

ago) was to see if he can persuade the Americans to release papers (due to be published in 2 years' time) which would give him the evidence required to defend himself in his 'action'.[58]

 15

[MARIE-THÉRÈSE TO BRIAN]
Tuesday morning, 10 August

I spent quite a pleasant day yesterday with Fr Brian[59] who came to tea. He's on the hunt for a French and History Master. Do you know anyone suitable? The man must be very good at French and passable at History. Yesterday evening I went to the pictures with Rosalie and a cousin of hers. Apparently, the 'girls' broke up in confusion, as Eva's brother was operated on Sunday morning for peritonitis. So Eva went home and Con is coming tomorrow.

Mama misses you too, and I'm so busy keeping her amused, that it helps keep me distracted.

If you're speaking to Mrs Frauenfelder about Switzerland again – the Swiss family that are our great friends in Lausanne are the 'Cardiz',[60] he's a doctor. I gather that American hospitality is not a legend but a fact.

P.S. Tell the Jap[61] that I think his views on marriage are dangerous!!

---

58   In 1953, in a series of articles in the *Leader* and *Irish Press*, Desmond accused the war-time Irish Minister to Spain, Leopold H. Kearney, of having been a Nazi collaborator. Kearney sued him and the two publications for libel. Despite Williams having been supplied with captured German documents by the British Foreign Office to boost his case and Kearney being refused the right to present Irish ministry documents in support of his action, Kearney won the case, which was settled out of court.

59   Brian (Fr Mathew) was headmaster of Glenstal at this stage.

60   The Cardiz were a Swiss family who looked after MT when Marie had to take care of Theo in Switzerland. Their daughter, Jeanne-Marie Cardiz, became a life-long friend of MT's, who named one of her firstborn twin girls (Naomi's twin who died) after her.

61   The Japanese student who didn't seem to care about his wife.

P.S. LOOK OUT FOR SNAKES

16

Well the English test you recalled was a bit queer. It was given in book form and, with each question asked; one was given five possible solutions and marked a stroke through the appropriate solution. Then, to correct the papers, one placed a sheet with holes punched in the correct spaces on top of the answer book and so could count the number of correct answers.[62] There were various sections: in the spelling, one had to pick the words wrongly spelled from a group of five: in punctuation and capitalisation various parts of a paragraph were underlined and one had to mark whether a capital, full stop, comma, semi-colon (or nothing at all) should be added. The longest section consisted of short pieces of prose followed by questions whose answers (it was presumed – wrongly I think) could be deduced from the passages given. Then there was a silly question on style, in which one had to pick out the better way of expressing something, and also had to arrange groups of five sentences into a paragraph.

It doesn't really matter about the notes, and, by the way, isn't the story about Desmond very like the one I heard in which it is Desmond's American guest (Henry Steele Commager[63]) who asks the train to wait for them?

Last night I went with a couple of others to Carriers (he is a lecturer in English here) to hear him read some poetry and have an informal discussion on American literature. But the last lines I thought were very personal to me – this poem was about a man driving home, who stops to look at the landscape and finds the soft snowy wood lovely, dark and deep: it seems he might plunge

---

62 American standard form of testing.

63 Henry Steele Commager (1902–98) was an American historian. He wrote extensively and helped define modern liberalism in the US. In the 1940s and 1950s he was noted for his campaigns against McCarthyism and other abuses of government power.

into it or else stay watching as the night turns cold. 'But I have promises to keep and miles to go before I sleep.'[64]

And that's how it is as I climb into bed that I wonder what time is it in Ireland and what are you doing (and think how wonderful you must look – brown as a berry and with lovely eyes of palest blue) or remember our times together, like a walk over Killiney, or the Conferring dance, or your weekend meals. Somehow I seem to be so much more secure and content thinking of you, that I just drowse off into sleep without any worry.

It's now about 10.10 a.m. on Wednesday and I haven't yet posted this because I thought I might hear from you this morning. Yesterday we left for Poughkeepsie at 9 o'clock and visited first of all a big printing works that does many of these coloured comics – including Disney's Mickey Mouse stories. It was quite a fascinating place, especially where the artists and engravers were at work. They also do paper-back pocket books, and I saw a cover of a novel by Ben Kiely[65] (remember Engl. Lit and 'Irish Press') being processed.

We then went to IBM – a very well-known American firm which makes electronic brains (none there now, though), accounting machines, and electric typewriters. We had a picnic lunch in the grounds of their country club – a fabulous place – dance hall, swimming pool, recreations of all kinds, restaurants, lounges etc. It is all set in lovely surroundings. Unfortunately, IBM is one of the 'paternalistic' business places where the president calls people by their Christian names and gives them everything to make them contented and happy and leave them no soul of their own. The plant was very fine, but dotted all over (even in the lavatories) with notices saying 'THINK'; as someone said, all very 1984-ish and straight out of Huxley's Brave New World.[66]

....

64 From 'Stopping by Woods on a Snowy Evening', a poem by Robert Frost.

65 Benedict 'Ben' Kiely (1919–2007) was an Irish writer and broadcaster from Omagh, County Tyrone.

66 Very insightful considering it's 1954, and in the light of the hi-tech ethos today.

Today almost everyone has gone off to Westpoint to visit a power plant, but I thought I'd stay to do some work in peace and quiet. This shouldn't be too difficult as it's only about 60 degrees today and the library is open for us. I still haven't told you much about the personalities around here, but I'm afraid that must wait for another day.

Thursday, 12 August (the glorious 12th)

Aunt Agnes had a card from Neil[67] and he'll be back next Monday and will be up to see her next week. So she plans to get back to Little Mary Street by the second week in September.

The weather here (while we're on the subject of weather) is un-mentionable and, in my opinion, winter is here – the neon lights were on in Dublin at 6 o'clock this evening and it's raining almost all day. So on this damp note let me end, warmed only by my love for you, which I send with this letter.

[MARIE-THÉRÈSE TO BRIAN]
Friday, 13 August

Despite the ominous date, today has been very pleasant. This morning I spent half an hour chatting with the buyer (of materi-als) in B&Ts,[68] who is getting me some glamorous material for a

---

67 Neil Porter (1930–2006), was a member of staff in Experimental Physics at UCD from 1958–89 and Professor of Electron Physics at UCD from 1963. He was a close friend of Brian's and shared digs with him in Little Mary Street. They both shared the same passion for DramSoc. Stephen Hawking once referred to Neil as the 'Irish Savant'.

68 Brown Thomas Department Store.

house coat. Then coffee with Sheila, Con and Pat Glaser[69] – after which Pat told me the glad news (which I actually knew) of the 'expected one', then home, umbrella-less in a torrent of rain, and spent the afternoon making an adorable nightie! Mama is, thank goodness, better now. We sent Nancy,[70] with a cheery goodbye, on her way at 3 pm, and spent a pleasant evening together. We expect a new girl tomorrow lunch time.

Of course I trust you and us – if I didn't, life would be pretty meaningless, just a series of doubts, worries and fears. I'm trying to improve myself, because the Marie-Thérèse you know is still very selfish and much too hard, but without your company it is very difficult not to be hard! Anyway, you'll correct that for me, I know.

Dearest, it's a dreadful pity you can't see my hair now! It's great fun – like an untidy, curly mop – my own cut and everyone loves it – lord knows what it will be like by next spring! Yes, I'm quite brown still and wear no make-up, just lipstick, with great success, of course no stockings! So you see I'm not much changed! And my love for you is always and everything that is – Marie-Thérèse.

 19

The weather has suddenly become very damp, although yesterday was lovely and Tanglewood was a really wonderful experience. We drove down in magnificent sunshine through an almost English

---

69 Pat Delamer, wife of Otto Glaser. Otto was one of the refugees brought into Ireland thanks to Theo Dillon's efforts to help Christian Jews escape Nazi Europe. During WWII, Ireland did everything possible to prevent Jewish refugees from seeking haven on its shores. So Theo Dillon found a loophole and brought in Jews with a Christian connection. Otto was born in Vienna. His father was an Austrian government minister of Jewish descent (he was sent to a Concentration Camp) and his mother, Anna, was devout Catholic. Dillon guaranteed Otto's board and schooling at Blackrock College and used his influence to bring the young boy safely to Ireland. Otto became a well-known inventor and entrepreneur in Ireland.

70 The girl employed to help Marie Dillon.

landscape, and after a picnic supper settled on the grass just in front of 'the shed'.[71].This is literally a shed, a huge barren structure that escapes being ugly, since it is so lacking in pretension.

The enormous audience was very varied. There were long-haired music students complete with scores, a few brash jazz fiends left over from the Friday night 'pop' concert; plenty of ordinary picnickers, tourists and 'music-lovers', and a fantastic number of young people necking madly underneath great piles of blankets. We got back about midnight and I'm quite tired, having got up to go to 9.00 Mass. Today nothing particular planned, but I have to write the general student appraisal of orientation, which we spent two hours discussing on Friday, as I told you.

The Tanglewood experience, dearest, was wonderful, and yet, in all-this great crowd, and with this really unique complex of atmospheres, I just stared up at an early star and thought of you. The moon came out full and round, as we have so often seen it hanging over Dun Laoghaire as we wander home. All that was missing was you, with that wonderful glow you have when you're really enjoying yourself. Look after yourself and your mother, my pet, give her my love, but keep all my love for you.

 20

[MARIE-THÉRÈSE TO BRIAN]
Sunday, 15 August

My Dearest Brian,

Having played a little game of 'hide-and-seek' with the sun, I've settled down indoors and am going to have, I hope, a pleasant day with the S.E.P.[72]

---

71 In 1938, Finnish-American architect Eliel Saarinen designed the fan-shaped Shed (now known as the Koussevitzky Music Shed or simply 'the Shed'). It has 5,100 seats, giving the Boston Symphony Orchestra a permanent open-air structure in which to perform. Broad lawns extend beyond the Shed, providing space for concert-goers.

72 Sunday evening paper.

I had a very pleasant 'windfall' yesterday of £21-0-0 – returned by British income tax, which paid off all my debts. So I now face the coming few months with a clear conscience.

Yesterday evening I went to see Maggy Doran (Mrs O'Reilly's[73] sister) and was received very well. May, her daughter, has taken over executorship of the will.

I looked in Rosalie's diary and I see that Easter Sunday is on April 10th next year! Very near to the date we got engaged, and isn't it your mother's birthday around then? Oh, when is Aunt Agnes's birthday?

Betty[74] is instated here now and she is a pleasant, willing girl – Mama likes her, anyway.

You'll be glad to hear I'm thinking of taking Rosalie, Con and Eva to the theatre for my birthday. That will be a pleasant party. The Gate is doing a Thurber play which is, I believe, v. good.

 21

[MARIE-THÉRÈSE TO BRIAN]
Monday, 16 August

You poor lonely men! I hope the Jap gets very homesick before he's finished! And your letters don't take me for granted. I feel I'm beside you as I'm reading them. The English 'Test' sounds childish – the sort of test for sorting mentally deficient from imbeciles – but maybe I'm just anti-test – and certainly I'd have failed dismally!!![75]

No, Dear, I'd be very unhappy going out with anyone till you take me out again! For more reasons than would fill 3 aerograms! I'm not sending mail surface, as it only costs 3 pence less than an aerogram, and takes ages!

73 Maria O'Reilly – known as Lia – was the woman who stepped in when Elizabeth Mathew (Theo Dillon's mother) died in 1907, and was housekeeper and mother to the Dillon family.
74 The woman employed to help MT and her mother.
75 MT was dyslexic and as a result found tests very challenging.

P.S. LOOK OUT FOR SNAKES

I'm delighted to see it's getting cooler. Here, just for today, the sun is shining! Con and I spent yesterday in Killiney and got soaked and today got sunburnt. As the evening draws in, I'm sitting in the drawing room with my Saturday E.R.[76] and some peppermints. (But never fear, I've lost 1 lb since you left, despite the holiday, and won't be any fatter when we meet!)

Last night Con and Rosalie came in to play cards. I lost every game because Radio Paris was playing 'The Rosen Cavalier' (Remember – the opera we saw in Manchester 1½ years ago). I couldn't play the cards because I was perfectly happy, wrapped in a daydream of memories.

Good night, sleep well. Don't, of course, if you are reading this at breakfast, follow the last bit of advice!

P.S. Don't have anything more to do with that Jap! He sounds a dangerous element among you nice, lovely men! Love MT

 22

[BRIAN TO MARIE-THÉRÈSE]
Monday, 16 August

A wonderful morning with two letters from you, darling, I'm writing this in the sunshine – brilliant again today – then I shall carry on some work on American diplomacy. Tomorrow I hope to get to Hyde Park for a few hours and maybe I'll find some material of interest there.

Yesterday was very quiet. I visited the De Grés[77] and was shown their war game. It is quite fabulous: a huge table littered with miniature toy soldiers, tanks, airplanes and factories. The rules are quite involved and do resemble some aspects of warfare. Still, even despite this, I feel a grown man might derive

---

76 Evening rag (newspaper).
77 Professer Gerard de Gré lectured in sociology at Bard, and also developed rules for ancient war games.

greater satisfaction than playing toy-soldiers.[78] Of course, de Gré is a sociologist.

After supper I watched Mike and Abe playing 'Scrabble',[79] which is a word-game played with squared letters on a board. They were showing me what are called 'boys' rules' (the girls' rules[80] are much more simple). Mike made me some 'Turkish' coffee – a very sort of dry, sandy mixture – and I went off early to bed.

About the pyjamas,[81] darling, they really are wonderful and superbly comfortable. So far they wash very well, but I have washed them myself and do not know what a laundry would do to them, so I think I should wait and see. How is Sheila Coakley and what news of Billy?[82]

 23

[MARIE-THÉRÈSE TO BRIAN]
Wednesday, 18 August

Yesterday, I met Pat Glaser[83] for coffee and Sheila Coakley joined us. After coffee I spotted a sweet nightie (£5 5/-), took it home, copied it last night (material costing 2/-), and returned it this morning (saving £5 3/-that way!)

---

78   Ironically, one of Brian and MT's younger sons, Theo, who used to play war games, with miniature soldiers, as a young teen, went on to make a very successful career as Professor of War in the Modern World at Kings College, London.
79   Invented by an American in 1933, the board game Scrabble was first sold in Great Britain in 1954.
80   Gender discrimination upon which the older Brian would have seriously frowned, but which the younger Brian doesn't deride.
81   MT designed and sewed him pyjamas for his trip
82   Billy Kingston, adjunct professor at TCD Business School, Dublin, originally a DramSoc friend from UCD, remained a lifelong family friend, and is godfather to MT and Brian's son Theo.
83   Wife of Otto Glaser (the German refugee/Irish inventor).

P.S. LOOK OUT FOR SNAKES

This morning Con and I went to a new café in South Anne Street called the 'Coffee Inn'[84] – very new – with a machine which produces fluffy coffee (Italian style) – very pleasant.[85]

 24

Another letter from you, darling! How on earth do you manage it? Well, last night a new student, John Mbiti – a theology (Prof) student from East Africa arrived. I was more or less showing him around when I was told that arrangements had been made to take me to Hyde Park to see the Roosevelt Papers.

So at 7.45 am Mrs Frauenfelder drove me down to Rhinebeck and from there I drove with the librarian and two other members of staff to Hyde Park.[86] There is a Roosevelt museum, and then this carefully filed and cross-indexed collection of several million documents. The greater part (of course, the collection dates from the beginning of the century) is accessible, but many of the files I examined were incomplete, since some of the papers are in the restricted part of the collection. However, I did gather some small amount of detailed information and hope to go to Hyde Park again in the very near future. Perhaps I shall go tomorrow, although a field trip to Albany (the capital of New York State) is planned to start at 8 am tomorrow morning.

Today was really lovely and the drive down was magnificent – even the Hudson (a rather muddy river) seemed blue. The sun was

84 The Coffee Inn at 6 South Anne Street (1954–95) was an Italian snack bar run by Antonio Gentile. It was very popular with the art, student and music set of the 1970s and 1980s. Patrons included Phil Lynott of Thin Lizzy.

85 MT's first cappuccino.

86 The Franklin D. Roosevelt Library was the first of the presidential libraries and was built in 1939 and 1940 to house the vast quantity of President Roosevelts's historical papers, books and memorabilia, accumulated during a lifetime of public service and private collecting.

blazing in a beautifully clear blue sky, but fortunately the Search Room, where I was working, was air-conditioned. The staff was very pleasant, and a Mr Roach[87] – who is in charge of the papers – has invited me to come over to his home sometime. However I'm not sure I'll have the time.

 25

[MARIE-THÉRÈSE TO BRIAN]
Thursday, 19 August

My Darling Brian,

Tanglewood (what a lovely name!) sounded very pleasant. Last night I came in from having been to 'The Heart of the Matter' with Con and Sheila and then supper in Con's, where we had a long discussion on the fine distinction between love and infatuation, and when should children 'know' and how much they should 'know'? And found your 2 letters and postcard!

I notice that you are doing lots of work on American Neutrality – are you doing this outside the summer school course? And does that mean you are thinking of using it for a thesis or as preparation for your work at Harvard? If you do an American subject instead of an Irish one, will that affect this year's grant from UCD? Or have you a way around that? Sorry about all the questions, but I love to hear about your work – otherwise I get a little out of touch and will have such a lot of ground to cover next spring!

Next Monday I'm going up to Geraldine O'Connor Kelly's[88] to meet her sister who is going home to Denver next week and she

---

87 First appearance of George Roach, archivist of the Roosevelt Papers in Hyde Park, and soon to become a close friend of Brian's.

88 Gerry (Geraldine) worked as a checker in Larhams, the clothing factory where MT worked. She was originally from America and had moved to Ireland with her family when she was twelve.

P.S. LOOK OUT FOR SNAKES

knows Mary Seidensticker[89] (Papa's cousin) quite well, so I am looking forward to it.

(Friday morning) The phone never stopped ringing last night; first Shawn[90] to say he's sent you photos (by surface mail, as the other way was too expensive!!) so if you don't get them before going to Virginia I suppose they'll be forwarded to you. Then Neil[91] – he's coming out to see us on Sunday. Then Myles asking me to lunch next Monday (can't go) to meet the professor of English literature in Harvard, but I am going to see him tomorrow instead. He must be the man Pat McHugh[92] was speaking about.

Mama got a letter from Julian[93] (the Polish man who was a great friend of Fr John Lavery[94] and who was correspondent for the Times Herald Tribune). He's lost his job as the paper was sold, and is doing temporary work for some publishers. Julian says he'd very much like you to contact him, if you are going to Washington, and I know he meant it.

I'm looking forward to a very full and pleasant birthday tomorrow[95] – only it won't feel complete without you. This time next year will be much pleasanter, please God.

....

89 Mary Seidensticker was the daughter of Mary Elizabeth Dillon (granddaughter of John Blake Dillon, father of John Dillon) and Edward George Seidensticker from Colorado.

90 A college friend, not to be confused with Shawn Dillon.

91 Neil Porter, physicist and friend.

92 Wife of Roger McHugh (1908–1987), Irish academic, author, playwright and politician.

93 Not sure who Julian is, he could be one of the Jewish refugees saved by Theo Dillon during the War, or Julian Stryjkowski, a well-known Polish journalist. The court is out, and anyone who can throw light on the matter, I'd love to hear from them.

94 Friend of Theo Dillon.

95 MT's birthday is 21 August.

26

Addressed to 'Miss M.T. Dillon, c/o Larhams Ltd (Blouse Factory),
George's St., Dun Laoghaire, Dublin, Ireland.

My Dearest,

It's another warm but not really blazing day and I hope to finish this in time for the afternoon post. Last night I spoke to one of the Semantics group and he told me he was a member of the Irish 'Civil Liberties' organisation!

I'm really sending this to you at Dun Laoghaire, because I want to tell you something about Myles. Really I suppose I shouldn't, but it is rather interesting. Among the papers on Ireland in the Roosevelt collection at Hyde Park I found a memo on a request made by Myles to Gray[96] (the American Minister) in 1943, asking what he could do to help the war effort. This request was apparently shuffled to and fro and so the memo came through F.D.R's office. Myles[97] is described as a Prof. at either Chicago or Wisconsin (I forget which), and it is suggested that he work with the Dept. of Psychological warfare. It's really nothing to talk about, but I know how you like to keep full files on your relatives.

Saturday(same letter)

---

96 David Gray was appointed minister to Ireland in February 1940. In Gray's own words, his appointment was nepotic, as he was First Lady Eleanor Roosevelt's uncle through marriage. Gray consistently tried to get Ireland to join the war against the Nazis, though Ireland refused. De Valera went so far as to ask the US government and Franklin Roosevelt to remove Gray from his post because of opposition to Irish neutrality, though the US government never did.

97 Myles taught at this time at the University of Wisconsin at Madison and, being a linguist, could offer some help in the war effort. As it turned out, he was a sort of double agent, and was roped in to finding out what Gray was up to, the suspicion being that the Americans were trying to overthrow De Valera's government and thus end Irish neutrality. To this end, Myles had to slip into Ireland in the middle of the war, via London. (This information was passed on by John Dillon, Myles's eldest son).

I'm sorry, pet, but Charles Muller whisked me off for a drive to Poughkeepsie yesterday afternoon, and in the evening we all went down to Rhinebeck for their celebrations. These celebrations (really a racket to bring tourists and trade to the town) were officially in honour of Levi P. Morton,[98] who was a local yokel and became vice-president of the US, and as American Minister in Paris accepted the Statue of Liberty.

The whole thing was quite a shambles. First, we all strolled (couldn't possibly describe it as marched or even walked) in procession with people in all sorts of fancy dress and period costume. Then we came to a great park where (horror!) we were each called out by name (fortunately the audience was bored and just ignored this part of the proceedings) as we were presented with a 'Queen'; these were local girls all dressed up in hick, tulle dresses. We each sat with our Queen (making feeble attempts at conversation) while we had speeches from the Mayor, a pep-talk from an Air-force captain, a rather vicious war-scare harangue from a local politician, beseeching people to join the airplane spotting unit. Then we had 'concert' items – half of them performed by our students: they included a wonderful (local) representative of Ireland (I believe he's really a Canadian who has settled in Rhinebeck) who sang Stephen Foster[99] songs. Meanwhile I was sitting – almost crawling on the lap of my Queen – a ravishing beauty from Red Hook whose brilliance and lustre cast a spell. WHAT IS GOING TO HAPPEN? For further adventures of Casanova Farrell wait until our next broadcast, and meantime be good. With all my love, Brian.

....

98 Levi Parsons Morton (1824–1920) was the twenty-second vice-president of the US (1889–93). He also served as US ambassador to France, as a US representative from New York, and as the thirty-first governor of New York.

99 Stephen Collins Foster (1826–1864), 'the father of American music', was a songwriter known primarily for his parlour and minstrel music. He wrote more than 200 songs, including 'Oh! Susanna', 'Hard Times Come Again No More', 'Camptown Races', 'Old Folks at Home' ('Swanee River'), 'My Old Kentucky Home', 'Jeanie with the Light Brown Hair', 'Old Black Joe' and 'Beautiful Dreamer', and many of his compositions remain popular today.

[MARIE-THÉRÈSE TO BRIAN]

(1 am) 21–22 August

My Darling Brian,

You are the cleverest Darling imaginable! Last night I got a very pleasant letter posted on the 18th, with no mention of birthday wishes, and so I resigned myself to the fact that you had forgotten. Then at 10.30 this morning, a very small boy appeared on the doorstep with a huge box full of flowers. Pink, Blue, Mauve, White, Red, Yellow and Orange – I filled every vase in the house. There are red and white gladiolas in the drawing room, Mauve and Pink ones in Mama's room and white Sweet-peas in my bedroom. You are a darling and very clever. Thank you for the wonderful surprise.

I got a card from Ethnea[100] and family, and one from Aunty Agnes and from Eva.

The Dillons all forgot![101] I spent a very pleasant afternoon in Myles's, nevertheless, and find that family very pleasant – my small cousins[102] are highly amusing – and will probably go there soon again.

In the evening Con, Sheila, Rosalie and I went to the theatre – 'The Male Animal' starring Sheila Brennan and Godfrey Quigley, a Thurber play that is every bit as good as his best stories.

Sunday – Brian (OSB[103]) came to coffee and wished me a belated Happy Birthday – his visit was very pleasant and we had a most invigorating fight about James.[104] I am now writing this in the afternoon sun (rather cool!) and expecting Neil to tea – so hope to have more news to conclude before the end of my letter.

---

100 Brian's younger and only sister.
101 A fact she finds charming.
102 John, Catherine, Elizabeth (Bim), Peter and Andrew are MT's cousins and in many ways were more like the younger brothers and sisters she never had.
103 Order of Saint Benedict. Brian (Father Mathew).
104 James Dillon, Theo Dillon's younger brother. He was a Fine Gael politician, at the time Minister of Agriculture in the Coalition Government, who sometimes pushed MT's buttons – she loved to argue with and about him.

Am closing now as Neil will post this in the G.P.O.

All my love, and thank you again for the wonderful birthday surprise!

Marie-Thérèse

PS Mama sends her love, and says that the maid is really very stupid but honest!

 28

The story continues: at the end of the 'concert' a dance was started on boards about the size of a small living-room. I really thought that sitting there watching people being trampled to death was too much – especially since my 'Queen' wanted to join the merry throng. Fortunately Charles and Mike came to say that we had to drive right back! However, the problem remained of palming off 'Queen' on somebody. Luckily Schumann came along, moaning that his woman had gone home, so I brought him over and with an introduction – 'This is Daniel Schumann from South Africa; he's full of racial problems and he dances' – I withdrew and we sat around Bard.

Yesterday afternoon as I was in the middle of laundry (which today is beautifully white and dry) I was told someone was looking for me on the campus, and found George Roach[105] (the man who works in the Hyde Library I told you about) with a friend and a 1953 Cadillac (I quote the year because John Kelly's is a '54). He invited me to a concert of chamber music, and so we drove about 80 miles into Massachusetts to South Mountain, where we were in time to catch the last half of the concert. It was all fairly recent music, including a first performance. I found it interesting rather than 'enjoyable' strictly speaking. The concert hall is really a large, barn-like building, but we sat on the heather-covered

---

105 Archivist at Hyde Park.

hillside outside and enjoyed sunshine as well as music. We drove down into a village called Lee – where we had a pleasant supper, over which we dawdled for about two hours, and left about 8, arriving at Bard at 9.15 or so.

At Bard, we joined the party that was going on at Zabruski Mansion – a large manor house about half a mile from the houses proper. We had dancing, singing, bridge, chess etc. One of the Germans and I played four games of chess simultaneously, I won three. We had a very pleasant time until about 1 a.m., when Mike drove me back to the college, as I had to rise at 8.00 this morning.

After Mass, I did a little work and then started to write this. Today most of the students were taken off to spend the week with American families, so there were only about a dozen of us left. We spent the afternoon sitting on the lawn listening to records. The high spot was José Ferrer on a long player in 'Cyrano de Bergerac'. Now after supper we are again on the lawn. What do you think we are listening to? 'Rosenkavalier' – quite a coincidence isn't it, pet?[106] It takes me back to that week in Manchester – especially since I'm wearing your green sweater for warmth.

Tomorrow more students are going off for the week, and I'm setting off for Harvard so I can arrange my accommodation. I expect to be back before the weekend and D. V.[107] will spend the last couple of days with George in Rhinebeck – that way I can spend some further time at Hyde Park.

Perhaps it's time, dear, that I said something about some things over here that impress me. One undoubtedly is the way in which food is served. Use is constantly made of paper cups, napkins, etc. ... and always one has a paper table mat. So there is no worrying about whether or not things are clean. The food here

....

106 Brian and MT shared a lifelong passion for opera and classical music, and in later
    years (from 1980 on) went regularly to the concert hall in the old UCD building on
    Earlsfort Terrace.
107 Deo Volente – God willing.

P.S. LOOK OUT FOR SNAKES

is of course 'institutional' but good. However, I think your palate is better educated than mine for savouring new dishes. The roads (which have a constant stream of 35–50-mile-per-hour traffic) are wonderful – very straight, but with great rises and hollows, as they tend to go over rather than round the little hills on the way. Yet drivers here seem very careful, and the width of the roads makes for greater safety.

The newspapers are frightening in size, and I now seldom look even at the headlines. New York is very strange – nobody seems to speak either American or English: there is a great deal of really bad, broken English – even in the small towns around here. Despite the enormous numbers of immigrants, however, there is terrific curiosity about foreign lands and people's impressions of, and questions about, Ireland are really amazing.[108]

Food is dear: a glass of milk or tea/coffee/mineral are all around 10 cents, but milk shakes, ice-cream and ice cream sodas are 25 cents (as are cigarettes, which isn't too bad). Meat is very dear, but fruit is plentiful and reasonable.

Fashions – what I have seen of them – are uninspiring. Around here there is great informality and many women (not just girls) wear jeans or shorts with check or plain shirts, often not tucked in. I didn't see that much of N.Y., but by and large there didn't seem any great variety. Of course, the heat doesn't help, for I'm sure that dark dresses or costumes would be unbearable and would probably fade quickly.

The people are very pleasant, but one meets a lot of apparent bad manners – actually it's a matter of different behaviour. Round here the children are really beautiful – brown, chubby and very healthy looking, and small wonder, they have a wonderful time on a campus like this, where everyone pets them and plays with them and I'm sure most of them are 'spoiled', at least when they are younger.

....

108 Interesting to note that despite the large number of Irish immigrants in America, especially in the Boston area, original Irish were an exotic attraction to most people.

Everywhere one notices fire precautions – hydrants, pumps, bells, ugly fire-escapes – all arising from the tremendous number of frame (i.e. wooden) houses and the fact that there have been so many tragic fire disasters in this country. Perhaps I should have expected much of this, but these are some of the things that stick out most in my mind.

Of course, it would be silly to generalise: for instance, around the Hudson area, almost all factory workers arrive in cars (and there are enormous numbers of cars here), but the parking problem in N.Y. is so bad and the traffic so heavy that most stockbrokers go to and fro by the subway! Incidentally, in this locality (Poughkeepsie and Rhinebeck) they have parking meters and you pay 10 cents to park for an hour, and – also rather strange, but I think very sensible and practical – they have toll bridges on the big highways which run you straight into the heart of N.Y.

 29

Today has been beautifully sunny, and by sneaking out now and then, I'm managing to keep quite brown. I'm sorry if you aren't brown, do try and get a tan while you are with John,[109] it will see you through the winter. Four weeks today since you flew off, 1/8th of the time covered!

(Tuesday) Have had a most interesting evening discussing my trip to America with Gerry's[110] sister Maureen (from Denver); she advised me strongly against travelling alone tourist class on the boat. She said the chances were I might be sharing a cabin with people whom I didn't like, and, as it would be very rough in March, it could be quite an ordeal. Also, tipping is a very necessary

---

109 Kelly, Virginia.
110 Gerry O'Connor, factory friend of MT's, originally from America.

P.S. LOOK OUT FOR SNAKES

practice on board and comes to 15% of the fare (about £75=), as against the flight you went on, out of season, which would be only £5 or so more – (single fare). She also said that, if we wished, we could get to Denver by 'grey-hound' bus for £10, and that it's a lovely way to see America. We might consider it for a honeymoon come Easter Holidays! Mary[111] has said in her last letter how much she'd love to have us stay, but of course it all depends on how long you are free from College.

I met Ronan[112] last night, on his way home from the library studying. He's doing the Brooke,[113] £50 for the first three years at the Bar. He'd love a card from you and says he'd answer it. You made my Birthday very happy, darling.

 30

[BRIAN TO MARIE-THÉRÈSE]
Boston YMCA, Monday, 23 August

There is no place like home, dearest, except Boston with local elections brewing: all over the place are posters for O'Connors, Foleys, Murphys etc. I arrived here at 6.30, having hitchhiked about 250 miles from Bard (which I left at 10.00 this morning). However, in justice to myself, I must admit to spending two hours in Springfield, Massachusetts. As I was walking to the outskirts of this city, a police car picked me up, heard I was from Ireland and promptly brought me out about two miles to a crossroad, where the very next car stopped to give me a lift. Amongst others, I had a lift from a horse-dealer, an ardent young Baptist and an

---

111 Mary Seidensticker, her cousin.
112 Ronan Keane , flat-mate and friend of Brian, was Chief Justice of Ireland (2000–04). He delivered a touching eulogy at Brian's funeral in 2014, quoting 'Heraclitus by William Cory' – "They brought me bitter news to hear and bitter tears to shed..."
113 John Brooke Scholarship – Highest Overall Mark in the Examination leading to Admittance to the degree of Barrister–at–Law. This prize originates from a gift by Mary, Margaret and Elizabeth Brooke, three sisters of the Rt Hon. John Brooke QC, an esteemed Bencher, who died in 1877.

engineer still (at about 40) going to night school to get his degree. Incidentally, almost without exception, everyone giving me a lift claimed some sort of connection with Ireland. It was a lovely day, very hot and plenty of traffic. Fortunately, I followed my planned route here nearly all the way: the change was in the last 40 miles, when instead of following along the road I had travelled for 140 miles and which runs on into Boston, I was brought up to a four-drive road, which not only ran straight into Boston but actually passed the 'Y' – and I was brought right down it in one lift.

Boston is much more quiet than N.Y. – in some ways maybe quieter than Dublin – though some shoe and drapery stores stay open until 8/9 o'clock. There is a huge Irish population here, but I also noticed a lot of Negroes[114] (at least in one area). The subway from the centre of the city emerges above ground just outside here, which is really a gift!

If I can manage it, I hope to start my journey back on Wed. and I shall D.V. stay with George Roach in Rhinebeck for a couple of days, and so get into Hyde Park for some more rooting around the documents.

 31

[BRIAN TO MARIE-THÉRÈSE]
YMCA Boston, Tuesday, 24 August

Mission completed. I spent the day in Cambridge, which seems a really wonderful place. I found the 'Negotiations' and one parcel of papers (the postage must have cost a fortune, pet) waiting for me in Keppler's office. Most important of all, I have a pleasant and quite large room which is almost inside the main college area

---

114 The word 'Negro' is socially unacceptable today. But back in the 1950s it was how most black Americans described themselves. The turning point came when Stokely Carmichael coined the phrase 'Black Power' at a 1966 rally in Mississippi. Then in December 1988, Jesse Jackson announced that members of their race preferred to be called 'African-American'.

– about 100 yards away, in fact – at only $7 per week, with a fire escape just outside the window.

The buildings are clustered around Harvard Square, but as far as one can see the University owns the whole of Cambridge: down all sorts of side streets one finds research centres, administrative offices etc. Also on the square is a subway which takes you straight into Boston for 20c.

The people at the Foreign Students office seem very pleasant and are obviously able to handle red-tape. While I was there, a man from Iraq, who has just spent four years at MIT without ever contacting the Aliens' Dept., came in to register at Harvard, and a girl who had dual US and Norwegian citizenship, and has been treated as an alien at Vassar College, arrived. I also went to the Russian Research place which Langer[115] runs (about three minutes' walk from my digs), but was told he wasn't expected until Monday.

It's been a hot, 'sticky' day and all these posters asking for votes on behalf of O'Donnells, O'Connors, Sheehys were slightly nauseating. I can well believe that Boston politics are really crooked.

 32

[MARIE-THÉRÈSE TO BRIAN]
Thursday, 26 August

We had rather a bad night, last night! I came back from a very pleasant evening in Noeleen's and found Mrs Jones[116] (no. 6 and 4) a Mrs Ward from no. 3 (a trained nurse), the priest upstairs anointing Mama,[117] and the doctor on his way. Dr Roche arrived

---

115   William Leonard Langer (1896–1977) was the chairman of the History Department at Harvard University.

116   MT and Marie's neighbours on both sides (of no. 5) were called Jones, one family was protestant and the other catholic, but, despite different religions, they were very kind and good people.

117   Marie Dillon had failing health, which deteriorated dramatically during this time.

shortly and gave Mama a strong injection of Luminal[118] – apparently she has got Coronary Thrombosis. She only called me three times during the night, but it's hard to sleep when you are listening for the bell. So I got this morning off and, having slept late, did the shopping and made lunch – thank goodness Mama seems to be over this attack. But she's terribly weak. The Dr is coming again today, so I hope he'll settle her comfortably. Mrs Jones (both of them) were terribly kind and Mrs Ward promised to come over and help should anything happen again.

Your wonderful long letter (to Mama and me) arrived yesterday evening. Who was the 'Queen' referred to in the letter? (at the concert!) I'm delighted to read that George Roach is such a nice person, and I hope you'll have a lovely holiday with him. I'm dying to hear what accommodation you've got at Harvard! I hope you'll have pleasant room-mates – don't go on your own or you'll be lonely.

Will write a happier letter tomorrow. Darling,

 33

[BRIAN TO MARIE-THÉRÈSE]
Bard, Thursday, 26 August

Back again, darling, to your letter of Sunday. How is Neil after his Italian trip? I left Boston this morning about 9.45 and took a street-car to the outskirts of the city. I got my first lift about 10.15 and arrived back at Bard 5.45. I would have arrived sooner, but for the fact that one of the roads we travelled was under repair for several miles and we were in a long, long string. Also, in a little town called Westfield I had to wait 25 minutes before getting a lift.

In answer to some of your questions: Alice Hermes and Mike Rado are not the Frauenfelders – they are the two members of the speech-training staff. As for the Roosevelt Papers, I'm merely doing

118 Luminal works by controlling the abnormal electrical activity in the brain that occurs during a seizure. This medication is also used for a short time (usually no more than two weeks) to help calm patients or help them sleep during periods of anxiety.

60   *P.S. LOOK OUT FOR SNAKES*

some examination of first-hand diplomatic material while I have the opportunity. I have started on American and Irish diplomatic relations during the war, as a likely, small field which I know something about (N.B. there is a glowing pen picture of Frank Aiken[119] as one of the most intelligent members of the government.)

Thursday 3.00 pm [same letter]

Have just arrived in Rhinebeck – it's only about 6 miles from Bard, but it took about 20 minutes to get a lift down this far. Charles wanted to drive me down, but I find hitch-hiking (but only while I have some time to spare) great fun.[120] For the next couple of days I expect I shan't get any mail, but it will be all piled up waiting for me when I get back to Bard on Sunday D.V.

 34

[MARIE-THÉRÈSE TO BRIAN]
Friday, 27 August

Now feeling much happier, I'll settle down to give you some news. Mama is better and is using the electric fan and loves it – says the purr … puts her to sleep.

Joan (Fitz) Costello[121] has had her baby – 6 weeks too soon. But I believe she's all right – the baby John is in the Coombe (Bill's[122] looking after it) and Joan is in Hatch Street Nursing Home, and the poor girl hasn't seen the baby since he was born – I hope to go to see her tomorrow. Also, Noeleen heard in Bundoran in the Railway Hotel Lounge from someone I've never heard of that 'Angela O'Connor's wedding dress was made by M.T.D and that M.T. liked the material so

---

119 Francis Thomas Aiken (1898–1983) was Chief of Staff of the Irish Republican Army. Originally a member of Sinn Féin, he was later a founding member of Fianna Fáil.

120 In later years, Brian liked to offer lifts to people, a sort-of payback from his Harvard days.

121 Joan was married to Declan Costello (1926–2011, barrister, judge and Fine Gael politician who served as judge of the High Court (1977–98), Attorney General of Ireland (1973–77) and President of the High Court (1995–98).

122 Bill Kidney, renowned Dublin paediatrician and husband of MT's closest friend Naomi. Naomi and Bill were godparents to MT and Brian's firstborn, Naomi, a surviving twin.

much she'd got the same for herself!' Ireland's remarkable! Well, it's nice to think my dress is news before it's made!

Funny, last night lying awake and listening to Mama, I remembered the first vigil I had with her – I was so frightened (trying to sleep in the corner of her room) and in the end getting the first 2 letters you ever wrote me from London, reading them and then feeling complete confidence. Far away, you still have that effect, but I don't have to reread the letters now – because I know them in sequence all by heart.

3 letters today – 2 from Boston – that trip down must have been great fun, but I'll be glad to hear that you are safely back in 'Annandale' [Bard College].

The letter to Larhams only arrived this morning. Now I know what the beginning of your story was – having received the second instalment first I was confused.

What's the news of your 'Council of Trent' friend?[123]

 35

I know it's very bad of me not to have written, but really there has been nothing to write about. (Or did I write Friday? Perhaps I did.) Anyway, Saturday was a lovely day and, apart from eating, I stayed in the sun, while I could. Today, when I came back to Bard, everyone said I looked fatter and more tanned, so I think the weekend was a real success. Of course with George's 5,000 gramophone records[124] on hand and two record players, even today's rain – it has now got much heavier – couldn't really spoil the holiday.

George, incidentally, is also a historian and has quite a tidy little historical library. So while I was in Rhinebeck I thought I would take up the study of social history in the mid-west. Hence I read

---

123 Reference to John Locke.
124 George Roach had a library full of classical records instead of books.

'Thurber's Country' and 'The Thurber Album'[125] – both very good.

This morning when I went round to 10.30 Mass I thought I was back home. The church was packed to the doors – mind you, it's a tiny church. I met Anna Martelloni after Mass and brought her back for a cup of coffee and Mozart.

This evening at six we were going to have this barbecue, I told you about, but with all the rain, and it really was heavy, nobody felt like settling down for a picnic. Anyway, if only for the sake of the food, we dutifully trotted over to Kappa House and, as it turned out, we had a really wonderful time.

Hamburgers were cooked out of doors and rushed in piping hot and there was more than enough for everyone. We were also given huge pieces of water-melon and slices of three-tier party cake. In next-to-no-time the party got into swing and we were going round shaking hands and mingling with people we hadn't met for a week.

By now nearly all the 'General Semantics'[126] groups have gone, but I found a relic of their 'fancy dress' dance, which apparently they held on Sat. This was a large cardboard shield with two loops of string so that it could be strapped on the arm. The top had a notice 'Modern Knight in Shining Armour' and on the bottom – again hanging on a string – was a roll of toilet paper with the motto 'noblesse oblige'. Not bad, eh?

I have sent off your Vogue and Reader's Digest (the last is considered a rather poor magazine over here), but I suppose it will take some time to reach you. Anyway, if you want to know about clothes, dresses and such like, just ask and I'll try to find out for you. Of course the greatest mine of general information is probably the Sunday 'N.Y Times', but that runs to a hundred-or-so pages.

P.S. could you send me some used commemorative stamps? Some of the children of the Faculty collect them. B

125   James Grover Thurber (1894–1961) was an American cartoonist, author, humorist, journalist, playwright and celebrated wit. He was best known for his cartoons and short stories, published mainly in *The New Yorker* and collected in his numerous books.

126   Alice Hermes and Mike Rado and Co.

[MARIE-THÉRÈSE TO BRIAN]
Sunday, 29 August

On Friday I saw Joan and Declan[127] – Joan looks very well and happy. She says the baby (John) is still in some danger, but they are facing it all very well.

(1 hour later) I've just stopped to listen to a play by Donagh MacDonagh[128] 'The Law of the Prophets', and the BBC did it extremely well. In many places the script seemed to be slices of the 'Playboy', but to anyone who didn't notice this, it was very good radio.

Mama is very weak since her heart attack. She has an injection of heart stimulus every evening, which gets her through the night, but she sleeps a lot during the day and doesn't get up at all. So instead of writing a long letter to me next time, could you address it to her? She'll love it and I'll read it after her.

Last night Rosalie, Eva and I went to see 'The Beggar's Opera' with Sir Laurence Olivier in the part of the villainous Highwayman hero – great fun – script by Fry and additional music by William Walton – after which we went for coffee in the Savoy – there the girls met 2 boys they last saw in Achill.

Darling, you are looking after yourself, I hope, and get those good winter shoes you need and a warmer coat. I've got your jacket cleaned and ready, so write when I'm to send it out.

Everything is very dull here at present, which accounts for this terrible letter. I miss you very much, and on these Sundays more than ever.

P.S. The story about Myles[129] is much too good to keep to myself!!

127 Joan and Declan Costello.

128 Donagh MacDonagh (1912–68), Irish writer, judge, presenter, broadcaster and playwright.

129 Memo in the Roosevelt Collection at Hyde Park on a request made by Myles to Gray (the American ambassador) in 1943 asking what he could do to help the war effort.

37

My poor pet – the post was late arriving today, but after all I got two letters – you aren't getting much comfort after your holiday. I understood your mother is feeling better, but I know how worrying all this is for you – in many ways, dearest, it brought us so close together that day you called me in the Hibernian.[130] I do hope that by now everything has passed.

I think my letters are crossing, but on the accommodation at Harvard, I am in a rooming house for students as things stand, so, although I shall have my own room, I won't strictly speaking be on my own. Anyway, I may share an apartment with Stan Kalkreuth and one or two others.

Today we settled back to work and I spent the afternoon reading 'Munich – Prologue to Tragedy'.[131] In the evening we had a meeting of the Students Union and a film show. About 10 it started to rain quite heavily, and when Charles Muller, Marion Dixon and I drove down to Annandale for a snack (our own coffee shop is closed evenings this week), it was pouring down.

Have you read 'The Cruel Sea'? I remember you talked about it, but if you haven't read it, I could send you a cheap paper-back edition. Do let me know, pet, if I can get anything while I'm around N.Y. area – altho' Boston is also a huge shopping area, of course. It's very late now, dearest, and wet and dark and I suppose you are trying to sleep while worrying about your mother, and there's little consolation in my writing to say that I share it with you – but

---

130 The Royal Hibernian Hotel, Dawson Street, Dublin, goes back to 1751, making it the oldest hotel in Ireland.

131 *Munich: Prologue to Tragedy* by John. W. Wheeler-Bennett is an historical interpretation of European developments during the eight months from March to October 1938. Wheeler-Bennett, a British historian with practical diplomatic experience, was one of the editors of the captured German documents.

I do – as I want to share everything with you, most of all my time, but soon we will be together again and real life will begin. Brian

P.S. Just since I had the space I thought I'd ask how the factory is getting along – do they still keep in line for you?[132] B

P.P.S. A little bit more space, so a question. Did I ever get round to telling you that I miss you and love you? B

 38

I'm delighted about your safe return to Bard and that you had such a good time with George. But am frankly terrified about the hitchhiking! I only hope American drivers are very safe!

I'm afraid yesterday was one of the worst days since you went. I suppose my nerves are rattled after Mama's attack, and Mama's nerves aren't much good after it either, but Mama said 'sorry' to-day in a very nice way. She offered to go to a hospital (M.M.Ms[133]) and let me off to join you before Xmas! But I refused for the present. I hadn't the heart, though it almost killed me to say 'no', because it would be such a long time for her! Anyway, we agreed that she'd go next spring.

Your mention of 'corn on the cob' (in butter) made my mouth water. The Cardiz grew it in Switzerland and it's so delicious and messy! Good night and God bless us both, all my love, Marie-Thérèse

---

132 Brian was very fond of puns. MT was managing Larham's clothing factory in Dun Laoghaire.

133 Medical Missionaries of Mercy, Drogheda. Mary Martin, its founder, was a close friend of Marie Dillon and godmother to MT. Mary Martin became friends with Marie and Theo Dillon at Leysin Sanatorium, when she came out to nurse her brother who was suffering from TB.

P.S. LOOK OUT FOR SNAKES

Chapter 2

SEPTEMBER 1954

We knew within two weeks that we were perfect for each other. We were both very ambitious and shared a similar background in that we both came to Ireland at an early age. It was a very strange courtship; we must have known within six months that we were going to get married. We also knew it was going to be for the long haul.

❧

Marie-Thérèse, talking to Donal O'Donoghue
(RTÉ), 2005

1

Booterstown, Wednesday, 1 September

My Dear Brian,

Well, Mama seems to be back to her cheerful self again and I'm feeling better too. My throat isn't hurting so much and seems to be clearing. Ethel Martin[1] was over this afternoon and they were discussing the possibility of Mama going to Drogheda. If all goes well, Mama is happy to go there in March, which would mean I'd be over in exactly 7 months! Though where I'll get the odd £100–£150 between this and then is quite a question!!! You won't mind if I bring no clothes? That would save some money!!! Anyway the main thing is Mama's cheerful about it all!

We're back working 8.30–6 pm! Just when I had hoped for short-time too! You can't count on anything. Mr Needham[2] is like a man with a constant hangover which doesn't help.

Darling, there are lots of little things I'm curious to know, such as, what sort of clothes do you wear most? Are you putting on weight? Are you developing a better appetite and an American accent? How far does the pocket money go? And is there anything in your flat that you are kicking yourself you've left behind?

No, I am not becoming nunnish! But maybe retiring, which in moderation always attracted you in women, and to help me attract you even more, don't forget a copy of the 'Vogue' next time you're in town. I'd love it. That is if you don't consider it outrageously expensive.

So Darling, I'll end this miserable little letter which is just to say you've all my love and my Heart – Marie-Thérèse.

---

1   Mary Martin's younger sister.
2   Boss of the Larham's clothing factory in Dun Laoghaire.

2

My Dearest,

Yesterday we went to a reception given by President Case, which was very pleasant and then after supper we had our farewell party. This consisted of a dance, buffet supper and a short concert – everything went off very well, but I left rather soon and spent a couple of hours talking to one of the Bard students, who is interested in theatre (they have a drama department here).

This morning we had a 'commencements exercise' (the American term for presentation of degrees), at which we were each presented with a certificate stating that we had fulfilled the orientation programme. Almost immediately afterwards the exodus started and continued throughout the day. By lunchtime we were reduced to about 25–30 students and tonight there are only 14 or so left.

In the afternoon I had some final things to tidy up and your two letters (both arrived this morning) to reread. Later I went for a quick swim and then a small group of us went round to the Carriers for our final poetry reading: today we were reading the work of a man called Stevens,[3] who is vice-president of some insurance company or other, but is also a really fine poet. After supper I drove to Annandale with Alice and Mike for an hour while they consumed steak: on another Friday this might have been a real temptation! Fortunately I was already stuffed up with corn. I went round to the Frauenfelders for a couple of hours (incidentally they both admired the photo of us and thought you looked lovely – I'm rather inclined to that opinion myself – pause while you throw something at me). Then we all foregathered in Alice's apartment for a long talk and gossip.

---

3   Wallace Stevens (1879–1955), American modernist poet.

So now, my darling, it is 2 am (and so really Saturday) and I haven't answered any of the questions you asked in your letters, but later on today, please God, I'll do that. I was really delighted to hear that your mother is feeling better again and that Joan and the baby are doing well. I hope the Abbey is good, though I rather doubt that it will be, but now I find I'm almost asleep, my dearest, and so sending you all my love and with a little prayer for us, I think I'll turn in for the night. Sleep well, my lovely and beloved pet, and keep yourself well and lovely for your ever loving, Brian.

 3

[MARIE-THÉRÈSE TO BRIAN]
Friday morning, 3 September

Your very welcome letters arrived this morning. I was beginning to feel neglected and a little lost as Mama has been feeling sick all week, which is so upsetting. And then there has been no post since Monday, which made me feel worse, but I'm a new girl now after your letters and as cheery as a trout!

Yes, I would love to read 'The Cruel Sea' – this weekend I'm buying the second book in the series 'Don Camillo'[4] – having re-read the first book during the week.

Myles rang me for a chat last night – he had just recorded a discussion (for Radio Éireann) on 'population' and said it was most amusing as one of the people kept referring to the Bishop of Cork[5]

---

4   Don Camillo and Peppone are the fictional protagonists of a series of works by Italian writer and journalist Giovannino Guareschi, set in what Guareschi refers to as the 'small world' of rural Italy after the Second World War. Don Camillo is a parish priest and the character is said to have been inspired by a Roman Catholic priest, Don Camillo Valota (1912–1998), a partisan who was imprisoned at the concentration camps of Dachau and Mauthausen.

5   The Bishop of Cork, Cornelius ('Con') Lucey, was a notorious figure in the 1950s. He delivered his views on a wide variety of topics, without any basis. James Dillon (Myles's brother) clashed with Lucey on a number of occasions.

as his authority (much to the rage of the director of broadcasting, who was making angry gestures behind a pane of glass!).[6]

Did the hurricane come anywhere near you? It seemed to have swept the American coast from Boston to N.Y. I think it was responsible for the delay in receiving your letters.

Let me know if you want to see those friends of Louie Bennett's[7] in Boston, if you send your address in Cambridge, I'll pass it on to her but do say if you'd rather not, as they might be terrible bores.

So if you pick up any good books, cheap, I'd love to read them after you. Especially Dorothy Parker books, I love their delicious American-New-Yorker-style humour!

  4

[MARIE-THÉRÈSE TO BRIAN]
Saturday, 4 September

My letters seem to be arriving as sporadically as do yours! Your letter of Wednesday arrived last night (making yesterday's haul 3 in all!) enclosing your photo which I'm delighted to have, thank you very much dearest. I'm delighted that you are going to George's and hope that you get all the sun you can stand and plenty of rest!

Mama had a very bad night again. Last night Sheila, Con and I went to a dreadful picture 'Trouble in the Glen' (not my choice) in the Savoy and when I came home she was quite well but, while I was in my bath, she rang and she could only breathe with great difficulty when I got to her room. I got to bed at 12.30 and at 4.00 her heavy breathing woke me and she was having another attack.

Aunt Agnes and I were to have gone to the Abbey next Monday,

---

6   In the Report of the Commission on Emigration and other Population Problems, published in 1954, Lucey delivered his view, in criticism of the policies of Sean Lemass, 'that the neglect of agriculture for industry in recent decades is not only socially and morally indefensible, but demographically unjustifiable as well' . The director is furious that Lucey is being used as a legitimate source.

7   Irish suffragette – Mark DeWolf Howe, Professor of Law at Harvard was married to her niece.

but I'm writing her a note now to say we'll put if off because I haven't the heart to go out much these evenings. I rang the doctor and he says Mama's condition will not improve and she will go on having these attacks from now on, so I'd better make life as pleasant as possible for her. I think, but I may be wrong, that she is worse the evenings I'm out!

A very funny thing happened at lunch today (wish you'd been here to enjoy it too!). Betty[8] and I were eating in the kitchen when I heard a gentle rustling under the sink ('mice', I think), so creeping to the sink I look under and find … a pigeon – meditatively looking at the saucepans and cooing to itself! So remembering that the boys in no.4 had a pet one, I called over the wall and yes they'd lost theirs and came to collect it then and there! I hope they don't start keeping white mice or hedgehogs if that's where they end up!

Well, I'm settling down to read the S.E.P.[9] and also 'Don Camillo and the Prodigal Son' – which I treated myself to today.

If you get a moment write Mama a long letter (I'll see it after her), it will give her so much pleasure! For the present all my thoughts are with you, and I'm enjoying your 'American Holiday' in your company so don't forget it, your Marie-Thérèse

P.S. will notify you if I'm putting any money in the bank but as I've only £14 saved towards my fare (which is about £120 to £450) I'll not do it yet.

 5

[BRIAN TO MARIE-THÉRÈSE]
Rhinebeck (22 South St), Sat – Sun, 4, 5 September

Mike and Alice drove me here at about 10 pm and stayed with us till about midnight listening to records. As a result of two late nights, I was glad to have a sleep-in and went to 11.30 Mass. We had a pancake lunch at about 1 o'clock and sat in the sun (not very

8   The maid.
9   *Sunday Evening Post.*

clear sky but quite warm), reading the Times and I started a book on the 'Age of Jackson'[10] by a Harvard man. We ate a late, but very fine supper, and then sat by the pond for an hour chatting.

Now, dearest, to answer some of your questions: about hitch-hiking – I knew you might be worried, but I told you because I want to tell you everything I do. Actually, it's quite safe because in this state, even on the great Parkways, the speed limit is 50 mph. Re money, so far it's been working out well, but I can't really tell you until I've spent at least a month in Harvard because up to now I've had relatively few direct expenses. The room I have is for boys only, but don't worry I shall make arrangements for us, darling. I think I should be able to live within my $170[11] a month without pinching!

While at Bard I've been wearing mostly either shorts or my old gab pants and your check shirt or a T-shirt. On Sundays, and for more formal visits, I've used my grey suit. Occasionally I wear my tweed jacket and sometimes in the evening I put on a pullover, but most of the time a shirt is enough. I seldom wear ties. At Harvard, I expect shorts will be out (usually are in cities), but jackets and ties will scarcely be de rigueur. About your clothes, pet, you need very few in the warm weather and a couple of washable dresses are the most important part of a girl's wardrobe (sometimes you might need to change twice).

So now, pet, after all that comment, there's very little space for me to ask how your mother is, and how you are keeping. I know how you feel about leaving your mother, but I hope the next seven months fly away very quickly. I do wish you wouldn't call your letters 'miserable', when they have so much of yourself in them, my darling, and, when reading between the lines, it's obvious that you are putting on a brave face and I'm so proud of you. Lest you should be afraid that I would change even a little bit, I am happy

....

10   *The Age of Jackson* (1946) by Arthur M. Schlesinger Jr is a Pulitzer Prize-winning interpretation of the era of Jacksonian democracy.

11   Provided by his scholarship.

to report that I am not developing even a trace of an American accent of any kind – Brooklyn, New England, Texan or Southern. You see, my pet, I'm staying really the same as ever, only I am trying to be a better person for you.

[MARIE-THÉRÈSE TO BRIAN]
Monday, 6 September

Just after I put down your letter, who should appear but Father Mathew![12] We chuckled over him being described as 'a slim, small man'.[13] He said that Christopher Preston is going to Glenstal as French and History master. I said that you didn't think he was very good. Fr. M. said that he didn't expect he was but as long as he could control the boys he (Fr. M.) would be happy!

Mama is a little better these last two days, but I'm exhausted from watching her and not leaving her alone, even when she is dozing! I'm looking forward to Aunt Agnes's visit tonight.

[BRIAN TO MARIE-THÉRÈSE]
Rhinebeck, Monday, 6 September

Dearest,

Today was not such a lazy day. It was beautifully warm and we started and finished a project, which consisted of laying down a small stone path towards the pond. In the middle of proceedings we took time off to have a swim. After that I carried on reading 'The Age of Jackson'; in many ways a typically American work. Quotations, drawn from many sources, spatter the pages and give a certain structure of impressions from contemporary viewpoints, but, while this adds colour and humour, it tends to weaken the

12   Fr Mathew – Brian Dillon – then headmaster of Glenstal school.

13   Fr Mathew was far from slim.

analysis of the historical process. That's a rather typical professional outburst I'm afraid, darling, but you are well used to them.

This evening after supper we went to the local (604)[14] to see a 'bang-bang'; Spencer Tracy in 'Broken Lance' in cinemascope. In fact, the screen was about half the width of the Savoy's cinemascope. The photography was excellent, but the film was rather typically Western.

Being Labour Day, there appears to be some kind of fun and games going on in Kingston across the river. Anyway, there are fireworks and general bangs coming from over that direction.

Rhinebeck is a tiny place; founded in 1688, many of the houses date back to 1710 or so, and the 'Beckman Arms' claims to be the oldest hotel in the U.S. One of the churches intrigues me; it has tall windows but the shutters are in sections, so that by opening or closing just some shutters, they can almost change the shape of the building. The Catholic Church is tiny, and 11.30 Mass yesterday was packed.

By the way, dear, did I tell you I sent off 'Vogues' and 'Readers Digest'? I suppose they'll take a fortnight or so. How's your mother now, dearest, and how are you finding the long Sundays that we always found so short and fleeting? Time lies heavy here too, but I think of you and look forward to the spring and dream of the future and remember the past. And always I send you all my love and prayers. Brian.

 [MARIE-THÉRÈSE TO BRIAN]
Monday, 6 September

There's no doubt but you are a very clever darling! At work today, I got your consoling letter, and when I got home Mama was crowing with delight over hers, and the fact that none came for me on the same post added greatly to her pleasure, so I said nothing about mine!

14   American Federation of Teachers, Local 604.

And 'my' letter said all the things I feel. I'm not able to put feelings on paper, pictures yes, but not feelings – and rereading a letter (to see will you ever understand it!) I often say 'how cold this all sounds, will I tear it up and start again?' and then I decide you'd rather have it the way it comes, bristly rather than a 'polished edition'. Yes, I do worry a little, and then I try to realise that it's all for the best. You and I are working for the same 'end', and that in itself is such a wonderful feeling, it can make time fly and bridge any distances.

Aunt Agnes came out this evening and we had a very pleasant walk around the estate and gossiped till near eleven. She is wonderful company and looks very well and cheerful. She'd just come from Little Mary Street, where she met Neil[15] and Frank D.[16] (who is staying there), and Neil is off to Harwell (England) in 3 weeks' time! He's delighted, of course. He told her he'd ring me sometime, so I'll get his English address (in case you are writing to him within the next six months!).

 9

[BRIAN TO MARIE-THÉRÈSE]
Rhinebeck, Tuesday, 7 September

My Own Dearest,

At about 6 o'clock this morning, I was awakened by the most tremendous thunder and lightning. The storm, of noise and light, lasted about 15 minutes, and then rumbled off into the distance and only then did the rain start, a short, sharp and heavy shower. This was my first experience of summer storms and it really was rather frightening – this afternoon, between 4.00 - 5.30, we had more of it. At present one headline in the news is about 'Edna' – a hurricane about 300 miles out in the North Atlantic. They christen hurricanes every year starting with an 'A' name. So this is the 5th.

15 Neil Porter, Physics Department, UCD.
16 Frank D'Arcy, a college friend, later settled in Derry, where he had a lifelong involvement in adult education

Today we set out to finish off the path, but there wasn't very much left to do, so George showed me some of his book reviews – he does Roosevelt books for one of the historical journals. I must say I was very impressed!

 10

[BRIAN TO MARIE-THÉRÈSE]
N.Y., Wednesday, 8 September

Arrived here today at about 12.30 and checked in at International House. It is really very pleasant and worth the extra 50 cents a night. I did find the Y (Sloane House) so depressing. International has the advantage of having about eight of the Bard contingent staying here at present, but has also a double disadvantage, in being just in front of Harlem and being at 125th Street (it's really on Riverside Drive and quite open), and so rather far from the centre of N.Y. However a subway express takes one to Times Square for the usual 15 cents. The lounges here are pleasant and the laundry facilities really wonderful – use of a washer-rinser-dryer all for 25 cents.

This afternoon I walked down Broadway from 125th to Times Square (which is between 42 and 43). En route I took the opportunity to have a haircut, a mere 90 cents! This evening Marion Dixon (the English woman at Bard with me) and I took a walk around. She is about 34 and is connected to the Education Department of Sheffield University and various training colleges. So it's quite politic for me to pump her on information for the future.[17] She is going to Chicago.

Tomorrow I'm due to leave Penn station at 5.25 (4.25 railway time i.e. Eastern Standard time), and I'll reach Charlottesville about 9.30, D.V. By the way, George tried yesterday afternoon about the photos, but they are still not ready.

Do you know I haven't had a letter since Friday? Actually, this is

....

17   Brian believes that he has no future in Ireland and that he'll have to teach in England.

probably due to Labour Day weekend and my moving from Bard, so I'm looking forward, as I always do, to your next.

 11

Not having John's address, I feel a bit 'at sea' as where to address this – Bard, George's or Harvard? But I may wait and see is there any post from you this evening.

Thank God, Mama is a bit better and is quite cheerful. Fr Brian called again on Monday but I missed him. I heard that Roma Beauregard[18] (my cousin from Washington) is coming home with her baby for 4 months, on the 15th Sept., so if we see anything much of each other, I may ask her to be my maid of honour next spring!

Last night I got to bed quite early and I was just dozing off, when I started remembering – a taxi ride after the conferring dance, a small bottle of brandy that brought me to DramSoc, going to Manchester to meet your family, that day in Skerries ... oh, and that wonderful outing to Powerscourt (remember Tommy[19] arriving hours later having walked 5 miles) – all very pleasant to go to sleep to.

Darling, please answer this in your very next letter. I'm sending off your short jacket, as soon as I get an answer to this question, am I to send any woolies, books, papers or clothes (left in the flat)? Write, if and where am I to send it – remember; it will take 4–6 weeks.

I do hope you've left those filthy slacks to the cleaners somewhere, or will, as soon as you reach Boston, along with your sports jacket and brown pants, so they will be clean when you want them. There is a very good cleaning service (ask John about it), where you can leave your clothes in one city and they will deliver them clean and pressed at your university, wherever it happens to be.

---

18   Daughter of Elizabeth (Nano) Dillon, Theo Dillon's sister.

19   Tommy Owens was one of the DramSoc crowd (see illustrations) and a good friend of Brian's in UCD. He ended up being Sheriff of Monaghan.

P.S. LOOK OUT FOR SNAKES

This is especially for students returning to college.

Did you read about the terrible crash at Shannon airport – a super constellation (Dutch airways) came down on the mudflats in Shannon estuary 2 minutes after take-off and wasn't discovered till 2½ hours later![20] The inquiry will be very interesting because there are a lot of things to explain. No report of the check point, no making radio contact 5 min after take-off. Junior staff reporting to control tower that the take-off looked backward and being told to mind their own business! I'll send you the paper when it starts.

 12

[BRIAN TO MARIE-THÉRÈSE]
Cismont ,Virginia Thursday, 9 September

My Darling,

As you will see by the postmark of my last, I forgot to mail it in N.Y. I left Penn station at 5.25 and travelled by coach to Charlottesville -- passing through about five states and a very-darkened Washington – and arrived here about 10.40.

On the train I sat beside an American English Major (a student of English), and over dinner on board, I met a young cleric called Murphy! John met me at the station and drove me the odd 8 miles or so to Cismont. Apparently, the house consists of

20 KLM Flight 633 was a passenger flight from Amsterdam to New York City. On 5 September 1954, immediately after take-off from Shannon Airport, the Super Constellation Triton ditched on a mudbank in the River Shannon. Twenty-eight people were killed in the accident. Even though the crash occurred less than one minute after the plane took off, airport authorities remained unaware of the disaster until the mud-caked third pilot (navigator) of the craft, Johan Tieman, stumbled into the airport and reported, 'We've crashed!' That was 2½ hours after the plane fell. Mr Tieman had swum ashore and floundered painfully across the marshes to the airport, whose lights were clearly visible from the scene of the crash. It was not until 7 o'clock in the morning – 4½ hours after the crash – that the first launch reached the survivors, who were huddled on a muddy flat in the river.

John, his wife Betty and mother-in-law Mrs Wagner and a large dark-haired poodle.

The house seems quite spacious (about 5 bedrooms I'd say), and I have a lovely bedroom on the ground floor with a four-poster! Also attached, is my own toilet and bath plus shower. In John's study, upstairs, there is a wonderful set-up for records (about 4 tables) with speakers in the ceiling.

I'm promised breakfast in bed tomorrow, so though it's 2.30 am, I thought I might write this and give it to the maid to post tomorrow morning, with the other (forgotten) letter, for which my really deep apologies, darling.

The journey up was quite pleasant, and the dinner ($1.80) good but, both on the train and in N.Y., the heat was oppressive. Of course, here in Virginia it's normally warmer than in the North; notice I say 'The North' – it's almost another country: these people still think in terms of 'the war between the States', that's the American Civil War.

 13

[BRIAN TO MARIE-THÉRÈSE]
Cismont, Friday, 10 September

Dearest, while I posted your letters in Cismont, I feel that there might be quite a time lag in getting them to you. The village of Cismont, in effect, consists of two gas stations and a post office. Here in Virginia there has been a tremendous drought. John claims it hasn't really rained since they gave a garden party for the county about two years ago, and the grass and trees are looking very yellow and dead.

Betty (John's wife) is very pleasant and, I find, intelligent. Mrs Wagner (her mother) is about 76 and behaves rather like that. The regime of the house is very free, and my breakfast appeared on a tray at 10 o'clock this morning, and, by the time, I had eaten it, bathed, shaved and unpacked properly, it was already noon. I walked into the dining room to find Betty and John at breakfast.

This afternoon was very heavy, cloudy and sultry, due to the imminent arrival of hurricane Edna. John and I drove past the university, which is a fine old red-brick with white colonnades, and had lunch in the country club (very fashionable, very county) on the other side of Charlottesville.

This evening after an excellent dinner (salmon trout), we sat around talking to a neighbour just back from holidays. Then we watched television for a while. The programmes were moronic but the news was, to me, fascinating. It was sponsored by some beer company, which had about four 'plugs' in the 10 minute or so news reading; also after the commentator had spoken about an issue, one was shown a television screening of some of the events described.

The house is very lovely and I'm sure I'll have a very relaxing time here before starting at Harvard, but I'm really geared up to go, and am reading quite a lot of American history in preparation.

 14

[**BRIAN TO MARIE-THÉRÈSE**]
Cismont, Saturday, 12 September

The weather -- despite the threat of hurricane 'Edna' – remains very dry, hot but overcast. Today John drove me over to look at the University,[21] which was designed by Thomas Jefferson. It's all red brick with great white pillars and looks very attractive, but more like a Country Club than a college.

Last night one of the ex-college boys (he was kicked out, not graduated) was over for dinner. I was frankly fascinated. He was stupid, uninformed, almost non-English speaking (in the sense that he controlled barely two hundred words) and very, very

---

21   University of Virginia (UVA) is regarded as one of the most beautiful and prestigious universities in the world. In 1987, UNESCO named the university a World Heritage Site.

Southern. So he talked about 'Negroes' in a paternalistic-patronising- brutal sort of way. He wasn't even a 'gentleman' in the Southern sense; his breeding etc. must be most peculiar.

Cismont, as I have told you, darling, is completely isolated and nobody seems to do very much. Most of my time I spend reading, but we talk so late into the night, that I'm always late in rising. However it is quite pleasant, and I'm really intrigued by my four-poster bed and the general luxurious lifestyle.

I had a note from Stan (Stanislaus Graf von Kalkreuth[22] is the full treatment), to say that he and Grommers have an apartment – 3 rooms, kitchen, bath – at $85 a month, and so I intend to move in with them. The address while I think of it is 146, Upland Road, Cambridge, Mass.

 15

[MARIE-THÉRÈSE TO BRIAN]
Sunday Evening, 12 September

I'm sitting by the radio and fire, Mama and I had tea in her room. I've put what's left of the autumn flowers (after heavy rain) in her room, and I'm half listening to 'Radio Newsreel'. It's been a very empty day without you, but then, please God, it's the end of another week apart, and brings us a week nearer to being together. I've never been so happy to see the days drawing in – come winter, come spring.

I'm delighted that you are getting to Washington D.C. so soon. Unfortunately, 2 of my letters will reach John's after you leave – so I hope Betty will forward them – by now you should have found other letters; that reached George's after you moved to N.Y. and Virginia. You should be receiving 5 per week, if not do let me know!

22　Stan was on the orientation course at Bard with Brian, who later learned that Stan was the nephew of Colonel Claus Schenk Graf Von Stauffenberg, one of the officers who tried to assassinate Hitler.

You were asking Mama about the new girl,[23] and Mama insists I answer. Well, she's very, very good! Stupid but untiring in her wish to please – she seems to be very fond of us both and does everything to make us comfortable – when I started taking my 'Multivites' again, she used to follow me about the house, after meals, complaining that I hadn't taken my pills! But she's very stupid, the other day we got some mint leaves from Switzerland, and Mama decided to have mint tea. Betty had never made it before, so having carefully followed Mama's instructions; she threw out the tea and served Mama the stewed leaves. She won't do it again! She's also got more used to Mama's attacks, and I can go out with some degree of confidence, when Mama's not so well.

 16

[BRIAN TO MARIE-THÉRÈSE]
Cross Meadows, Cismont, Sat, Sun, Mon 11–13 September

I'm wondering in a way, how I possibly fit into this society here (though I'm not at all worried about it). Maybe it would help, if I gave you some sort of impression about the 'social atmosphere' here and the people involved. Albemarle County (in which we are) is said to be the third richest county in the country – not just in this state. Wealth in fact is the obvious dominant note, but it is coupled with a set of social prejudices, which seem quite complex – some about schools, birth, North or South etc. Sometimes something is said, as a joke (presumably!), such as, that the Randolph's resented having Jefferson's daughter in the family: need I say that Thomas Jefferson was one of the great 'revolutionary' patriots – Declaration of Independence, President, Founder of Virginia, University etc.

Much of my difficulty, in understanding all this, lies in my own completely different background, prejudices etc. But there is also

23   The maid.

the extremely loose terminology, which makes comprehension almost impossible. So, 'white trash' and 'the wrong side of the tracks' are phrases having a more or less definite connotation, but here they may be applied to, say; the vice-president of a big bank, someone who didn't go to the right school, practically anyone who doesn't come from money.

Of course, this kind of society is very strongly and traditionally Republican, and this makes political discussion difficult. For there are Conservative Republicans, and many are not just anti-Ike, but anti-all – what they term – left-wing Republicans. The term communist is synonymous with; 'party member', 'Marxist', 'socialist', 'liberal, radical and even 'British'. On the really hot issue, they are strongly pro-McCarthy!

Of course, much of these talks are carried on in a bored, blasé and cynically indifferent way. Yet so much of all this appears as 'typical' Southern rigidity, prejudice, conservatism, ignorance etc., while, in fact, many of the people, round this immediate neighbourhood, are not only non-Virginians, but in fact New Yorkers.

Yet I find Betty and John very kind and thoughtful as hosts, and really enjoyable company (though they are part of all this), and, although, I do enjoy – but only, I think, in a temporary way – the high-living, I don't believe I could reconcile myself to a permanent round of 'brunch', social calls and cocktails, dinner (always served on silver) by candlelight, with all the trimmings. Also, the weather is too changeably hot perhaps, and too much gossip after dinner.

You know, darling, this is where you lose in a letter, in that you can't change the conversation. Really I should never have embarked on this subject, but since I have, I may as well try to carry it through. So, at present, the great local debate centres around the Keswick Country Club, which is, apparently, on the rocks, and in which several people (including the Kellys) own 'lots' of land – just a token couple of acres, I suppose – for which they paid $2,500; a lot! I'd say about £800. They also pay dues etc. and are members of several other clubs, including the Farmington (one of the golf clubs in the South), which is about a ¼ hour by car; the Keswick is about half that distance.

 17

I hope that by now you are 'knee-deep' in my letters, of course, that all depends on whether or not George knows John's address! I imagine that a lot of my post must be chasing you around North America.

Yesterday evening Aunt Agnes and I went to the Abbey (The Caretaker[24]), and, although the acting was first class, I've decided that they have completely lost any sense of theatre or drama, and I wonder why? Anyway, that didn't take away from a very pleasant evening. Aunt Agnes is very well, and showed me your letter (made me feel spoilt because you write me such lovely long letters almost every day!). Poor Mama wasn't so well when I got home, and still isn't so good this morning!

My 'children'[25] are up to mischief again (I'm writing this at work), and every now and again there is a scream or howl of laughter from some part of the building. Those scarves are boring work, so they make their own fun.

 18

I've been scanning the paper for any 'local' news that might interest you, and all I can see is that – Mr Smyllie [sic][26] died, the Prime Minister and President are away on holidays (they must be sure

---

24 Harold Pinter play.
25 The workers in the clothing factory managed by MT.
26 R.M. Smyllie(1894–1954), editor of *The Irish Times*.

of their positions), and the foreign news frightens me every time I look at it! What is the general view held on the International situation on your side of the water?

Of course, I'm terrified of the chance of there being another war, but that's all in God's hands.

Darling, how well do the women dress that you are meeting at present? I've got 5 dresses lined up for next summer, and I'm wondering will that be enough? Do they wear jeans and T-shirts in the morning? If you get a chance to pick an iron up cheap, it will be a good investment. I can foresee a lot of ironing and washing next summer!

P.S. I held this open in case there was a letter, but 'Edna' must have disrupted the post (slightly). Mama was sick again this morning and is very uncomfortable poor pet! Best love, M.T.

 19 ....

[MARIE-THÉRÈSE TO BRIAN]
Thursday, 16 September

Well, yesterday Con and I went to Sheila Coakley's for tea, and afterwards I was fool enough to suggest she take us for a drive (she has her brother's car at present). Sheila's a terrible driver! We went to Bray via Killiney village. In Bray I found a totaliser machine[27] that was paying dividends (obviously broken) so we had a pleasant hour at the amusements. The homeward road was hectic because Sheila had obviously never driven in the dark and couldn't judge distances. We called into a 'ye oldy worldie' place in Stillorgan village for coffee, and then Sheila's car decided it had found a home-from-home and wouldn't leave. Finally, after taking half a gate with it, we got going. Con and Sheila went off to the theatre but I decided to get home early as Mama's so sick this weather. I'm afraid she never seems to get much peace at present – she's a lot weaker and hasn't the stamina to stand up to these attacks.

....
27   Slot machine, commonly known as a one-armed bandit.

P.S. LOOK OUT FOR SNAKES

Sheila and I were reminiscing about the last time we went any-where by car together: Sheila was driving us to Michael's[28] cottage 3 or 4 years ago. We were lost in the Dublin Mountains, passing through a hamlet at top speed. Sheila said to me: 'What's the name of this place? Can you read that notice?' I replied confidently: 'Yes, it's called Bonified'[29] – I've certainly told you that one before.[30]

 20

[MARIE-THÉRÈSE TO BRIAN]
Friday morning, 17 September

I do hope my letters are arriving by now! I write every day except Friday or Saturday – so if you're not getting them, try George's. I think the postal communication between John's and the outer world mustn't be very good.

Do tell: does the long-haired poodle eat his dinner off silver plates too?

Of me there is little news – yesterday evening I spent in Mama's room – she's having a hard time. This evening I'm hoping to see the Model Homes exhibition and to visit Uncle Myles – he's in hospital having had a hernia operation (Bessie[31] rang to tell me and to ask after you.).

Yes, I'm looking forward to you starting at Harvard. When will that be? Somehow your college news is always more interesting than 'Highlife Down-South' (which seems to bear a resemblance

---

28   Michael Gorman, a lifelong friend of Brian and MT from UCD.

29   Bona fide houses utilised a legal loophole – a hangover from the days of coach travel – that allowed a genuine traveller three miles from his place of residence to partake of alcohol outside normal hours. If you lived in Dublin city, the limit extended to five miles from your habitual residence. Famous Dublin bona fides included Lamb Doyle's in the foothills of the Dublin Mountains, Walsh's Sandyford House – then known as the Widow Flavin's – and the Dropping Well in Dartry.

30   MT was hinting, 'Let's stop for a drink!'

31   Myles's wife, Elizabeth (Bessie) Mary La Touche. Bessie was like a grandmother to MT's children.

to the French court of Louis XIV!). No wonder they back up McCarthy – they know that should the Commies come they would be the first to suffer.

 21

It now seems possible that we go to Washington D.C. tomorrow, but nothing is really definite. Today we went over to Keswick for lunch and sat around most of the afternoon. There was a rain shower for about 5 minutes, but I'm afraid much more will be needed to revive the grass.

I forgot to tell you that on 'Person-to-Person' (TV show) last night we saw Mrs Perle Mesta:[32] she is the original 'host-ess with the most-ess' of 'Call me Madam'. I had thought that Clare Boothe Luce[33] (present US ambassador to Italy) was the archetype of Ethel Merman, but apparently it is based on Mrs Mesta's carry-on as US representative in Luxembourg. Incidentally, I did hear a story of Clare Luce having a private interview with the Pope: it lasted about half-an-hour and as the Papal Chamberlain came in to announce the end of the interview the Pope was heard to say 'But, Mrs Luce, I am a Catholic.'

About this eating and menu thing darling – my favourite dish remains the famous 'M.T. Dillon week-end mixed grill', and I have no great yen for American dishes. Anyway Cismont is by no means typical of the US. The television set (including aerial) cost about $750 (say £250), and, as far as I can see, Betty and John have invested capital.

32 Perle Reid Mesta (née Skirvin) was an American socialite, political hostess and US ambassador to Luxembourg (1949–53). She was known for her lavish parties for Washington DC society – attendees included artists, entertainers and political figures. She was the inspiration for Irving Berlin's musical *Call me Madam*.

33 Ann Clare Boothe Luce was an American writer, politician, US ambassador and public figure. She was the first American woman appointed to a major ambassadorial post abroad.

P.S. LOOK OUT FOR SNAKES

Your letter of Thursday morning (impossible as it may seem) arrived this morning, and I was delighted to hear that Sheila Coakley was still around (you do tell everyone I was asking for them, don't you dear?), and I hadn't heard the wonderful 'bona fide' story. I'm sorry I'm not with you, dearest, especially now, when your mother isn't well, but please God she will recover shortly.

 22 [MARIE-THÉRÈSE TO BRIAN]
Saturday Night, 18 September

Bill Kingston rang me at 5 o'clock and asked me to a small party he was giving for his Boss (Lloyd's – the market research people) tonight. There I met Dr Geary, who congratulated me on my engagement! Then I was speaking to Bill's Boss's son, who is a History student at Princeton University – that was very pleasant … because I could quote (and I'm sure misquote) you all night. He seemed a simple youth, his main interest was drink, and as one would expect, he plans to make a 'go' at politics. Oh! I also met some girl who said that she read of your scholarship to America in some paper – was it in the papers? I didn't remember it!

Roger McHugh[34] was asking news of you and, as I said before, it was every bit as pleasant as if a room full of people were saying: 'Where's Brian? We miss him – but hope he's enjoying it all very much.'

Sunday (same letter)

Mama had a slight breathless attack last night while I was out, but Mrs Ward (the neighbour who is a trained nurse) came in and gave her an injection so she's not too bad today.

34 Roger McHugh (1908–87), academic, author, playwright and politician. He received a BA (UCD) in English and History (1928), an MA (UCD) in English and in 1947 was awarded a PhD. He lectured in the history department at UCD (1930–31), but his main career was in the English department (1934–78). He was the first Professor of Anglo-Irish literature and Drama in UCD. He had a great interest in Irish theatre and wrote four plays; his best known, *Rossa*, won awards.

Re: 'The Age of Jackson' I was discussing this book with the American youth, and he said it was written by a superior of Roosevelt's to show how alike their two policies were (or something like that), and he argued with you that as a historic study it was a failure ... Roger told me to tell you to look up John Kelleher[35] (I think that's his name) some Prof. at Harvard.

P.S. 'Edna' has made Headlines here too. 'She' seems to have caused havoc in America. I do hope 'she' didn't cross your path! Love M.T.

 23

My Dearest, today was a real scorcher – well into the 90s – and I thought I would pass out at Mass this morning in Charlottesville: Mrs Pine (a neighbour) drove me over to 12 o'clock Mass and on the way back I discovered she was – guess what? – a Sacred Heart girl![36] (Manhattan Ville High, I think she said).

The afternoon was so hot we simply had to stay in. Besides there wasn't a breath of air (actually over dinner we had a fairly violent thunderstorm for about half an hour), so most of today was spent watching TV. The reception was very good and the standard of programmes much higher than anything I've seen so far. We saw a number of those parlour game shows ('The Name is the Same' and 'What's my line?')

Now about travelling: I leave tomorrow, D.V., probably by the 3.00 train and I shall take an overnight break at either Washington

---

35 John Kelleher (1919 – 2004) was [emeritus] Professor of Irish Studies in the Department of Celtic Languages and Literature, first came to Harvard in 1940. Although he spoke with a stammer, Kelleher was able to lecture and read aloud without impediment, and his deep, finely modulated voice could bring out meanings in a poem through nuance alone.

36 MT attended the Sacred Heart School, Leeson Street, Dublin.

D.C. or N.Y. (depending on the weather etc). One way or the other, I expect to reach Cambridge not later than Wednesday morning. I'll post this letter on the way, as it will almost certainly be faster than posting it here.

 24 [MARIE-THÉRÈSE TO BRIAN]
Sunday Night, 19 September

The week-end has been very lazy, I made my 'little something' (and very pretty it is too!) but that's all, the rest of the time I just sat in Mama's room and read my SEP. Oh! I do love my nylons – getting them with a letter, mentioning Myles, reminds me how I got my first pair of nylons ever: Myles sent them, from the States and wrote me a letter on the price tag (about one inch square!), seeing his handwriting you can understand. The pair you sent me, are a perfect fit and colour – made by Gordon Regal was printed on them, but no size. I suppose the assistant could help you, if I want more.

At present Mama is considering going into hospital for Xmas – we agree that Xmas at home could be ghastly for both of us, and should she get very sick over the festive season, we'd be badly stuck – Betty would have to go home for some time off and that would tie me to the house. Looking after Mama is a full time job, and she's been pressing to go to hospital for some time now, so by the time Xmas comes I feel she'll be just as glad of the change. I'll go and stay with friends – and we'll all come back to the house after the New Year – that is the plan anyway. The Poor Darling is so much weaker than when you left, and I think sometimes would love the feeling of security one gets in hospital!

I'm going down to Aunt Agnes's tomorrow night – I know I'll feel a little sad. The last time I was in no. 13 was a few days after your departure – to collect the notes – everything was cold and empty about the place. I hated it!

25

On the move again, dear, I left Charlottesville on a bad train, and it took about 3 hours to cover the 110 miles or so to Washington D.C. I arrived about 9.30 and went straight to the YMCA. This is by far the best 'Y' I've been in so far (but at $3 a night), though not as good as International House I think. It has the great advantage however of being about 4 minutes' walk from the White House. Last night I walked by there – it looked quite well in the lights (floodlighting I think might spoil), and is well set-off by the flanking Treasury and State Dept. buildings.

Well, you were I think right about the Louis XIV atmosphere. Yet I did enjoy myself, and Betty, John, Mrs Wagner and the poodle (no silver for him) were very kind. I almost fell when Betty kissed me goodbye! In front of John though, so it was safe enough. She insisted on our going down to Cismont, if we can make it (and if they are not in Italy).

I'm leaving for Boston on 'The Senator'[37] at 12.00, D.V. I hope to get there 8.30.

 26

My Darling, this is to say how much I loved your letter (of Thurs). I couldn't write back amid the dust and chatter of the factory, but waited to be curled up in front of the electric fire in my room, where it's much easier to focus! As I've often said to people (who tactfully say: 'you must be lost without him' – or: 'six months, how will you stand it?'), as long as your letters are frequent, full of

---

37 The Pennsylvania *Senator* was a regional passenger train that served the heavy commuter market in the Northeast between Washington DC and Boston.

P.S. LOOK OUT FOR SNAKES

life, fairly happy and you are well, I'm extremely well off thank you! The other side of the picture is filled in by a popular song of last year – remember 'Any place I wander … ' every time I hear it there's a very hard lump in my throat. Strangely, I'm not a bit scared of either of us 'going off', but the thought of war, ill health and accidents quite terrify me at times. [38] Thank goodness it's only things that are in God's hands. I suppose it's rather terrible to not (seemingly) trust God, but to trust you – but then I know we want the same things. Having got that off my mind, I'm off to bed – sleep well, my darling, with all my love, Marie-Thérèse.

 27

[BRIAN TO MARIE-THÉRÈSE]
Washington, Wednesday, 22 September

My Poor Pet, you were almost really neglected. I was so tired when I arrived here at 12.10, that I thought that I couldn't lift a pen (actually I missed the earlier train and didn't leave Washington till 3.00). But on arrival I found a letter of yours postmarked 3 Sept., and, as always, I have to respond to your charming writing. The apartment seems good value and pleasant but I won't report on that fully for a couple of days.

Now about Washington D.C: the 'Y', as I told you, was beside the White House (incidentally this morning I saw the Oberkirchen Children's Choir – 'The Happy Wanderer' – mob going in) so I walked up to the Capitol Hill. The building, despite its size, is beautifully proportional and since the roads all around are lined with trees it simply springs at you very impressively. As I was walking by a little squirrel ran to within six feet of me; he played around for a while and then calmly crossed over the path right in

---

38 MT constantly worried about health and war. Explained by the following events in her life; her father (who had been a TB patient) died suddenly when she was seventeen. She had witnessed at close hand refugees from war-torn Europe and her mother was very sick when she was writing these letters.

front of me. Then the rains came and lasted for some time, however I did glance at the House of Congress and walked past the very impressive Supreme Court and so over to the huge Union Station.

From what I saw of it, I liked Washington D. C. It was clean, dignified (with its buildings and wide roads), and had a settled, little-rushed air about it – despite the hundreds of taxi cabs. Also I saw for the first time these big buildings which are used for car-parking. Going back to the station I passed through a 'China Town' full of restaurants, chow houses, laundries and Chinese characters (letters rather than people). Then I walked into a rather shabby Negro area that was discouraging. Yet my general impression was more favourable than that which I got in passing through either Boston or N.Y.

 28

After a good night's rest I went down to do some shopping and bought butter, milk, bread, 'spam', spaghetti etc. We have our own ice-box (lent us!). After lunch I went down to Keppler's office, and got all the notes (3 parcels), book and the Theatre Magazine (for which much thanks).

This business of choosing courses is quite a headache but I'm working on it.

I came back for tea, and in came Anna Martellous and Jussila (Finn from Bard). So we went over to Boston and walked around there for a while, and I came back about 9.30, since then I've been doing some reading. While talking about going to Boston I'm sure you're wondering (or will ask) about transport. So as always, pet, I do my best to anticipate, though I seldom succeed. Well from here to any part of Cambridge by street car costs 13 cents.

Actually dear I went to see Langer[39] today and found him very pleasant and friendly, but I don't really think I shall get into his seminars (I'd prefer you not to say that to Dudley as Desmond mightn't like it). The main reason is that my own impression is that they are too advanced (mainly for students working on PhDs), and there is this language problem. However, I might change at Christmas. As I told you, I am thinking of concentrating on American history, and hope to meet various members of the Dept. on Saturday morning when they will be advising students.

Also today I phoned John Kelleher (Roger's[40] friend), since he wasn't in his office in the really lovely Lowell building. He sounded non-committal, but suggested I see him at his seminar on Irish history on Tuesday.

Today, for the first time, I ventured inside the huge Widener Library.[41] It's very big, impressive and airy, in fact an excellent library, and I expect to be allowed access to the stacks (which will save me from having to wait for porters or boys to bring up the books).

I'm surprised that you enjoyed 'Hobson's Choice' (set in Salford – not Manchester – I'm almost sure Neil told me); must go and see it.

Well, my dear, I'm afraid this isn't a very newsy letter, and has none of your touch (the sketch of the new maid could almost be Thurber). By the way, I would love to have my coat, and could you send me the External Affairs Booklets (about 2/- each) on 'Theatre in Ireland' (MacLiammoir), 'Poetry' (Austin Clark), and can you think of something I could send to Betty[42]? Sleep well, my own, and good night all my love, Brian.

PS Maybe some linen table mats?

....

39 William Leonard Langer, history department Harvard.

40 Roger McHugh – English Department, UCD

41 The Harry Elkins Widener Memorial Library houses 3.5 million books. It is the main library in Harvard and was constructed by Widener's mother after his death in the *Titanic* in 1912.

42 John Kelly's wife

When I got back I found your letter Tues/Wed waiting for me: I quite agree with you, and worry even less in so far as – a) I know I take care of myself and trust you to do the same – b) traffic accidents are rare in Cambridge (in the paper the other day it was announced Cambridge's 300th day without fatal auto accidents), but I take no chances with all the cars on the road – c) I really don't believe we'll have a war, at least for another couple of years: U.S. and Russia (and perhaps China) will make the decision, and despite the reactionaries over here, it would be difficult enough to get U.S. back into a major struggle. In Russia, they are probably worried about the comparative war potential of East and West. And moreover, all 3 powers are worried about the use of atomic and fusion bombs.

Today I went to see Prof. Owen, the chairman of the History Dept. He was much younger than I expected and really quite charming. I am not to take a degree here, and will not be too tied down (most people have 14 hours and upwards of lectures per week, even in the Graduate School). Tomorrow I hope to discuss research projects with various people, and also sign on for German A (elementary, emphasis on reading; which will be 5 hours a week).

I can see why people fall in love with Harvard: it is a lovely place. Crowded together are the main college buildings, and then stretching out in all directions (and embracing several styles, though there is general consistency of style in given areas) are various other halls, houses, museums and so on. The new houses over towards the river are really magnificent. Here, too, squirrels are found running all over the place. Really the whole place is charming.

By the time I register on Monday, I hope to be finished with the bureaucratic machine, and should be able to get down to something like real work before the weekend. Meantime I am working

P.S. LOOK OUT FOR SNAKES

on American style (reading), and also reading a volume of Halévy's 'History of England' in French for practice.

Some things occasionally cross my mind that we might start thinking about. The most important is the question of what I am going to do when we get home, and, at this stage, it seems to me more than likely that teaching in England is the only real solution. However, God knows, anything may happen. Another possible alternative is that I may be offered another year here, but it seems that in view of your mother's condition this would be out of the question.

 30

[**MARIE-THÉRÈSE TO BRIAN**]
Friday, 24 September

I feel anything but neglected, as 4 of your letters arrived this morning – yours of Sat. Sun and Tues and Wed – Boston post arrives much quicker than any other, I've already noticed.

Re Myles, he's well and at home. He's planning to go to Vienna on the 8th October, so do write, as he rang last night enquiring news of you. He knows already about your experiences so far, but is very interested, and I told him about Gray's memo re him! He was very pleased! Mama loves news of you, and I sometimes give her one of your letters to read.

I took the liberty to ring Dudley,[43] who said they'd not yet heard from you and I said that you were only getting to Harvard this week. He said you could submit the thesis anytime, if you've applied formally through the History Dept. for an extension.

Mary Murphy rang and was very interested in all your news. I'm to go over next week for supper to meet Anne McCabe (and fiancé) we'll see how I feel, I've taken the step and arranged to be vaccinated[44] sometime next week. Dr Roche comes to the house so regularly

---

43   Dudley Edwards, Modern Irish History Department, UCD.
44   The smallpox vaccination was a requirement for entering the US.

that it would be silly to get anyone else and work is so easy at present. I want the scar to be as small as possible by spring!

Now, that you are in the flat, eat well, plenty of eggs and try your hand at making omelettes and make-up powdered soups (veg and oxtail) put in an egg just before removing from the fire and eat with buttered rolls - very nourishing!! I suppose meat is a terrible price.

 31

[BRIAN TO MARIE-THÉRÈSE]
Cambridge, Saturday, 25 September

Now for some good news, it seems that I am not going to be tied down to any courses at all, this is obviously a real History Department; drawing up deliberate blinds to fool the administration. This morning about 20 members of the Dept. sat around at various desks waiting to be consulted, so I trotted round to three or four for a chat (I had already signed on for elementary German A). The 17–18th centuries English History man, Dr Perkins, was very pleasant (as indeed they all were) and said he might be able to find space for me in Lowell House. But I would have to take it for the full semester and couldn't continue there after Easter. Anyway we shall see.

I am now trying to find a good topic for a thesis; the latest possibility that crossed my mind was something on Anglo-American relations in the Roosevelt-Chamberlain era – say post-abdication to the war. However, I am also thinking in terms of political theory (taking Locke as a central figure), and hope to talk to Perry Miller[45] about that.

The degree of informality in clothing is fairly slight here and in fact ties are quite useful since it gets quite cold about 6.30–7.00 in

45 Perry Gilbert Eddy Miller (1905–63) was an American historian. He specialised in early American history and took an active role in the revisionist view of the colonial Puritan theocracy that was cultivated at Harvard.

the evening. Autumn is well in now and the ever-present squirrels are busy laying their store.

 32

My Dearest,

The Boston to Dublin postal service is very good! I hope the Dublin to Boston is as good, if so you should receive: the 2 books, coat, Saturday Irish Times and present for Betty very soon. The present is very small but good. The assistant recommended Damask Table Linen as being unobtainable and very popular in America so I'm sending ½ dozen Damask table napkins – I hope you think they are suitable. I'm sending the Irish Times because I think the article about 45 Mary Street will amuse you. If you think of anything else let me know, you know how I adore shopping.

This morning I had coffee with Mary Hamilton, she is preparing a 'funny' programme (called: 'We're just Plain People') for Radio Éireann. Apparently she used to write sketches for the 'Players' (TCD), and she submitted a ½ hour radio programme (sketch, songs parodies etc) to R.E. and they offered her 120 pound for 6 programmes – so herself and a friend are working nightly – deadline being Xmas!

I'll ring Miss Bennett and give her your address for those friends. Writing to Myles is a very good idea, and can you remember McHugh's[46] friend's (English lecturer I think he was!) name. I'm sorry you can't do a degree there, but we didn't have much hope! Anyway I bet Desmond would rather get some credit by you doing it under him.

P.S. When choosing a course don't forget the college grant (£100 isn't to be sneezed at) I'd much rather we had it than UCD! Love M.T.

---

46   Roger McHugh, English Department, UCD and his friend was John Kelleher, Irish Studies, Harvard.

33

Well, today was really very pleasant. I went to 11 Mass in Cambridge and bought the Sunday New York Times (it costs 25 cents but has over 300 pages), and went over to the Graduate Centre – a very modern building which makes Store St. look really old-fashioned. They have a lovely lounge and waiting room plus grand piano, and I think I'll start taking lunch there; it's 85 cents but is said to be very good and you can get as much as you want.

While there I met Fels (German) and Scimeni (Italian) from Bard. After a while they both played the piano, but we were looking for a record player to try out some of Eberhard's new records. So we decided to go across to the International Students Centre. This is a small but friendly house run by G.S.A.,[47] and we stayed there talking to people from all over the world (including Americans) and had supper there. In the evening there was a talk on the American Mind and Foreign Affairs by a man from the 'Christian Science Monitor' (quite a big paper), so we went along and then we walked home.

Tomorrow I'm due to register at Weld – did you ever get the map of Cambridge I enclosed with some of the Magazines? Without it you will never understand what I'm talking about half the time – for 300 courses i.e. Reading and Research. The system here is quite elaborate: you must get your instructor to sign your study card and so on. However, I am really on a 'fix' as Professor Owen said simply to bring the cards to him and he'll sign them or arrange to have them signed.

You know, dear, the more I think about it, the better this Chamberlain/Roosevelt appears. Even if I can't get State Department stuff (they've only published up to 1935 or so), I

---

47 General Services Administration.

could make use of papers at Hyde Park, and by staying with George a few weeks on and off I would certainly save money. Anyway I want to read around it a bit more before broaching the subject with Langer.

34 [MARIE-THÉRÈSE TO BRIAN]
Monday night , 27 September

At the cost of repeating myself: you are the cleverest, most thoughtful Darling possible – the 2 bridal Mags arrived tonight and I'm devouring them! Of course my dress will be much nicer than any of them, but certainly they have good ideas, I must admit!

Tuesday Morning

As I hoped 2 letters arrived this morning with all the photos – I left Mama enjoying them (the photos). Poor Mama is not at all well – she called me again during the night and I was an hour helping her to sit up and breathe. Luckily I'm getting quite used to getting up during the night now, and it takes very little out of me (good practice anyway!)

As for plans for the future, Mama told me the other day, that after their Honeymoon she and Papa had exactly 50 pounds in the world, and (no home) so at least we will be a little better off than they were!

35 [BRIAN TO MARIE-THÉRÈSE]
Cambridge, Wed morning, 29 September

Really I have relatively little news except that I did go to see John Kelleher[48] (Roger's friend) yesterday. He has an office in Lowell

---

48   John Kelleher, Professor of Irish Studies at Harvard.

and apparently Dan Binchy[49] was also in Lowell when he was over. Actually Kelleher was giving a Seminar in medieval Irish history – he also lectures in Yeats, Casey and Synge. However I don't intend to do a course with him, but this shouldn't affect my £100 from College, as technically I shall claim to be doing (some) research in Irish history on the 1689 Parliament. After quite a long chat, Kelleher and I had cup of coffee. His stammer does make conversation a little difficult, but (as Gerard Murphy[50] said) he mimics easily without impediment.

If I do take up the Chamberlain subject, it struck me that it could be very convenient if I left the Hyde Park material to the end. Then we could perhaps stay with George for a month or so, and you could see Hudson and the Bard community. Also from there we could go to N.Y. for a couple of weekends. This would perhaps simplify the housing position. But it would give rise to some difficulties: a) I might need to get on to this material sooner b) the village of Rhinebeck is very isolated c) I would be expected to stay on here for some of Easter to June period (on second thoughts, I don't believe this is true). This type of programme would however mean that we would be making a personal temporary home here. We have time to think about this, but do let me know how you feel on this subject.

Did I tell you that I phoned the Irish consulate? And the under-consul asked me to drop in when around Boston! Actually I wanted more dope on the emigration report, but I hope to get a copy through them out of External Affairs.

---

49   Daniel (Dan) Anthony Binchy (1899–1989) was a scholar of Irish linguistics and early Irish law. He was awarded a senior fellowship at the University of Oxford, where he and Myles Dillon became two resident Irish Celticists. He took up a visiting professorship at Harvard University in 1954. He was the uncle of the author Maeve Binchy and the academic William Binchy. When Theo was alive and living in Killiney, Dan, Michael Teirney, John Lavery and others would gather to discuss philosophy every second Saturday and Marie would serve them tea and homemade cakes.

50   Irish scholar and close friend of Theo Dillon.

P.S. LOOK OUT FOR SNAKES

How are things with you, dearest? We are having something of an Indian summer though, thank God, there's also a cool breeze. News here, in general, is concentrated on the murder of a young baby sitter in Massachusetts over the weekend; the McCarthy report seems to be leading to a counter-attack by McCarthy Republicans on Watkins: the election campaigns are getting under way and Vice president Nixon is speaking in New England – however so far indications are the House will be Democratic and possibly also the Senate. Of course, anything may happen to upset the political scene: Ike is staying very quiet, and it is noteworthy that one Democrat candidate is plugging an 'I-don't-like-Ike' line without losing support (most Democrats attack administration but not Ike himself).

Chapter 3

OCTOBER 1954

The facilities at Harvard were extraordinary. It had the biggest library in the US after the Library of Congress, so books were widely available and much more so than they were in Ireland at that time. I found the year I spent there very exciting, but I wasn't over-awed because my good UCD education enabled me to hold my own.

Brian Farrell

1

Cambridge, Friday morning, 1 October

Last night I had my first introduction to Irish society in Boston, when I went to a farewell meeting and concert for Lady Valerie Goulding,[1] run by the Boston Friends of the Dublin Remedial Clinic (for polio children). Also over was a Dr James Hanlon,[2] who was an ear-nose-throat specialist, before he contracted a disease from a patient, becoming blind and stone-deaf: he has taken up physiotherapy. After the meeting I met an elderly man called James Barry[3] (need I say from County Cork), who seemed to know everyone there and introduced me all round.

Although these people are very 'Irish', they were coo-ing at me just over and asked for my address and gave me theirs and so on. Incidentally they are obviously well above the 'lace-curtain Irish'.[4] This man Barry was very pleasant and invited me to a meeting of the Irish Society on Sunday. These meetings, by the by, are held in the Sheraton Plaza, which is very luxurious.

1   Valerie Lady Goulding (1918–2003) was best known in Ireland for her work with the Central Remedial Clinic, which she co-founded in 1951 to care for children stricken by the polio epidemic. She was an English aristocrat with 'the common touch' who cut a dash in Irish society in the 1950s and 1960s, using her title and her connections with the rich and famous to help the sick and the underprivileged. She served as a nominated Fianna Fáil senator in the late 1970s. The poverty of Dublin in the 1940s shocked her: '... the slums, malnutrition, unemployment, abysmal social conditions. Tuberculosis was rife. There were barefoot children, and that really got to me.'

2   Dr James Hanlon (1949–2014) was known as 'the blind doctor'. He was a prominent ear, nose and throat surgeon in Dublin in the 1940s and contracted a disease from a patient which caused him to go blind. The subsequent treatment destroyed his hearing. He went on to become a prominent physiotherapist and worked with polio victims.

3   James (Jim) Barry ended up standing in as 'father of the bride' at Brian and MT's wedding.

4   'Lace curtain Irish' and 'shanty Irish 'are terms that were commonly used in the nineteenth and twentieth centuries to categorise Irish Americans by social class. Neither term was complimentary. Aside from financial status, the term 'lace curtain Irish' connoted pretentiousness and social climbing, while the 'shanty Irish' were stereotyped as feckless and ignorant.

The time is now 9.30 and I'm writing this in the Widener as I intend to go to a lecture at 10.00, it's a course I may follow on the history of the South.

Today, the first day of October, began with rain but it is still terribly warm and sticky and now the sun is up again. However, I suppose we mustn't complain and so I shan't. Anything I haven't told you that you wanted to know, dearest?

For now I'll close. Do remember me to your mother. Look after yourself and don't you work too hard at Needham's Treadmill. Love Brian.

PS Fortunately I haven't posted this: I've only just remembered that, as part of the drive for Polio, there was an Irish fashion show during the week. Inevitably, your Richard Alan[5] woman was showing stuff and also Nellie Mulcahy.[6] It got a great write-up in the papers. So bye for now, Brian.

 2

[MARIE-THÉRÈSE TO BRIAN]
Saturday, October 2

You are very good to write daily, it helps me to face the days more cheerfully, but I have no news, except that Mama is not getting on very well. The Doc came on Thursday evening, and when he had finished with her, insisted on examining me and has given me a 'nerve tonic'. It's like drinking perfume and seems to be rather strong, but I suppose I'll get used to it and then I won't feel so tired. Last night Con, Rosalie and I went to the R.E. [7]concert. It's the new Brian Boydell[8] Violin Concerto and is terrible. I'm so glad the poor man

---

5   MT studied dress design in Dublin and her first job and work experience was at Richard Alan at the top of Grafton Street.

6   Nellie Mulcahy (1925–2012), Irish designer and one of the founders of the Irish Haute Couture Group.

7   Radio Éireann.

8   Brian Boydell (1917 – 2000), Irish musician and composer.

wasn't sitting anywhere near me, because I'm afraid I yawned notice-ably during it, so much so that Con got the giggles!

Having more a mercenary than an academic turn, I find, as long as we get the £100, I'm thrilled about the 'Chamberlain'[9] idea es-pecially if it means a prolonged visit to George,[10] if he'll have us – poor man! I suppose there'd be no room for me in the flat you are sharing – a single room that could be turned into one for us – or are you 3 boys sharing one room? It seems rather a shame to go to all the trouble to get a flat for us, if we'll only be there for a month or so. But how are you enjoying your flat anyway? You promised a description: flat-mates, food, fittings etc. I suppose I'll get it soon! And I'm dying to know our financial position, as far as I can see I'll only be able to scrape together my fare. Mrs O'Reilly's legacy[11] doesn't seem to be forthcoming and I can't depend on it. I've got £22 in the world. I had hoped to bring it up to £30 by the end of September, but I fell for some pretty dress lengths (and you did say that I need dresses!), and £10 went west! I think the best thing about our honeymoon (for you at least) will be the fact that I'll have no charge accounts anywhere in America!

Neil rang here last night when I was out and said he'll ring again this morning - so I hope to write you of his news in my next letter.

Does Alistair Cook[12] write for any American papers, or only for the Manchester Guardian and talks for BBC? His letters from America are fascinating and I've a feeling that he lives in Boston. Do find out if you can!

....

9   Neville Chamberlain, British prime minister before Churchill. MT is referring to the extra funding that Brian will get if his thesis has an Irish theme, such as American/ Irish neutrality.

10   Roach, secretary of FDR papers.

11   Maria O'Reilly, John Dillon's housekeeper, made a small bequest to MT in her will.

12   Alistair Cooke (1908–2004) was a British-born American writer whose work as a jour-nalist, television personality and radio broadcaster was done primarily in America.

                                         P.S. LOOK OUT FOR SNAKES

[BRIAN TO MARIE-THÉRÈSE]

Cambridge, Saturday, 2 October, 10.40 am

Over here, the dress-code is less free and easy than at Bard: many of the girls wear white socks and tennis or baseball shoes, but no shorts, slacks or jeans are seen around the university. The stated style for the college women this year is plaid with long stockings. In fact, there is the usual mixture of clothes that you'd get at home, although they must be much lighter. Today, for instance (Oct 2nd), you could sunbathe in spots – but I'm not going to do so.

Today's post brought an invitation to the History Graduates Club picnic next Saturday. As you can see, I'm finding my feet but I've no intention of getting caught up in any Dram. Soc.[13] Last night over dinner on Commons, I had: soup, 2 helpings of scalloped fish and potatoes (creamed), 5 glasses of milk – it was very warm yesterday – 2 or 3 dishes of ice-cream, oh yes and a little salad and coffee – cost of $1.15 say 8/-. Anyway, I spoke to the boy at the same table, John O'Reilly, are there any non-Irish here? He has just arrived at Harvard Graduate School from a Benedictine Liberal Arts College.

On the financial set-up, by the end of the month I hope to have restored (and transmuted) your £100 into about $300, or so, and I'll try to save as best I can, but don't worry. By the time I'm finished covering Boston-Irish,[14] we'll be all right. Yesterday, by the by, a letter from George saying: "I still hope that you will both come and stay here with me next summer after Harvard closes, for as long as you can."

---

13 Brian was very involved in DramSoc in UCD and ended up being the auditor in his final year. He loved it but it was time consuming, hence, despite the attraction, he fought the urge to get involved in drama while at Harvard.

14 Brian is referring to giving lectures to Irish/American groups and getting paid for it.

4

Today is the feast of the little flower![15] And Papa's birthday,[16] which was always most profitable for me as a child, because receiving a feast day gift on Papa's birthday meant I also had to get one on Mama's! All these memories flashed through my mind, when I saw the street hawkers selling roses outside Clarendon St. this morning.

Dearest, it's been really quite a pleasant day. After Mass I went up to see Mother Hogan,[17] she was delighted and said that being engaged obviously agreed with me, as I had grown years younger since she'd seen me 18 months ago. She's going to try and get Maureen Farrell[18] a job in France. Yes, Maureen is back after a month in Paris looking for a job, without success and she looks very pretty and well groomed.

Neil rang me this morning to say goodbye, he's off tomorrow but will probably be back at Xmas time and will ring me then. Aunt Agnes will be delighted to get at the flat, I don't know if this is to be a surprise for you to see on your return, but she's planning to get all the furniture re-upholstered and get new curtains. We

15 Saint Thérèse of the Child Jesus and the Holy Face was a French nun who was popularly known as 'the Little Flower.' She was canonised in 1927 and her feast day was 3 October until it was moved to 1 October in 1969.

16 Theo (TWT) Dillon was born on 3 October 1898.

17 Mother Hogan was a very kind nun at the Sacred Heart Convent Leeson Street where MT studied. When MT's father approached her to ask her to forbid MT from wearing lipstick, Mother Hogan told him that she'd better things to be doing with her time. The year Theo died, Mother Hogan encouraged Marie Dillon to send her daughter to the Domestic College in Edinburgh. Mother Hogan arranged everything and MT stayed with Sacred Heart nuns at Craiglockhart, which features in Pat Barker's *Regeneration Trilogy.*

18 Maureen Farrell (O'Farrell) (1930–2007) was a very talented member of DramSoc who went on to become Maureen Charlton. She was a successful Irish playwright, poet and broadcaster.

are going through the clothes you left and I'll take home any coats, jackets and suits worth cleaning and keeping.

Myles rang today. He's back from Cork and there's a good chance he'll be elected President of Cork University! There are three of them 'up' for the job and the other two are Cork men, but knowing how much Cork people dislike Cork people, and as the Senate elects them, I feel he's a good chance. Anyway pray hard, I feel that it might mean a lot for us. Myles is off to Vienna on the 8th October (or sooner!). He is coming out to lunch on Tuesday so I hope to have more news for you then.

 5

How is your mother? I worry about you, pet. I think the tonic is a good idea, as you are under a tremendous strain and must be very weary. Is there anything I can send you, or your mother, to brighten things up?

Yesterday after Mass I went back and had dinner (served early on Sunday) in the Graduates Commons, and then went on to the meeting of the Éire Society. Jim Barry again took me under his wing and introduced me to many people including the speaker, who was a thick called Daniel Lyne, a lawyer, I think, who spoke on 'Education in Ireland'. He talked like a Tourist Association pamphlet, and can you imagine? He represents educated Harvard at the Centenary celebrations; he's probably the only person willing to pay his own fare over. I also met the consul and some people from Boston University. At present I'm edging in the direction of getting this Éire Society to invite me to speak to them.

After the meeting Jim showed me around Boston: then we had a light meal in a delicatessen snack bar and went on to see an excellent double feature: Marlon Brando in 'Viva Zapata' (which

I'd call a good film) and 'Caesar and Cleopatra' (really excellent). Then, inevitably as we talked on and on, Jim got worried lest I miss my transport, so invited me to stay the night at his place.

He has a nice house outside Boston and lives there alone. We sat a long time talking and I was astonished when he said he was 65. He somehow reminds me of my Dad – perhaps when Dad was younger. Jim's great interests are Irish movements – and the Oblate Missions.[19] I think you might find him a little boring and possibly think he's inclined to boast but over here I've grown very tolerant (for me!) of kind, down-to-earth, people. Also I've come to realise that using a European or Irish yardstick to measure Americans is a mistake. One thing that you might steel yourself against, pet, is the conversation by and large. And incidentally 'Readers Digest' is scarcely read by anyone over here and 'Time' is also considered bad!

And now a little story[20] to cheer you up: the only excuse for introducing such a tale into a lady's boudoir is the fact that it is true. Vassar College is an extremely well-known and very good college for girls and some years ago the local mayor was there on prize-giving day. As the ceremony wore on and the girls lined up to receive their cups and badges, the mayor (a practical man) counted the number of names on his list and the number of cups and found he was a cup short. He called a friend over and asked him to hurry over to his (the mayor's) house and pick up one of the smaller cups there – the mayor was a well-known, all-round sportsman etc. Just in time, as the last girl stepped forward, the friend slipped a cup into the mayor's hand: a broad smile, a hearty handshake, the girl turned away with her cup, there was applause. She glanced down at the cup and fainted. The professors ran to her assistance and the mayor retrieved his cup. He too read the inscription: 'For the best straight-haired bitch in Vassar County 1943–4'!

....

19 The Oblate Missions celebrate the sacraments, feed and shelter the poor, care for the orphaned and nurture the sick and elderly.

20 Smells like an urban folktale.

Monday night, 4 October

Dearest, Mondays are 'funny' bitter-sweet days: they start the week's work, which is pleasant, you went away on a Monday, which is sometimes a little bitter but Aunt Agnes's Monday visits always make them much happier. She was a little late this evening as she had tea with 'the boys', Neil was off on the mail-boat tonight and Aunt Agnes had tea with himself and Frank [21] (who passed his MA). Her real reason for calling down, apart from to see them, was to see if that nice bookcase was gone, or was Neil selling it. As he didn't mention it and it was still there FULL of your books, she realised she couldn't remove it and we've got it for nothing! Did I ever tell you that she knitted me a super jacket of the same wool as your white jumper – and I'm living in it! I, at last, rang Miss Bennett today and gave her your address, her niece's husband is one of the most important law professors at Harvard and they are in a literary crowd. Miss Bennett will send your address and I hope you'll hear from them soon.

You keep saying how you are neglecting me but I've had a letter every breakfast for ages now, in fact, two arrived this morning.

The Boston-Irish sound a very trifling bunch! You certainly have great courage standing up to talk to them, and I'm thrilled about the $300; it takes quite a load off my mind – I'll be able to eat too – not just sit and watch you stuffing yourself! The food sounds delicious and I hope you're not too fat (I'm beginning to worry – you know everyone must recognise their 'type' and you are definitely the lean and interesting and not the fat and bored type) – jokes apart, here's to a very good winter and I hope you're well protected against the winter cold!

---

21   Frank D'Arcy.

7

Marie-Thérèse my dear, your letter, of Saturday, was waiting for me when I got back from a meeting of the Politics Club, you are in the dumps aren't you, my pet, and what can I say to help at all? Anyway, I'm glad the Doc is looking after you and try not to worry, dearest. After all we both thought your mother wasn't doing so well before and she has managed to pull through.

What do you do in the evenings? Now that it's getting dark so early and our Indian summer is slipping away (it's raining this evening) I must confess to being depressed myself. You know I miss you so much and even work doesn't seem to help. Long ago, I think I must have missed you, before I ever met you, but then I could find some escape from the emptiness of life. Now there's no escape possible – because I don't want any. So, my dearest, here we are in the same boat but, please God, time will slip quickly by.

Last night there was a meeting of Grads at Radcliffe addressed by the Dean of the Graduate School, who invited me to have lunch with him soon. That's one awkward thing about Americans, they constantly issue vague invitations. However I intend to take this one up. The meeting was followed by an informal dance. I talked; even had I wanted to dance, the distribution of females was poor – about 10 men to every girl.

As far as money, there's no point in worrying about it, we'll manage to live all right, though you poor pet, our wedding is getting smaller and smaller and the honeymoon may turn into a subway ride.

Last night I met one of the Harvard Dram Soc people and discovered that Mrs Howe (Louie Bennett's niece) is somehow connected with dramatics here. Do you think I should ring her?

I'm afraid my letters will grow erratic as time goes on. Time is somehow difficult to manage and words are even more so: all the things I never needed to say when I was with you seem to

P.S. LOOK OUT FOR SNAKES

jumble themselves up in my head. But as the night gets darker I just stretch my arms around you so very far away and we are home again, for home is wherever we are together. Goodnight my love and God Bless, Brian.

Tuesday night, 5 October

We had a very pleasant visit from Myles for lunch. He is off to Vienna (to give 3 months of lectures on Thursday week), but his plans are in rather a mix-up, because the boat he (and all his books) was to have taken to Holland, was rammed (and sank) in New York last week. Now apparently this is the third time in succession that this sort of thing has happened to him,[22] (each time a week or so before he was to sail somewhere), and each time he's had to fly – so once again, he flies to Austria!

Myles asked after your news – work etc., and was very upset that you weren't doing an MA or PhD at Harvard, yes he knew (everyone tells me about it) that you sat your MA paper here (note Mary Murphy told me 2 weeks ago that she knew about your MA all along), but told me to write and advise you strongly to try and start a PhD at Harvard – something you could finish in Dublin (or wherever you might be the following year) – otherwise (he said) you might look back at this year as wasted. So now I've delivered the message – don't forget Cork! The election[23] is on the 14th Oct.

Louie Bennett rang this evening to say she'd just sent off a letter to her niece. I do hope they are nice and do please write me a word description of your flat-mates. I'm most curious.

If you should reconsider the question of work (if that's still possible), in the light of what Myles said (he was very strong about it),

22 The family used to tease him that the ships always sank after they'd dropped him off at his destination.

23 Myles is running for President of University College Cork (UCC).

please don't think about my visit. I'm coming out to be with you but not to monopolise you. If you have to go to the library, I can be patient till your day's work is finished and anyway, if we were at Hyde Park, a pleasant garden is quite good company in itself.

 9

[BRIAN TO MARIE-THÉRÈSE]
Cambridge, Wednesday, 6 October

Your news, re Myles, in your letter of Sunday is interesting; I actually wrote him a note yesterday. Is Harry Atkins still running for the job?[24] Sending George a postcard was a wonderful idea and of course I'll look after the Ridge Boy[25] – what's he in? Obviously he's stupid not to have haunted you more consistently, but I will try to tolerate this lesser mortal!

On the Consulate thing, today I got a note from Michael Flynn, the vice-consul, and he's taking me to lunch tomorrow. Possibly I'll go on to Bard (Rhinebeck) over the weekend as Flynn has offered me a ride there and back, Friday to Tuesday, so we'll see. Also in today's post was a note from the Widener to say that they are giving me a stall i.e. a desk in the stacks. Also there was another postcard from Keppler,[26] inviting me to a reception for foreign students on October 15th.

By the way, just to put you in the picture, the Supreme Court decision abolishing segregation[27] in schools has caused some trouble (though relatively little force) down South. In some States, moves are being made to make the public schools private and to supply them with State funds and then leave the Negroes in their

---

24   President of UCC.

25   Reference to the young man MT met at Billy Kingston's party.

26   Counselor for foreign students at Harvard.

27   Brown v. Board of Education of Topeka (1954) was a landmark decision of the US Supreme Court in which the Court ruled that state laws establishing racial segregation in public schools were unconstitutional, even if the segregated schools were otherwise equal in quality.

own. Among other reasons given, is a reluctance to allow Negroes to see the poor housing of white schools. Even in Washington D.C. there has been some boycotting.

Alistair Cooke, to the best of my knowledge, does not do any large scale commentary over here, but have I told you about Westbrook Pegler?[28] He writes for the Hearst papers – in a scandalously libellous way – particularly about Eleanor Roosevelt and the Roosevelts in general, Democrats, anti-McCarthyites and Labour Unions. The mildest of his terms of general abuse is 'traitor'. But now, dearest, paper runs out (and it is 11.40 pm) so goodnight, God bless and all my love, Brian

 10

[MARIE-THÉRÈSE TO BRIAN]
Wednesday evening, 6 October

I'm just starting this while drying my hair, before going over to Naomi's[29] at 8.00. Yesterday I started my house-coat and Mrs Ward popped in to see how Mama was. She spotted the material and evidently thought I was making my wedding dress. She claimed that she'd never seen such lovely material and kept saying 'are you going to cook bacon and eggs in "that"?' I didn't like to say that I had high hopes that someone else might be getting my breakfast now and then! She wouldn't believe it was washable and crease resistant and ended up taking a piece of it home to show her family! Yes, I think it's wonderful material too and I hope you'll like the 'effect'!

We are working 9–5 again. It's very pleasant and long may it last! Mother Hogan rang me today to say that she found a job for

28 Francis James Westbrook Pegler (1894–1969) was an American journalist and writer. Pegler supported FDR initially but, after seeing the rise of fascism in Europe, he warned against the dangers of dictatorship in America and became one of the Roosevelt administration's sharpest critics for what he saw as its abuse of power. Thereafter he rarely missed an opportunity to criticise Roosevelt, his wife Eleanor Roosevelt and Vice President Henry A. Wallace.

29 Naomi Kidney, MT's closest lifelong friend and wife of Dr Bill Kidney.

Maureen Farrell[30] and that she was to contact Shawn S.J.[31] I passed on the information, so hope something will come of it.

Later: Naomi's was most enjoyable. She has got quite fat, maybe an addition,[32] maybe not! Too early to tell! Anyway am settling down to dream of us in the past and future. Good night Darling, Marie-Thérèse

Thursday P.S. No news of you! But I hope this means you are working hard and enjoying every moment of it all.

Mama is just about the same, which isn't very good! She has bad nights and days now. I'm much better though my medicine is like drinking perfume! Horrible, Love M.T.

 11

[BRIAN TO MARIE-THÉRÈSE]
Cambridge, Thursday, 7 October

Well dear, you are wonderful! Your gay letter of Tuesday was waiting for me, as I got back on this very cold night, to warm me up again. Today was really lovely: a bright, clear, blue sky but a very cool breeze and in fact forecasts are that the weather will be down to 20 degrees tonight. What on earth did I say about the Boston-Irish to make them sound so 'terrifying'? The ones I met are harmless old fogies.

Today at 11.40 Michael Flynn, the vice-consul, a tall young fellow from Galway, picked me up in Cambridge and drove me over to Boston where we had lunch with an Irish-American called Joe Gannon. It was all very pleasant and the conversation was good. Over here there is a general tendency to avoid 'hurting' people by arguing or discussing touchy subjects, which tends to stultify conversation. It is all part of a general movement towards conformity and is rather depressing.

30 Maureen Charlton, Irish playwright.
31 Shawn Dillon, MT's uncle.
32 Naomi Kidney was probably pregnant as she ended up having twelve children.

After lunch Michael took me to see the Athenaeum library in Boston – a lovely place with a staff (I should think) somewhat larger than the National Library! On Saturday, he is driving to NY and giving Egbert[33] (Grommers – the Dutchman) and myself a lift up. I shall probably drop into Bard and spend the rest of the week-end with George. We'll return on Tuesday.

About my fat: Sorry pet, but I just can't find it! I'm eating well and so on but I'm sure you only have to worry about my remaining the interesting, 'thin man', who will remain a per-manent feature.

Today I spoke to Langer's secretary about the Anglo-American subject, and she promised to mention it to him when he returns from Princeton. Meantime I'm delving into Hooker[34] and Locke[35] again (one of the best essays you ever made me write during your slave-driving weekends), and also into an early attempt at an Anglo-American rapprochement.

And now for you and your bitter-sweet Monday; you know, dar-ling, for a realist, (you always say you're a mercenary, materialist, hard character) you're just as sentimental as I am and I love you for it – for that among a million other things.

 12

[MARIE-THÉRÈSE TO BRIAN]
Saturday Morning, 9 October

I was delighted to get your two letters yesterday morning. Now don't be cross, but are you developing an American accent? Your

---

33 Egbert was one of Brian's flatmates.
34 Richard Hooker (1554–1600), Church of England priest, important theologian of the sixteenth century.
35 John Locke (1632–1704), English philosopher and physician. He was commonly known as the 'Father of Liberalism'. His political theory of government by the con-sent of the governed as a means to protect the three natural rights of 'life, liberty and estate' deeply influenced the Founding Fathers. His essays on religious tolerance provided an early model for the separation of Church and State.

letters are rather Americanised. If you're to address any meeting, won't it be far more effective in an Irish accent?

Yes pet, there is something I'd love for Xmas – ½ doz pairs of Nylons – you see American ones are better than anything I can get here and they should last me ages, till I come to you in fact. (I take a size 7 shoe (American fitting) with very long legs – I think a size 10½ would do!) as for colour – natural not pinkish – anyway you decide what you like.

Now for my news I was vaccinated last night! I rang Doc. Roche to say I was giving up his horrid tonic because I hated it! He retaliated by suggesting I come out and be vaccinated! So here I am full of germs and awaiting the worst! I'm afraid it's in the arm. You won't mind will you? But had I had it in my leg I couldn't have had a bath for 3 weeks. THAT, I said, would certainly kill me if the vaccination didn't! So that's a step nearer you.

I'm absolutely thrilled about all our money! And I think your idea about going to George's is super. If we won't be too much for him, I'd far rather we keep him as a friend, which I fear he won't be after having us both for a MONTH!

 13

[BRIAN TO MARIE-THÉRÈSE]
Cambridge, Saturday, 9 October

By the time this arrives, Aunty Agnes will probably have told you about my invitation to speak in a Boston high school of some kind on Thursday, and since then I've had an invitation to go to Vermont, leaving Thursday night, until Saturday, to do the same sort of thing. This is all in honour of United Nations Day next weekend. The Vermont people won't pay for my talk but they do give me travelling expenses and feed and lodge me so I think I'll probably accept.

Well today I worked in the Widener (it's open until 5.30 on Saturday) and then had a good dinner; listened to records and came back here to do some more work. I have knocked off now (10.50) as I want to go to bed. Tomorrow I'll go to 9 Mass, please God, as I have an invitation to breakfast! Isn't that a barbarous idea! Anyway the three of us[36] are due to go to the other side of Cambridge at 10.00 to have breakfast with the Cushmans[37] – apparently she is something in the International Centre.

 14

[MARIE-THÉRÈSE TO BRIAN]
Sunday night, 10 October

How is your vaccination scar now? This is very important to me as I'd like to speculate how mine will be by the time I get out! As yet there are no ill effects but I've a week to go.

This has been quite a pleasant weekend; on Friday before going to Doc. Roche's I took myself to Danny Kaye's new picture 'Knock on Wood' at the Ambassador[38] – a delightful picture house, small, well-lit and well ventilated. The picture is tremendously funny and I'm going again to hear the jokes I missed by laughing too much! Yesterday morning I had coffee with Mary Murphy, who was in rather cranky humour. She seemed somewhat displeased about Myles going for the Cork appointment but I felt that something (quite else) had 'rattled' her. After lunch I walked Dun Laoghaire pier with Con and then got on the Killiney bus and called on Miss Bennett for tea. This was a great success! Without you to take the limelight, yes she has obviously lost her heart to you, dear, and in your company I can never again hope to gain all her attention – to this I'm resigned!

---

36 Brian and his two flatmates, Stan and Egbert.

37 The Cushmans epitomised American hospitality. They offered MT a home before their wedding and supported the young couple in every way they could. They became lifelong friends of the Farrell's.

38 The Ambassador Cinema (1897 – 1999), at the north end of O'Connell Street beside the Rotunda Hospital, was Dublin's longest running cinema.

This morning after Mass, Con and I met for coffee in Dun Laoghaire. We plan to get as much fresh air as possible, as the weather at present is wonderfully balmy and warm. Pet, thank you for that little story which I 'lapped-up' – have you met any 'straight-haired bitches' lately? Or ladies, I mean of course! Re-accommodation for me and us: I'd much rather a bed-sitter than a small hotel! Because we'd probably like quite a lot of freedom, hence I think a bed-sitter would be more suitable. I'd love to come out 10 days before Easter and will probably manage it. I could maybe stay in a small hotel near you, or flat for that time but don't forget to make friends, between this and then, with some priest and do find out do we need 'Letters of Freedom' because they take quite a time to get. But I definitely leave with you the final decision as to how, or where we'll live, because you know the 'way of life' there now better than me.

 15

[BRIAN TO MARIE-THÉRÈSE]
Rhinebeck, Monday, 11 October

My Dearest, Forgive these spasmodic letters over the weekend but I ran out of aerograms and somehow didn't get round to writing yesterday. Sunday, after Mass, we discussed going to Yonkers[39] but finally I decided to stay here and go through some of George's books on Roosevelt.

Today at 9.20 I got a lift up to Bard, from Mrs Bourne (a friend of George's who teaches there), where I attended two classes; this morning a history class in which I created a favourable impression of erudition without any intention at all. Then I went to see Mr Gumery (do you remember the pleasant people at Barrytown who were the first to invite me for a meal when I arrived), and he was

---

39 Yonkers is a city in Westchester County, New York, the third most populous city in the state.

P.S. LOOK OUT FOR SNAKES

very pleased to see me and brought me off to lunch. I met quite a number of students, who had been around Bard during the summer, and had a pleasant time.

After lunch I went to an 'Introduction to Philosophy' class and then had a long discussion with Lensing[40] on philosophy of history, Swift, Bard, Ireland etc. Also one of the students (whose name I don't remember) is trying to arrange for the Social Studies Club to invite me down sometime next month. It's still very tentative but I'm considering speaking on Irish Nationalism. I got back from Bard in the Doctor's car, he lives in Rhinebeck.

Tuesday morning – still not finished, dear, but I'm trying hard. One thing, this weekend has been really warm and N.Y. is in the 80s today! George has lent me sheets, blankets, and so on. Up to now I've been using the landlady's but this will save me quite a few dollars. I hope to see Alice[41] and the Nathansons[42] in N.Y. but we're to meet Michael Flynn at 7.30 and so I might not have time.

  16

[MARIE-THÉRÈSE TO BRIAN]
Tuesday night, 12 October

I'm afraid it's a very tired little girl writing tonight! I've been dancing attendance in Mama's room for 3½ hours and it's killing work! I hate to think what will happen when I get sick! But looking on the brighter side: I'm having 2 days holidays as there is no work so I get Tues and Wed off! This morning I continued making my house-coat (I started it last night while Aunt Agnes was here and she wound her wool so we'd a very pleasant active evening). Knowing that this was my evening 'on duty'[43], I took myself to a Doris Day picture and a little shopping. Tomorrow Noeleen and

40 William E. Lensing was professor of philosophy at Bard from 1949–81.
41 Hermes – speech trainer.
42 Nathaniel L. Nathanson, Lecturer at Bard and his wife, Leah.
43 MT stayed up nights to look after her mother.

I are having tea in town and going to another picture in the evening. I'm beginning to think a little amusement is as important as saving the money. It makes the rather strained conditions easier to bear, not that Mama's cross but she seems a lot sicker and as result slower and needs more attention.

This evening I rang the C.C.[44] about my (lost) Baptism Certificate and he says he'll draw up a form for Mama to sign and get my Letters of Freedom prepared and I'll have them sometime before Xmas. Darling, can I do anything about getting yours? It wouldn't do any harm getting a bit organised as you never know what hold ups might occur or what might happen. On Saturday, I'll bring my Birth Certificate to the British Embassy and see can they get me 2 copies.

I hope you didn't keep yourself to the task of rereading all my letters. They are best forgotten! The most sensible words I wrote you, as far as I can remember, were: 'look out for snakes!' and the ones I meant most deeply are: 'I love you, Darling, very much' and that's really all I can say so, for tonight God Bless, Marie-Thérèse

 17

[BRIAN TO MARIE-THÉRÈSE]
Cambridge, Wednesday night, 13 October

My poor pet, so you're frightened about me getting an American accent! Don't worry dearest; most people think I'm British and there's no trace of American in my accent – though I may have picked up one or two Yankee phrases. But I shan't change, my darling, just you wait and see. Even if I become pure Yank, you know I would never ask for anything else but you, and I don't. So don't worry! I'm my usual, spoilt, difficult self.

Today I received, in the post, my cleaned jacket (thank you!), the napkins, which seem very expensive, and your letter.

---

44   Local curate.

How is the vaccination? Mine is fine (though still red but sun tan will fix that). I also got a letter from Desmond,[45] he said that Maurice O'Connell got firsts in his MA, so I presume that I've passed. I've been busy in the Widener today as I have to see Langer tomorrow. By the way Desmond said Myles 'is regarded as having an excellent chance of becoming President of Cork before the end of the month.'

I arrived home from George's with sheets and blankets, which will save me money. We drove along the Merritt Parkway leaving N.Y. about 9.15 – all through Connecticut, arriving in Cambridge about 3 a.m. so I'm rather tired. Did you have a chance to explain to Myles about the research-cum-degree issue? I feel it might at least be diplomatic to do so and I think you can handle that sort of thing much better. I am quite thrilled to find Miss Bennett is a fan of mine, should I get my secretary to send her an autographed photo from my fan-club!

Really I'm in good form from the weekend. Please God I'll find Langer co-operative in the morning otherwise I'll have to turn to another field.

 18   [MARIE-THÉRÈSE TO BRIAN]
Wednesday night, 13 October

After a rather 'tragic' night (TRAGIC: because during it I woke up to find myself scratching my vaccination and I fear that I've caused great damage!), I've had a really funny day!

First: there is a chance that, for all my wishing to be married in America, I may have to be re-baptised! Mama is the only living witness to that memorable ceremony and the local C.C. says that he'll do all he can to draw-up an impressive looking document

45   Thomas Desmond Williams, Professor of Modern History at UCD.

for her to sign but we may have a baptism[46] on our hands! Then I popped in to enquire from the British Embassy about my Birth Cert (2nd copy) where I met a very pleasant chatty man, who was horrified to find me carrying an Irish passport and claims that I am really a British subject![47] In fact he tried to hi-jack me back to a British passport! They must be hard up, I felt like asking him how much it would be worth to him, if I did change back.

Your letter from Rhinebeck arrived this afternoon and of course you know better about the method and degree etc., but I would love a good argument sometime – well that's just one more thing to look forward to as well.

 19

[BRIAN TO MARIE-THÉRÈSE]
Cambridge, Thursday, 14 October

This is a very rushed note, darling, and yet has some information I want you to know, and also to pass on to Desmond Williams. Could you phone college and ask for the History Department? And tell Desmond:

a) Today I saw Langer and he agreed that I should start research on Anglo-U.S. relations in 1938–9. Really I intend to study 'Official American Reactions to British Policy'. My starting point will be the question of Eden's resignation.

---

46   MT had a big row with the parish priest who claimed that her Baptism Certificate wasn't 'kosher'. She was born and baptised in Vienna (where her father was furthering his medical studies) and her godparents were not present. Since they attended by proxy the parish priest didn't accept it. MT argued that it would make a great joke if it got out that the godchild of Mother Mary Martin (the founder of the Medical Missionaries of Mary} and Brian Dillon, the headmaster of Glenstal, had to be re-baptised. On achieving her goal, she said 'where there's a will, there's a way!'

47   MT's father had a British passport as he was born in England. Hence MT was registered on a British passport originally. It was more useful to him for traveling purposes so he never changed it.

P.S. LOOK OUT FOR SNAKES

b) Desmond also wanted to know the name of the Director of the F.D.R. Memorial Library, Hyde Park, N.Y. It is Dr Herman Kahn.

I got Desmond's letter yesterday. Tell him that I'll write soon and that I'm also 'auditing' courses in U.S. history.

As you may guess I'm quite keen to make a thorough start (thank God, it's a field you know about too, so I shan't bore you too much). I had letters today from home and from Aunty Agnes – who is worried, I think, about my egg flips. I feel fine, D.G.[48] and am only taking them to be on the safe side.

P.S. Desmond didn't give me any information about applying for an extension on my MA. Would you ask him to whom I apply and is it to be a formal letter? Love, Brian.

 20

[MARIE-THÉRÈSE TO BRIAN]
Friday, 15 October

Darling, I came in tonight and looking, as always, to the corner of Mama's bookcase where the post is put, I saw 2 letters from you. You can't imagine the effect of your letters on my life at present. They colour my days and nights and they are such happy letters from Rhinebeck, which make them even better. George is a worthwhile friend, he thinks of everything. What on earth will we give him for Christmas?

A certain 'Black Bird' who rings a rather 'sharp' 2nd fiddle to Miss Green rang me tonight: first bit of news: Yvonne and John are officially engaged – having met John yesterday (he was walking about 2 feet above street level) I should have realised. Second, Myles won two votes in Cork University and the Dublin and Galway senates have still to vote. Mary Murphy thinks he has a jolly good chance as the other 3 candidates (Cork men) are unknown outside their native city.

---

48   Deo gratias – Thanks be to God.

I forgot to tell you that on Wednesday evening Noeleen and I went to see 'The Green Scarf' an excellent English picture (after the book called 'The Brute') you must see it, if you get a chance. You'll like it very much.

 21

Mrs. O'Reilly's[49] £50 came, hurray! I was hoping I'd get it sometime before leaving for America, but never expected it so soon. This brings my savings up to £83 but I'm not sending anymore out to America till I have £120 put away, that should be the price of my ticket roughly.

It made up for a nightmarish evening, which involved going to, waiting at, and returning from Doc. Roche's! I left here at 8.30 and I was home at 11.45 and only saw him for about 10 minutes! Anyway the vaccination has taken 'very nicely' and today, I wouldn't need him to tell me, that a slight headache and pain in the arm speak for themselves.

How long has 'Hazel'[50] affected you? We heard all about her progress through Carolina, Virginia, Washington on last night's radio newsreel but no mention of Boston so I do hope she'll leave you in peace.

I'm to meet Maureen O'Farrell[51] for coffee this morning but really it's only the delight of banking my £50 which drags me to town.

---

49   John Dillon's housekeeper.
50   Deadly hurricane that struck the east coast of the U.S.
51   Maureen Charlton, playwright.

P.S. LOOK OUT FOR SNAKES

22

Cambridge Monday, 18 October

Addressed to: Miss M.T. Dillon, c/o Messrs. Larhams Ltd,
George's Street, Dun Laoghaire, Ireland.

My Own Darling – Isn't it terrible that I forgot to ask all about your horrible vaccination till I got (real red-letter day) your two letters today. Anyway, dear, I hope that by now you have got over the worst of it. Don't worry about the scar – mine is now slowly disappearing and you'll find that yours will do the same.

What do you mean about Myles getting 2 votes in Cork – do you mean a majority of two, and who are the opponents? Congrats about your inheritance – you moneyed woman you!

My research is coming along nicely but I wish records of British Cabinet meetings were available. However even without them, one can piece the story together. The Eden resignation gives me a useful kind of introduction to the diplomatic world into which the new American Ambassador[52] (Kennedy) entered in 1938.

Do remember me to the Murphys and everyone – how did Ann Barbara[53] enjoy her summer? Here there's little news. As I told your mother 'The Rear Window' is extremely good and quite clever and amusing. I think you'll like it. Apart from that, I have little to report except that I am in good health, thank God, and that I've fallen in love with the most wonderful girl you could imagine and I miss her very much, and yet am willing to wait out my vigil over the winter so that no one can say that we are just another couple. Because we're not;

52 In 1938, Roosevelt appointed Joseph Kennedy as the US Ambassador to the court of St James (UK). Kennedy wasn't a good diplomat and didn't believe that the States should help England. It was said of him, "We have a rich man, untrained in diplomacy, unlearned in history and politics, who is a great publicity seeker and who apparently is ambitious to be the first Catholic president of the U.S." John H. Davis, *The Kennedys: Dynasty and Disaster* (1993).

53 Mary and Gerard Murphy's daughter.

we're something very special and wonderful and I hope, my dearest, that we shall come through a tough wait much stronger than ever before. And so, my love, for now sleep well, Brian.

PS I really send this to Larhams for variety for you, pet. B

Due to laziness as much as a rather stiff arm, your darling has taken a day off in bed! Poor Mr Needham, I hope his sympathy and good nature will never unbetter him!

Actually yesterday, the 9th day after the vaccination and a Sunday afternoon without Betty, Mama chose to have rather a bad stroke and I had to lift and turn her, which didn't improve my arm. She's been really very sick since and being a bit shaky myself I'd have had to stay home anyway. Dr Roche at last condescended to come (exactly 24 hours after he was called) and will come again tomorrow. So you see your letters (of 14th and 15th) were heaven sent.

I'm sure you're feeling well – I said so to Aunt Agnes – your letters are so cheering – and I'll contact Desmond tomorrow morning (it's now too late today) and I'm afraid Myles was away in Austria before I could relay your reply.

This afternoon I went over to Lowell to see Kelleher[54] and he brought me over to the Faculty Club for dinner. Inevitably we discussed Ireland, ranging up and down history and literature. It was all very pleasant and I went back to the Widener about 7.30 with renewed vigour until closing time.

54   John Kelleher, (Roger McHugh's friend), Irish Studies, Harvard.

P.S. LOOK OUT FOR SNAKES

How is your vaccine reaction? My scab affair lasted a long time and the spot is still red but getting much smaller and rather more pink. After that initial reaction I had no more trouble with it, so please God, by the time you get this, darling, you'll be feeling well again and bouncing around.

Today I had an invitation for tea from Mrs Howe[55] (Louie Bennett's niece) for Saturday at 4.30. However, as I don't know what time I'll be returning from Vermont, I'll phone her tomorrow and explain. One rather awkward thing about meeting her will be that I don't know anything about any of her plays, so I must be careful to steer the conversation away from the theatre.

Any further electioneering news? Over here a quiet has settled after last night's furor about Wilson's stupid remarks[56] about unemployment. Despite initial signs that the polling will be light and, presumably, therefore favour the Republicans, indications still point to a Democratic victory. What chances of Ike going Democrat?

 25

[MARIE-THÉRÈSE TO BRIAN]

Tuesday night, 19 October

We are all much better, thank you, Darling! Mama has survived 'this one' quite well and is sleeping sweetly in the arms of Morfia.[57] My arm doesn't hurt at all and my head is a lot better.

Aunt Agnes was here, yesterday evening, bringing us great cheer and she sat beside my bed and made me feel much better. Next week I'm going down to no. 13 to visit her. I was back at work today and all went well.

55 Mary Manning Howe, married to law professor Mark DeWolf Howe.
56 The newspapers on 15 October 1954 had a field day about the fact that Defense Secretary Charles Wilson had a genius for saying the wrong thing and that the President had been trying to explain what he (Mr Wilson) meant when he said he preferred hunting dogs to kennel-fed ones. The Democrats jumped all over Wilson and said he likened the unemployed to dogs.
57 Morphine – MT's rendering of the 'arms of Morpheus'.

In all my excitement on Sunday I forgot to mention the raid on a North of Ireland military barracks. The BBC is keeping such a silence about it that I felt sure you'd never hear about it. So today's paper cutting will amuse you --wasn't a van found in Raheny after the last raid with some rounds of small ammo? It sounds familiar. Anyway, as you can see, this raid was a failure -- but it does put the poor Irish government in a bit of a fix! Won't Costello[58] look a bit of a fool apologising to Churchill for something he didn't do?

There is no other news, Naomi rang last night prior to leaving for a few days to London and wanted to bring me a little 'contraband' and was asking after you etc. I rang Desmond (at History Dept. UCD) but he was away for the weekend and won't be in till tomorrow. I'll call again!

 26

[BRIAN TO MARIE-THÉRÈSE]
Cambridge, Wednesday, 20 October

This morning I went to my two lectures and had an early lunch on the Square then dived into the Widener and carried on muck-raking. You see, involved in the story is a tug-of-war between the F.O. and other branches of the Civil Service – especially the Treasury and the P.M.'s[59] office. There are hints about this and the honours list for 1938 announcing Vansittart's[60] new post is an obvious sign

58 John Aloysius Costello (1891 –1976) was an Irish Fine Gael politician who served as Attorney General of Ireland (1926–32), as TD (1933–43 and 1944–69), as Taoiseach (1948–51 and 1954–57), and as Leader of the Opposition (1951–54 and 1957–59).
59 P.M. Chamberlain.
60 Sir Robert Vansittart was a senior British diplomat in the period before and during the Second World War, from 1929 to 41. He was Principal Private Secretary to the Prime Minister (1928–30) and Permanent Under-Secretary at the Foreign Office (1930–38), and later served as Chief Diplomatic Adviser to the British government. He is best remembered for his opposition to appeasement and his strong stance against Germany during and after the Second World War. Vansittart was also a published poet, novelist and playwright.

P.S. LOOK OUT FOR SNAKES

that he's being kicked upstairs. At present I'm gleaning scraps of information from memoirs by various F.O. diplomats.

I had dinner at Harkness with some students in 'Regional Studies' i.e. intensive courses in the language, politics and economics of various countries (these are in Chinese and Russian). Afterwards, I went back to A-25, my stall in the Widener and read until about 9.30. Coming out I met Anna Martelloni and had coffee with her for an hour. She's very depressed about her work. Then I came back, washed my nylon shirts, half-dozen pairs of socks and some 'smalls'. Heavier things I take to an automat washing place and my shirts I send to the laundry.

Oh yes! Obeyed instructions at last, dear, and I picked up my sports coat from the cleaners this morning. They did a good job on it for only 5 cents. This afternoon before dinner, I phoned Mrs Howe to say that I didn't know if I'd be back in time on Saturday, so we put it off till the following Saturday. She seems a bit vague and Kelleher tells me she has bitter tongue but a good heart!

The papers have screaming headlines about a doctor accused of murdering his wife. So far they've spent three days, with a defence 'screening' prospective jurors (they have three out of twelve jurors to date) on the grounds that many will be influenced in their decisions by the sex angle in the case. Candidly, I feel that over here the jury system gives the guilty some hope, but God help the innocent!

 27

[MARIE-THÉRÈSE TO BRIAN]
Wednesday night, 20 October

Well, Dearest, I rang Desmond, again, this afternoon. He was pleased to hear about your choice of work, grateful to learn Kahn's[61] name and on the question of the letter, he suggests a formal application

61   Director of Memorial Library, Hyde Park.

on your part to him to ask permission to defer doing your thesis, and he'd like to receive such a letter as soon as possible.

Other news I have none! These evenings I take to my bed as my arm is still a bit swollen and my head aches at times. When we go out together again and I start yawning at 10.30 don't be offended, but that's your sweetheart's normal bedtime and it will take a little time to break the habit!

 28

[MARIE-THÉRÈSE TO BRIAN]
Thursday night, 21 October

You are, as always, inspired – how could you know that I was down to my last stocking? Now here's the joke of the evening: your note of Tuesday said that you had heard from Myles. Well, having rung Bessie (to find the results[62] won't be 'out' till Thursday), I can say you are honoured! Not even his wife has heard from him since his departure! Mama was 'tickled Pink'. Indeed, poor Mama, Dr Roche came today and prescribed oxygen for future breathless attacks and morphia at night from now on for always. It's all rather depressing. She says she loved your letter and sends her love but isn't writing any more herself.

Friday Morning (same letter)

Oh I loved that touch: your letter (to work) arrived this morning and signing off you said 'sleep well!' – and I do bless my stars for this job – there is no worry here and the Bosses are terribly considerate about everything. I'm wearing the new nylons today and they are a perfect colour and fit!

The two votes Myles got were for the nomination – there are 3 candidates – one man (the registrar at Cork) got 16 – and another got 6 or so.

---

62   The results of the election for President of University College Cork.

29

My Darling, Due to the fact that one 'over-flow' (a pipe running from the water tank attached to outside one of my windows) suddenly started gushing at 4 am this morning, thus announcing the fact that something was wrong – a rather spoilt night (cutting off water, running taps etc.) and a household drought: all added up to a rather shattered girl ... till your letter of Monday arrived this evening.

Amusing incident today: Mrs Ward's daughter came in this evening on a message and later on her mother came down to look after Mama. Mrs Ward said that her daughter (aged 17) came home to say that 'wasn't Miss Dillon smashing! She's just like an actress!'

Mary Murphy has invited me over for Friday week, she's trying to get Yvonne and John, Anne and the red-haired fiancé the same evening. I almost hope it falls through because the last time it fell through, it was very pleasant! Mary on her own is far better than Mary playing to a full house!

 30

Yesterday was rather hectic. We arrived at Beaver County Day School about 10.30 and after about fifteen minutes were given charge of various groups of about 40 students. I walked into my room to find teenagers (17–18 years old) from about eight different schools brought together. In introducing me, the Chairman, a faculty member, said I'd speak for about 15 minutes on what Ireland thought about the U.S. and then answer questions. In fact I turned it into a question-and-answer session very quickly and we talked about: Ike, McCarthy, Stevenson, The Quiet Man,[63] cars

---

63   1952 American romantic comedy-drama set in Ireland, directed by John Ford, starring John Wayne.

and roads, Irish population, politics and God knows what else. Then we had a buffet lunch.

After that we had coffee with the teachers from the various schools and discussed the whole set-up till about 12.30. Then one of the students (an ex-Navy type going to college next year on the G-I Bill[64]) drove me around Boston and dropped me at Worth Station. After dinner, I took a train to New Hampshire arriving at 7.40 (left at 5.00) and then came by bus to Rutland, where I was met by some of the teenagers and Mrs Rabbit (I stayed overnight with her and her husband – a doctor). The Rabbits are very pleasant and have a beautiful home here. Their daughter Betsie is also involved in the High School Club which asked me down here.

It's now 2.00 pm and I'm in Rutland High School (about 400 pupils), where I'm to have another of these question-answer routines on Ireland before the whole school at 2.30. On stage with me to ask questions will be about 15 teenagers.

But that's all for now – I'll let you know how it goes as soon as I have a chance – this morning I spent at the Catholic High School, I'm going out to dinner tonight and tomorrow I'm to attend a football match about 60 miles away. Forgive me if I don't write so soon, darling. I will try hard. God Bless and do look after yourself.

 37

I've just received your letter of Tuesday, where you mentioned dining with Kelleher, would that be John Kelleher? And isn't that the man Dan Binchy[65] can't stand? And if so, have you any idea why?

---

64 Eisenhower's GI Bill gave veterans an affordable college education.
65 Daniel Anthony Binchy, scholar of Irish linguistics, visiting professor at Harvard University in 1954.

P.S. LOOK OUT FOR SNAKES

You mentioned Wilson's 'Howler'[66] – it must have been pretty bad because Alistair Cooke devoted a whole ¼ hour to the subject, although he'd no reason to, because it's not very important in European eyes, but he clearly felt strongly about it.

Eva, Con and I went to the pictures last night and walked out after ½ an hour it was so dreadfully silly, something called 'The Actress' and then we went to see 'Where There's Life' – quite funny. Going into the picture I saw an ex-boyfriend of mine looking very moth-eaten – a pleasing sight – don't you dare ever to look moth-eaten – it's a sad thing to see!

 32

Back again, darling, to three letters (and your cuttings). The Vermont trip went off very well. I was staying with the Ravitts (not Rabbits as I told you) and they were very pleasant – Jews incidentally. Last Friday on stage, I was bombarded with questions, rather like my Boston experience of the day before. Then I went down to see the local newspaper and on to dinner with another family (who were careful to serve fish[67]). After that I played (and won – strangely enough) two games of 'Scrabble'. On Saturday, I was picked up at 10.30 by the Nassaus (Mr, Mrs and Bobby, about 13 – they also have a son in the army). We drove about 80 miles through Vermont to see my first American football game in which Vermont University gave Warwick (military academy) a terrible beating. After a lovely steak dinner (the steak was charcoaled outside on an open fire) at the Ravitts I went to the High School dance and talked to a lot of the kids and then back to watch wrestling on TV.

66 Wilson's remarks about dogs and the unemployed (see letter of 19 October).
67 The practice of abstaining from meat on Fridays was centuries old, but in 1985 the Catholic Church allowed Catholics to substitute it with another form of penance.

This morning I was badly caught out: 11 o'clock in Rutland was a 'Missa Cantata'[68]; the announcements and sermon took about 25 minutes; there was a special collection for Mission Sunday and a procession for the opening of the 40 hours.[69] So after two hours of religion and lunch, I left Rutland at 2.15 and arrived (all the way by bus) in Cambridge at 7.10.

Well what about Vermont? First of all, and you'll be very jealous and envious about this, darling, the weather was superb, brisk, bright, sunny, cloudless days – but for the bare trees it might have been spring. Vermont up beside Canada is a small, and not too prosperous state with a population of about 300,000 (I think). It lives on dairy farming, tourists, a certain amount of lumber and that's about all. It is famous for maple syrup and skiing. I saw a lot of territory as you'll have gathered, pet, and it's rather like the West of Ireland. The ground is rocky and barren; the roads are narrow and winding; only the mountains are covered with trees (apart from patches cleared for skiing).

The news that both my patients are feeling better was welcome and don't worry about the scar, darling; it will go in time. It was very sweet of you to phone Desmond so soon and I'll attend to that letter. As for answering Myles – I'll get round to that. The news about the I.R.A.[70] did penetrate here. Do you think John Costello will apologise? I don't see that he has to!

As for Christmas, I'll probably go to Rhinebeck and settle into the Hyde Park Papers if I have enough done here beforehand. I have no ideas about presents for Aunty Agnes or home and really with customs forms and transport costs I can't see myself doing much, short of sending books to everyone. What do you think I should do: just

....

68   Missa cantata is a form of Tridentine Mass defined officially in 1960 as a sung Mass celebrated without sacred ministers, i.e. deacon and subdeacon.

69   Forty Hours' Devotion, in Italian called Quarant'ore or Quarantore, is a Roman Catholic exercise of devotion in which continuous prayer is made for forty hours before the Blessed Sacrament in solemn exposition.

70   IRA raid on Northern Ireland barracks.

P.S. LOOK OUT FOR SNAKES

send nice cards and long letters or what? As for the damned dividend thing, I have it propped up in front of me but don't be surprised if I forget to put it in here – really I'm getting so absentminded!

About the M.A. exam, I expect I got it more or less but don't believe I did well as otherwise he'd have told me so. Anyway there's no point in worrying about that. Much more important is what I'm going to do next year! I possibly could get a job teaching somewhere in America but that would mean leaving your mother alone much too long, so I think we should get back to Ireland in June, D.V. and I'll scan the 'Times Educational Supplement' for teaching jobs in England. What do you think, dear? You must be getting very wise and more lovely than ever, with all those early nights and I'm sure I'll encourage you in the habit, rather than otherwise.

Rutland has at least three families willing to house us (and eager to see you, naturally enough), if we ever get up that far, but really it is a little bit too like Ireland. The villages we passed through going to Norwich are tired looking, semi-ghost shanty towns. Rutland itself is just a big town: the people talk about the town and each other and little else. Still I enjoyed my visit to a really rural area. The Hudson valley after all is too near N.Y. (and dotted with big cities like Poughkeepsie and Albany) to be really rural. So Rhinebeck is just a village but two/three hours by train and you're in N.Y. itself.

 33

[BRIAN TO MARIE-THÉRÈSE]
Cambridge, Tuesday, 26 October

Well what's new with you, dear? How is your mother? Perhaps the cooler weather will help? How is the poor old vaccination coming along? Tonight I went to the International Center from the Widener for a cup of tea at 10 and found a very pleasant letter from Miss Allen (the school teacher at Rutland who backs this International club). By the way, I did tell you about the dance on

Sat, didn't I? Officially it was a square dance session – 'stag or drag' (i.e. come alone or bring a partner) but the caller wasn't good and the kids simply did a rural version of 'The Creep'[71] all night. Instead of just sitting with the teachers, I wandered around and talked to groups of high school students. Two of the teachers going home by cab gave me a lift back to the Ravitts.

Apart from the changes in weather there's little news. The political set-up is really swinging and there's a great effort to 'get out the vote' and inspire the believers on both sides, but there is tremendous apathy. Even the argument that people should vote Republican in order to help Ike's programme doesn't help very much, since many Democrats are more pro-Ike (especially in foreign affairs and defence expenditure) than Republicans.

Some food notes: bread is cheap, very fresh but rather synthetic (though there are many varieties and the rolls they serve on commons are quite good). Fruit is very reasonable – 4 lbs of lovely eating apples, well packed, for 49 cents; bananas about 2 lbs for 29 cents; and tinned fruit and cereals are very cheap. They don't have butcher shops: the meat is cut, wrapped and priced in display refrigerators and you take what you want. As for packed food – you can get everything from whole canned chicken to deep-freeze chips (called 'French fries'; 'chips' in restaurants mean potato crisps). Biscuits are also fairly cheap and cigarettes are a quarter a packet – either king-size or normal; some filters cost a couple of cents more.

Other costs might interest you also: telephone calls are 10 cents but interior postage only 3 cents. Tea or coffee costs about 10 cents a cup and milk about the same. Milk-Shakes (usually bigger than ours) are 20–25 cents. Pocket books (paper backs) vary between 25–90 cents and have a great range of titles and subjects, for example: Mann's 'Buddenbrooks', Faulkner, Hemingway, Joyce's 'Portrait

----

71   A slow shuffle that was so popular with Teddy Boys that it led to their other nickname, 'Creepers'. The song 'The Creep' came out in 1953, written and recorded for HMV by Yorkshire-born big band leader and saxophonist Ken Mackintosh.

P.S. LOOK OUT FOR SNAKES

of the Artist'. Philip Hughes' 'Popular History of the Church', The Power and the Glory', novels by Colette; books on philosophy, language, literary criticism, history, detectives and science fiction.

Now I know this isn't up to Alistair Cooke's standard, dearest, but anyway these are some of the things I've noticed so far. Most of all I notice an emptiness, except when I settle down to write to you at night and even that's a little difficult knowing you get these in the mornings. Have a good day, my darling, and look after yourself for me.

[BRIAN TO MARIE-THÉRÈSE]
Wednesday, 27 October

Still no letter but perhaps tomorrow – I'm an old sentimentalist aren't I, dear? Well I heard two rather good lectures today. The second was quite fantastic: it involved a discussion of the establishment of various constitutional precedents and a brief account of their development. Anyway the lecturer plunged into critical asides on McCarthy (who was hissed) and Vice-President Nixon (referred to as a 'travelling salesman'). The whole lecture was punctuated by applause and hissing. Actually Buck[72] in the earlier lecture (on slavery in the South) had also taken a sharp dig at McCarthy. So as you can see the academics here aren't slow to unveil their political leanings. Of course, Harvard is in a very 'liberal' tradition and strongly Democratic (that is the staff – the students vary according to origins) and has in fact the reputation of being pink; President Pusey[73] crossed swords with McCarthy in Wisconsin.

72 Paul Herman Buck (1899–1978), American historian. He won the Pulitzer Prize for History in 1938 and became the first Provost of Harvard University in 1945.

73 Nathan Marsh Pusey (1907–2001), prominent American university educator and twenty-fourth president of Harvard (1953–71). He overhauled the admissions process, which had been biased heavily in favour of the alumni of New England-based boarding schools, and began admitting public school graduates on the basis of their scores. He was an early and outspoken adversary of Senator Joseph McCarthy.

This afternoon I spent in the periodical room of the Widener. They have about 60 book cases for periodicals with say 30 magazines in each case (quite apart from newspapers), so you can imagine what a wealth of material they get. Out of interest I checked to find they take in 'Studies', 'the Bell', 'Irish Ecclesiastical Record', 'Dublin Review' (really English), 'Irish Historical Studies'. I was working on articles and reviews in the 'Revue d'Histoire de la 2nd guerre Mondiale' (for a change, may I say, I'm not sure of the spelling)[74] which is very useful.

Tonight I invited Michael Flynn (Irish vice-consul) over for dinner and fortunately picked a good night – tomato soup, rolls etc., roast stuffed turkey and cranberry jelly, mashed potatoes, celery and raw carrots, ice-cream. We had a pleasant chat and he told me that the third candidate in Cork is, he thinks, Hogan (is this James H. of Cork or Jerry of UCD?). We also happened to notice an advert that Toynbee[75] is speaking here on Friday week so I plan to go along to that, please God.

 35

Friday morning, 29 October

As always, Darling, you are perfectly right: Harry Atkins got it. Myles, when discussing his own chances, felt Atkins was a formidable opponent and a dangerous man! I'd simply love to attend some lectures at Harvard. Do you think there's a chance? I thought UCD was the only place one could drift in and out of lectures at will.

There is little news, on Wednesday Noeleen and I went to the pictures. Last night was my night on-duty and we were expecting Roche, but of course he never came. Mama never gets up and eats terribly little. The poor thing always feels sick and, now and then,

---

74 A dig at MT's appalling spelling as a result of her dyslexia.
75 Arnold Joseph Toynbee (1889–1975), British historian and a leading specialist on International affairs.

P.S. LOOK OUT FOR SNAKES

looks terribly pale but thank goodness we haven't had to use the oxygen yet, because neither Nurse[76], Betty nor I are sure how to use it. And we'll probably blow the house up!

I'm off to Mary Murphy's for supper this evening so will give you lots of college gossip tomorrow.

 36   [BRIAN TO MARIE-THÉRÈSE]
Cambridge, Saturday, 30 October

Well dear, there's very little to report from here just at present. Tonight lots of kids are going around for Halloween and I looked in at the International Centre for a while. However, tomorrow Egbert[77] and I are going to a party in Radcliffe[78] so maybe it will be a little more festive.

Sunday. Thanks to the switch from Summer Time we get an extra hour today so it wasn't too difficult to rise for 9 Mass. There was quite a big crowd of students from St Thomas More Society and I got a lift up to the Graduate Commons where we had a 'Communion Breakfast'. There was a talk by some Jesuit on religious persecution behind the Iron Curtain but that was a bit too emotional to be of any real interest. I did have quite a long talk with a number of men. Of course, most of them are law students but one can usually find a topic to cover – inevitably of course, Ireland turns up.

After looking through the Book Section of the Times, the reviews really aren't very good, I came back to Upland Rd and spent the afternoon reading a book on the Axis. The last couple of days in the Widener I have spent reading the back numbers of the 'Revue d'Histoire'[79] but I'm sure I've told you this darling, haven't I?

76   Mrs Ward
77   One of Brian's flatmates.
78   Liberal women's college in Cambridge.
79   Brian was fluent in Irish and Latin and apparently could read French.

37

Murphy's was most pleasant last night, no one else was there. Mary reminded me that the chief librarian at Harvard is married to Michael Tierney's[80] wife's sister (McNeill would be her maiden name) but I can't remember his name – I met them, if Mary is correct, and they are a charming couple.

Sunday

It lashed rain all today – unlike our wonderful night two years ago when someone very dashing and very mysterious tidied up after the guests and stalked off into the dawn with my heart in his pocket.

I went off to a talk in the Gresham by Stephen Williams on Enjoying Opera and I enjoyed him but not his examples, he, almost deliberately, left out all my favourite pieces.

Mrs Campbell[81] babysat for me and then stayed for tea. So now while Mama dozes I finish this letter. I miss you very much but love to count the days rolling by – that make it now less than 5 months before we are together again, and this time for always, please God.

Mama sent you her love (before she fell asleep) (she's now snoring gently!!) and is in quite a cheery humour but doesn't go downstairs at all.

---

80 Michael Tierney (1894–1975) was Professor of Greek at UCD and then President of UCD from 1947 -64. He was a close friend of Theo Dillon's and was one of the group that met in Theo's house.

81 Mrs. Campbell was a neighbour of the Dillon's in Killiney and was one of Marie Dillon's few friends.

P.S. LOOK OUT FOR SNAKES

P.S. Look out for snakes

ILLUSTRATIONS

Brian and MT at their favourite picnic spot in Killiney, 1954.

DramSoc UCD December, 1951, taken when the final curtain went down on 'The Taming of the Shrew'. Left to Right - Neil Porter, Tommy Owens, Marie-Thérèse, Billy Kingston, Tommy Hayes (MT made his wife's wedding dress), Phil Irwin.

▲ Mary Murphy and Brian Dillon. Mary Murphy hated being photographed, so rarely smiled for the camera. She taught Irish at UCD and was Dean of women students. Brian Dillon, also known as Fr. Mathew, was at the time headmaster of Glenstal. He was also MT's godfather.

◀ Sheila Coakley went to school with Marie-Thérèse and studied at UCD with Brian. Sheila worked in the administration of UCD until her retirement. She was one of Brian and MT's oldest friends and a devoted godmother to David Farrell.

Agnes and Nick Stokes offered the ten-year-old Brian (originally from Manchester) refuge when WWII broke out. And as he used to say "I've been in refuge ever since." Agnes was Brian's godmother and his mother's sister.

George Roach was at the time archivist of the Roosevelt papers (Hyde Park), which is how Brian met him. They became close friends. George was a talented historian who died young in the early 1960s from leukemia.

► Ronan Keane was a brilliant law student at UCD and one of Brian's closest friends.

► Mother Mary Martin of the Medical Missionaries of Mary. Mary Martin was godmother to Marie Dillon, who had to convert to Catholicism before marrying Theo, and subsequently bridesmaid to Marie when she married Theo in Leysin. Later she was also godmother (in proxy) to Marie-Thérèse.

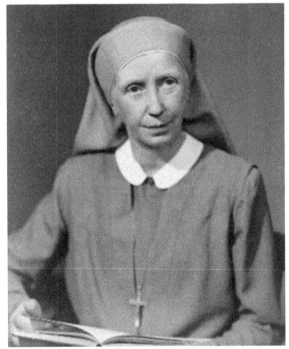

Myles, Marie-Thérèse and Theo Dillon taken in 1946.

Theo and Marie Dillon taken in Leysin TB sanatorium, where Theo was a patient and Marie Benninger his nurse. The photo was taken in 1924.

Brian reunited with his family in 1946, left to right: Brian, Frank, Kevin, Pearse (back row), Ethnea sitting between their parents, Francis and Teresa Farrell in the front.

Naomi and Marie-Thérèse, best friends for life, taken by Bill Kidney at Cobh, March 1955.

Myles Dillon (1900 - 1972) was a renowned Celtic scholar and was Senior Professor at the
School of Celtic Studies at the Dublin Institute of Advanced Studies from 1949 - 1972.

Wedding 11th April, 1955. From left to Right – Dom Bernard O'Dea, James (Jim) Barry, Brian, Marie-Thérèse, Mary Raleigh (Kotsonouris).

Newlyweds, Brian and Marie-Thérèse, Cambridge, 1955.

Chapter 4

NOVEMBER 1954

Mama was small in stature, stocky, dark with piercing blue eyes. She had a terrific strength of purpose and could will things to happen. She was very shy with strangers but she filled her home with her creativeness and courage.

Marie-Thérèse (Dillon) Farrell, talking about her mother, Marie Benninger

1

Cambridge, Monday, 1 November

Hello Darling, what's new with you? Here once again the weather is picking up and walking to College today, and back again for lunch, it was marvellous, just like spring, fresh and brisk. Really I didn't come back for lunch, so much as to pick up my mail, and found your letter of Friday. How did you find the Murphys? And how is your mother now?

Well the 'party' last night wasn't exactly high living in any sense. We were at one of the Radcliffe houses and I had about three good conversations, with the other men! American girls, by and large, seem incapable of conversation. They say 'yes', 'no', 'wonderful', 'gosh' but never say anything. Still it filled in the evening. Despite all the weekend parties, and, judging by the various sounds of revelry by night, there were plenty of them, 9 Mass was packed this morning.

About this blazer business a) I really think it's cheating for me to get one – after all my primary allegiance is to UCD not Harvard and I'm not really a Harvard man b) so far I've seen no one wearing a specifically Harvard blazer c) I think it would be very expensive.

The news of the election[1] wasn't after all so surprising but I should think Atkins is fairly old and probably won't have many years to go. The mere fact that Myles went off to Vienna suggests he didn't expect too much. Do you think this might be a trial run? Michael Tierney[2] will have to retire eventually!

By the way, dear, I got my two (green and light blue) college scarves cleaned – for 30 cents – and they look fine. As you can see my news content isn't high these days but really I'm quite busy and happy in my work as the formula runs. I had a letter from Brenda Hubbard (the little girl in the photo from Rutland) ending

1   Myles Dillon had run unsuccessfully for the presidency of UCC.
2   When Michael Tierney retires, Myles might run for the presidency of UCD.

P.S. LOOK OUT FOR SNAKES

with a delightful 'we sure would like to take you up on coming to Vermont for your honeymoon' – cute? And in case you think 'cute' makes me sound American, I'm not. Farrell of the neutral voice, medium long hair, tweed coat etc. ... remains firm as a beacon but still feels a long way from shore when you're so far away. However, let there be no panic, as Phil Irwin[3] would say, 'time passes like everything else' and soon I'll really be able to say 'good morning darling', so for now, God love you, (and me and us) Brian.

 2

Tuesday morning, 2 November

Strange and wonderful how closely our minds work despite 3,000 miles; all Sunday I couldn't get a question out of my mind: what would I ever do and what would happen to me should a lively American brunette draw you away from me? And then you write reassuring me. Speaking of romance, at about 5 o'clock yesterday evening, I met Mary Dwain and Frank D'Arcy on the bus to Dublin, they were on their way back from a walk over Killiney Hill – both looking very smug and dreamy. They told me that John O'D got his MA and that Sean White[4] is in Oxford, doing some further degree. Their news was bad, in one way, did you hear that none of the UCD people got the studentship (History) this year (some

3 Phil Irwin from a wealthy farming family in the West of Ireland, was a great storyteller and very popular in UCD. One of the actors in DramSoc. Years later, when Brian was part of the RTE team covering John Kennedy's arrival at Shannon, he bumped into Phil, who had brought his son to witness the historical event. Phil had settled down in the midlands, where he was teaching. He was much loved by his students. See illustrations.

4 Seán J. White (1927–1996), Irish writer, academic, broadcaster and journalist. He was an expert on the Burren and a regular attendee at the Merriman Summer School in County Clare and a good friend of MT and Brian. Brian and MT's daughter, Miriam and his daughter, Nicky, worked for several seasons on Liam de Paor's excavation on Inishcealtra, Lough Derg.

Cork or Galway person got it) so there'll probably be stiff opposition for you next year.

 3

I'm delighted to see that you are off to Bard again, I heard via Aunt Agnes, but do not hitch-hike or stroll out on streets to be picked up! During the winter I'm certain that driving is much more dangerous and it's too cold to be waiting for lifts, so go down in comfort by train and read a good book on the way!

Yes, Aunt Agnes came this evening. She's upset about the news from Manchester. Apparently, this visit to the hospital is more serious and I suppose anything serious is very serious with Pearse.[5] Darling, skip some of my letters and write home instead, you spoil me, at the cost of everyone else, I'm sure! And I can wait 3 or 4 days, as long as you are well, but some letters from you might take your Mother's mind off the present problems with Pearse.

Aunt Agnes herself is well and full of news, in fact she cheered up after a few minutes (a great gift of hers) and we had a snug evening by the fire. Mama is in quite good form too, but her room is terribly cold![6] I now keep my dressing gown on the back of her door and put it on every time I go into her room – people think I'm mad ... till they've been in her room for a few minutes and then they quietly turn blue or their teeth start chattering!

So, from the depths of a nice warm bed, good night Darling, your Marie-Thérèse.

---

5   Pearse Farrell (1919–1957) was the eldest of Brian's brothers. He died of heart failure in 1957. The family believed it was a result of gas poisoning during the Second World War. All of Brian's brothers – Pearse, Kevin and Frank were drafted at some point into the army during WWII.

6   Being a Swiss Alpine girl at heart, Marie Dillon loved the cold.

4

Sorry for the changed handwriting, darling, but I left my pen at home and I'm using a post-office, straight pen. The meeting on Monday night brought a very amusing speech from Owen, chairman of the Department, in which he described life 'in the chromium-plated gutters of the Graduate School'. Apparently, the History Department lets in 30–40 new graduate students per year and has about 120 graduate students altogether. He spoke about the rigidity of first-year graduate work compared to the freedom of the more advanced 301[7] courses, so apparently they recognised my work of last year[8] and consider me a 2nd year graduate student. I met quite a number of other students and had a pleasant time.

Yesterday, work, even in the recesses of the Widener, was difficult as loudspeakers urged everyone on their privilege to go out and vote. About 9 the results started coming in. The boys downstairs had an election party[9] and I went down there from about 10.00–2.00. At the present time, results are fairly certain but great interest still hangs on Case's[10] chances for Senator in New Jersey.

The weather here has gone all miserable again, it's very cold and wet. But today I got your weekend letter and now I'm ready

7   Classics 301 – Reading or Topics courses for graduate students whose individual needs are not met by the formal courses offered. This was the course that Brian was doing.
8   Brian had already completed one year of his Master's Degree in UCD.
9   The 1954 US mid-term elections were held on 2 November 1954, halfway through Republican President Dwight D. Eisenhower's first term. In the election, the Republicans lost the Congressional majorities they had won in the previous election. In the House, the Republicans lost eighteen seats to the Democratic Party, losing control of the chamber. Republicans would not retake the House until 1994. The Republicans also lost control of the Senate, losing two seats to the Democrats. Republicans would not retake control of the Senate until 1980.
10 In the Senate elections in New Jersey Republican Clifford P. Case defeated Democratic Charles R. Howell with 48.66% of the vote.

to face anything. You're so sweet (and so flattering) and leave the 'Vogue' thing to the boy. Re Connie's[11] efforts, I'll look but suggest she try the periodical rooms in the R.D.S. or the Royal College of Physicians (in Kildare St – between the Club and the National Library). Both of them should carry American medical journals. Of course over here, there may also be questions of recognition by the A. M.A.[12] and by the State bodies.

 5

[BRIAN TO MARIE-THÉRÈSE]
Cambridge, Wednesday, 3 November

Little news to report, dearest. On Sunday please God I'm going to the meeting of the Éire Society in Boston. I also have an invitation to tea at the English-speaking Union on the same day. Tomorrow and the day after are lectures from John O'Meara[13] (UCD) and Toynbee; before the latter I'm due to visit Mrs Howe. So as you can see it should be a busy few days.

Here great attention is being paid to the last couple of Senate seats, especially Case in New Jersey; he is Republican and was strongly supported by Ike but ran on an openly anti-McCarthy ticket. As things stand the Democrats will run the House comfortably, while the Senate will be about half and half. This will mean trouble for Nixon,[14] I suspect. Once congress meets the main focus will be the McCarthy issue but I wouldn't be surprised to see Wilson attacked by the liberal wing of the Democrats.

11 Previously, MT had asked Brian to look out for work in the medical field for her girlfriend Connie.
12 American Medical Association.
13 John J. O'Meara was Professor of Latin at UCD, from 1948 to 1984. In Ireland he played a major role in the effort to modernise education in the schools and universities, in particular the teaching of Latin and Irish, and the collaboration between UCD and Trinity College Dublin. His ideas were ahead of their time in the conservative, Church-dominated atmosphere in Ireland.
14 Nixon was vice-president at the time.

P.S. LOOK OUT FOR SNAKES

The murder-trial of Sam Sheppard[15] (which I mentioned some time ago) is only just beginning as one of the jurors had to stand down – he had a record! This after a fortnight spent in vetting the jury by both sides!

It really is getting cold here now and the central heating is wonderful. It's also getting late so I'll stop here until tomorrow, next thrilling instalment very soon.

3.00 pm Thursday. I've been working today on some things in political theory, just for a change. The post brought your letter of Tuesday, a letter from Neil, who seems in good form, and news from home and Aunty Agnes. It seems that Pearse is by no means well. It so tragic, just after they have moved to the new house! Pearse is in hospital but apparently very weak and only semi-conscious. Really I feel spoiled and mean, he is so intelligent and yet never had the chances given to me; yet he kept going in the face of rotten luck while I've been so very fortunate[16]. Please God he'll pull through but I fear the worst and feel very helpless so far away, but I'll pray for him and hope that God's hand will touch lightly, however it falls.

[MARIE-THÉRÈSE TO BRIAN]
Thursday, 4 November

Mama is much better and came down yesterday morning for the first time in 3 weeks, and today too! She loved your letter.

---

15   On 4 July 1954, Marilyn Sheppard, the wife of a handsome thirty-year-old doctor, Sam Sheppard, was brutally murdered in the bedroom of their home in Bay Village, Ohio, on the shore of Lake Erie. Sam Sheppard denied any involvement in the murder and described his own battle with the killer, whom he described as 'bushy-haired'. Facing two different juries, twelve years apart, Sam Sheppard was found guilty by one jury, not guilty by the next. Apart from the largely unanswered question of guilt, the Sheppard case produced a landmark U.S. Supreme Court decision on the right to a fair trial.

16   Brian always believed that he was lucky.

This evening I had a date at 8.15 with Alistair Cooke! All day I waited to hear him speak about the elections, instead he spent his full ¼ hour on a brilliant word picture of the Queen Mother's visit to Hyde Park and N.Y. and, tantalising, not a word about the elections. I'm looking forward to hearing George's impressions of her visit – is it next weekend you go to Bard?

P.S. Friday Morning – Aunt Agnes dropped me a card to say that Pearse is improving, Thank God, and that everyone is much relieved.

[MARIE-THÉRÈSE TO BRIAN]
Thursday night, 4 November

The news has just come of poor Ike's[17] defeat in this election! Aren't Americans mad? First they put a man in power and then they take away as much power as possible! Mad, I say! The papers yesterday showed Miriam Hederman,[18] complete with wig, being called to the bar and I also read that Ronan[19] got his scholarship and first place.

You asked about the weather, well it's much better than the summer we had, but it's seasonable, a bit of torrential rain and some clear lovely days. Actually, you can count on it not to rain after a fine morning, more accurately than during the summer, but the papers say the south west has had the worst floods since 1924 or so. At least 50% of the corn was still in the fields and no turf was saved, the farmers are ordering coal for this winter already.

---

17   In the election, the Republicans lost the Congressional majorities they had won in the previous election, thus limiting Eisenhower's power as president.
18   Miriam Hederman O'Brien (1932–), Irish barrister and academic, has held the posts of Chancellor of the University of Limerick and Director of the University of Limerick Foundation.
19   Ronan Keane.

Cambridge, Friday, 5 November

How are you, dear? I came home for lunch to see if there was any news but there wasn't, only an invitation to a short talk by Max Beloff[20] on Wednesday next. How is your mother feeling? Do give her my love. And ditto for you. Are you being careful to avoid colds and flu, watching the traffic (and the rain) and not working or worrying too hard?

Well last night I went to hear John O'Meara[21] speak. He got quite a crowd (110 odd) and we had to move to a larger room. After the lecture I walked him back to his house and we had a long talk about UCD, Ireland and so on. He is doing quite a long lecture trip until Christmas. Apparently Frank D'Arcy (who is now teaching in Belvedere) hasn't a hope of getting a job in UCD. But all news about College tends to be depressing anyway. I know you'll say 'don't worry about the future, darling' and I'm not really but neither am I particularly hopeful.

Since yesterday afternoon the weather has been very wet and now it's also getting somewhat clammy. Ugh, Ugh! Never mind, please God, you'll be here for only the sun and you do get sun over here.

This does seem a scrappy sort of letter but I'm rather worried about Pearse and this business of waiting for news doesn't help. However, between one thing and another I should be fairly busy over the weekend, and then next week I have my trip to Bard so that makes time move slightly faster for me. Now you, poor darling, don't seem to be getting around very much at all and frankly I'm not getting any great kick out of it. About seeing Taft,[22] I'll

20 Baron Max Beloff (1913–1999), English historian and political scientist and the author of numerous works on European history, US government and Soviet foreign policy.

21 John J. O'Meara held visiting appointments at the Princeton Institute of Advanced Study, Dumbarton Oaks (Harvard University) and Vassar College.

22 William Howard Taft III (1915–1991), diplomat who served as US Ambassador to Ireland from 1953 to 1957. He was a grandson of President William Howard Taft.

write to him over the week-end and then you can drift in any time, preferably 'phone' first to arrange a time. You can say what you like from my point of view; my end re the Fulbright people is untouchable. But I would suggest you see him soon.

 9

[MARIE-THÉRÈSE TO BRIAN]
Friday night, 5 November

Due to a strike of ground staff (fire-men) at Shannon for the last few days, all the post will have been delayed and will come in a bunch!

Tonight I have very little to tell, except that exactly 4 weeks since my vaccination the scab has fallen off my arm leaving a clean, small hole! Oh! I was quite naughty today: I showed your 'cuttings'[23] to Mr Needham, when he asked after you as usual! Being a divorcee [sic] and also being rather surprised at my gayness since your departure, fully expecting me to become morose and saddened, he was beginning to suspect that we were 'drifting'. He read it in an awkward silence and hurried off to town barely saying goodbye![24]

Suddenly the weather has become very dirty. Today getting off the bus, I stepped into a small lake up to my coat hem, hence decided the best place after tea was bed with magazines and chocolate. The rain beating on my window all evening keeps saying how right I was! How I wish you were here too! With all my love, Marie-Thérèse

Saturday Morning (same letter)

Your letter of Wednesday arrived this morning; considering the fire-men only went back to work late last night, it's a puzzle how it came! But I suppose our letters have developed a radar-beam by now!

----

23 I believe she is referring to Brian's most recent letters.
24 MT, to this day, still loves to get a rise out of people.

It's not quite clear, are you going to Bard this or next weekend? Anyway I suppose it's only for a few days, regards to George when you see him. Love, MT

 10

[BRIAN TO MARIE-THÉRÈSE]
Cambridge Saturday, 6 November

Well, dear, the Howe's [25] little party last night was quite fun. He is a small, quick, rather wrinkled, pleasant and intelligent man who is still working on the Holmes[26] papers (he claimed to have been an assistant director in Hollywood once and to have kissed Ginger Rogers – I wouldn't be surprised). She [Mrs Howe] is rather like her mother – somewhat vague, wide-open innocent eyes (and wide open ears for any little scandal), given to 'society' but again, fundamentally, very pleasant. There were about ten people there so it was quite a mixum-gatherum.

We got down to Memorial Hall to hear Toynbee (they moved him from the New Lecture Hall which only holds 800!) but by 7.45 the place was packed – in fact they were turning people away

25   Mark DeWolfe Howe (1906–1967), a member of the Law School faculty (Harvard) since 1946, was Charles Warren Professor of American Legal History. Upon his graduation in 1933, his life took a turn that was to have a lasting effect on his career. The late Mr Justice Frankfurter, then still in his professorial chair at the Law School, selected Howe to be secretary to Mr Justice Holmes. Howe was ultimately to become the editor of Holmes's letters and the author of Holmes's biography, unfinished at Howe's death. He published, in 1957 and 1963, two volumes of biography: *Justice Oliver Wendell Holmes: The Shaping Years, 1841–1870* and *The Proving Years, 1870–1882*. The two volumes brought Holmes only to his appointment to the Supreme Judicial Court of Massachusetts, but in them Howe made a permanent contribution to judicial biography and American intellectual history. In 1935 Howe married Mary Manning, a Dublin playwright and niece of Louie Bennett.

26   Oliver Wendell Holmes Jr (1841 –1935) was Acting US Chief Justice from 1902–1930. Noted for his long service, concise and pithy opinions and deference to the decisions of elected legislatures, he is one of the most widely cited US Supreme Court justices in history, particularly for his 'clear and present danger' opinion for a unanimous court in the 1919 case of Schenck v. United States.

by 7.30, I believe. Anyway I gather today that I didn't miss much although Langer apparently sacrificed his academic integrity by referring to Toynbee as a 'fellow historian' (tut, tut).

Today's post brought a letter from Desmond Williams. I had asked about my exam results; verdict 'a mark slightly under first class honours. What this means is that on your thesis you will have to get a mark above the maximum first.' Re the O'Cleary scholarship, he advised me to wait – if necessary to next year – as there are negotiations on foot to have it raised to £165. However, he says this is a 'provisional judgement' and that he will write me further on the matter. Anyway, I'll wait for now till I hear what's coming.

How are things with you, dear? The postal service here seems to have gone to the dogs (Desmond's letter was posted on Monday evening; my last from home Sunday), but maybe that will improve. I now plan to go to Bard fairly early next week and I may stay a full week in order to check on the Hyde Park papers. However I'm arranging with Stan[27] to have my post sent on to me as I can, at present, only say that I'll be at Bard from Thurs–Sun definitely. But now, my darling, I'll shut down for tonight: look after yourself, dear, and have a nice day and remember your wild colonial boy, Brian.

 11

[MARIE-THÉRÈSE TO BRIAN]
Sunday, 7 November

I was delighted to see that you'd extended your stay at Bard and with our old friend Locke and Hooker, and I hope you are now happily settled back at Harvard.

You mentioned colds, now you must avoid them, darling! I've had my 'first snuffle' but, by going to bed before supper every night, I shook it off very quickly. It's the only way, so you do that should you get one.

---

27   One of Brian's flatmates.

Yesterday I went to arrange about my new coat and it's a modified 'H' line, my own design, and should be ready in a fortnight. Then I'll go to see Taft! Here it is wet and cold at 4.30 and already completely dark, but still the garden is beautiful, wonderful golds and reds with the cherry blossom blooming.

Much later – I was just rereading your letter (with remarks about Owens) when, who should appear on the door-step but Tommy[28] and Ronan,[29] and I was so glad to see them. Ronan and Tommy rocked themselves merrily and told me 'titbits' – but they promised to write you so I won't spoil their letters. Apparently Billy and Avril are expecting an addition for February – that gives me an idea – if we were getting married in Boston I could ask Avril to be my matron of honour – but it's much too soon to do anything yet, let her get over her baby first.

I'll end here with 17 more Sundays to go and 17 past, please God the next 17 will fly. All my love, Marie-Thérèse

P.S. I am sending you a booklet produced by friends of Louie Bennett's, pass it on to James Barry in the Éire Soc., I'm sure he'll love it, M.T.

 12

[BRIAN TO MARIE-THÉRÈSE]
Cambridge, Sunday, 7 November

I'm just back from Boston, where I attended a meeting of the Éire Society and a rather vague talk by some priest. I met some people and of course Jim Barry. There was a big crowd. We went down to a 'Citizens for McCarthy' rally which was quite fantastic.

The meeting hall held about 2,000 and we barely squeezed in at 7.00 pm (meeting due to start at 7.30). Outside were another couple of thousand, I believe. The two main speakers were: some

28 Thomas (Tommy) Owens, friend of Brian's from UCD, he studied Law and became Sheriff of Monaghan.
29 Ronan Keane.

sort of Rabbi from New York – quite a rabble rouser on a sort of 'McCarthy for God' rampage and 'don't we all love McCarthy' – and the quieter but more effective Roy Cohn (McC's chief henchman). Of course this meeting was for the faithful and there was no attempt made to convince the other side, but I was amazed at both the vague treatment of the subject (everything and everyone involved was simplified) and the semi-hysterical reaction of the audience. Incidentally, this crowd of crackpots plans to join the protest meeting in Washington D.C. on Thursday. One of the minor speakers rather let one angry cat of 'McCarthyism' out of the bag when he dived into a bitter attack on crazy intellectuals who were 'stoogies' for the Communists; in effect, he appealed to some primitive and superstitious 'religious' conviction against any sort of rationalism. Of course, to be fair, I must admit that the anti-McCarthyites often tend to be just as bitter, narrow and fanatic on the topic. Also on the platform tonight was James Francis Curley[30] of whom I've heard a lot about ever since I came over. He was one of the old democratic politicians of Massachusetts and ex-governor and ex-mayor of Boston; he is also an ex-jailbird – convicted for some sort of racketeering. He's very old and apparently just waiting to see his youngest son ordained a Jesuit priest!

What sort of weekend did you have? I hope it wasn't as cold, Darling. Do try to get some fun, pet, and look after yourself. On the health topic, I'm still waiting to hear further news about Pearse, but none has come. I'm in an awful position of not being able to write because I don't know how things are.

....

30 James Michael Curley (1874–1958), Democrat politician from Boston. He served four terms as Mayor of Boston and a single term as Governor of Massachusetts. He was twice convicted of criminal behaviour and served time in prison during his last mayoral term.

13

146 Upland, Tues–Wednesday, 8 and 9 November

Well dearest,

Tomorrow I'm off on my travels again and I plan to stay until about Wednesday. Re-hitch-hiking, don't worry I'm going by bus. Today I went to a meeting of the Politics Club to hear Max Beloff speak on the possible abatement of Russo-American tension; he was very good but, as is apparently normal with an American audience, only the most stupid (and even in Harvard that means thick) asked questions. In fact Beloff became more and more high-pitched in discussing some things with one of these boys after the meeting proper.

The meeting was not published, simply postcards were sent out to members of the Club (I'm not in that august company, but had left my name and address when I attended their first meeting). The card announced that sherry would be served, but the meeting was held in Philips Brooks House and no alcohol is allowed there, evidently the donor was a puritan, so they served some kind of ice-cream sherbet instead.

After some more re-reading of Irish history, I then went over to hear McKay (he's a history professor) speak at the International Centre on the contemporary French scene; I enjoyed his talk, though he rather came heavy about 'informed circles in Washington' and 'when I spoke to the Ambassador'.

Apart from that I have little to offer you. I can't get your Vogue pattern in Cambridge but please God will try Gordon Marsh in Boston; the picture you sent is too small for me to decide about whether or not I like it but anyway knowing you I suppose I'd better send it one way or another (the martyr act; henpecked and hurt!).

Of news there is little. I still haven't decided what I'm going to say exactly in Bard, but guarantee that it will include Yeats, Frank O'Connor, Synge, O'Casey, Shaw, Joyce and the rest. In fact it may well turn into a litany of the patriotic saints and literary martyrs of modern Ireland. By the way, dear, did you know that your grandfather was apparently very fond of P. H. Pearse? He also spoke up in Westminster about the executions[31] of course. Naturally I'm not making any exhaustive study for the Bard people, in a sense it will be a very broad talk on modern Irish history. Still that period retains its fascination for me. For instance, all the criticism of Pearse's literary and historical and oratorical style leaves me unmoved. I still think his poems are pretty and touching and his speeches quite fine. Even the O'Casey setting of an exaggerated Pearse speech doesn't kill the nobility of the man.

One of the dominant notes in the period, naturally enough, is anti-clericalism.[32] Strangely, since I came over here, talking to people who know modern Ireland well, I find they have a strange hope that somehow a substantial anti-clerical movement will shake the stagnation of the general scene. Of course, the 'intellectuals' have good reason to be anti-clerical, I feel that the Magnificent Society in many ways reflects the feeling (also I hear that Michael Tierney is preparing to sell us up the river by getting us a charter as a separate University

....

31   John Dillon made an impassioned speech in Parliament on 11 May 1916 in the aftermath of the Easter Rising: 'I am proud of these men. They were foolish, they were misled ... (uproar). I say I am proud of their courage, and if you were not so dense and stupid, as some of you English people are, you could have had these men fighting for you, and they are men worth having ... It is not murderers who are being executed, it is insurgents, who have fought a clean fight, a brave fight, however misguided.' As a result of Dillon's speech, Prime Minister Asquith went over to Ireland that evening and put a stop to further executions.

32   The leaders of the Rising were Catholics who had a deep personal religious faith, but equally all of them were Irish Republicans who were opposed to the Catholic Church's interference in political matters. All of the leaders of the 1916 Rising, with the sole exception of James Connolly, were members of the Irish Republican Brotherhood whose constitution (Article 18) supported the separation of Church and State – 'In the Irish Republic there shall be no state religion but every citizen shall be free to worship God according to his conscience, and perfect freedom of worship shall be guaranteed as a right and not granted as a privilege.' Constitution of the Irish Republican Brotherhood – 1910 edition (Bureau of Military History, CD8/3 p.3).

P.S. LOOK OUT FOR SNAKES

in Stillorgan – but as a 'Catholic University': this, by the way, from an opponent of Tierney in general). I hope that some sort of amalgamation with Trinity comes off instead because, with a large Catholic University in Dublin, the present clerical half-Nelson on education would become a real strangle-hold. The whole secondary school system quo intellectual training is rotten but at least the teachers (except perhaps in smaller towns) are saved the complete humiliation of the national school teachers. Frankly at this stage I think any change would necessarily be for the better.[33]

 14

[MARIE-THÉRÈSE TO BRIAN]
Monday Morning, 8 November

Darling, I hope you are feeling a bit better now. I knew the news from Manchester would depress you but you've heard by now that he is recovering (Aunt Agnes dropped me a card to say Pearse was pulling through), and I do hope you'll neglect me a little in favour of home, please write them a lovely newsy letter to cheer them up.

Saturday I called in to 'the United States Lines': to enquire about sailings for March: the SS America leaves Cobh on March 15th (arrives NY March 21st) and I can get a passage for £60. If you have to book one return passage, this company expects a deposit, but they return every penny if one changes plans. If you have a look at a Tourist Deck Plan, try to get an 'outside cabin', so one has a window, sorry porthole! Make sure it is near public wash-rooms as the ones with private showers are just too expensive. You should be able to get one for about £73 per person, but do as you think best in this matter. I'll send money via your account, just before leaving, but I'm afraid I won't be able to afford much over £70. It's all so exciting and this booking brings March and April all the nearer.

---

33   Although a devout Catholic at the time, Brian Farrell bitterly resented the hold that the Catholic Church had on education – at all levels – in Ireland.

Now do tell me, and this is very important, can you afford to keep me from March 22nd till mid-June in America? It's a bit expensive isn't it? And also very important, plan a good Christmas for yourself, and answer me on what you would like as a present. I think we might leave off celebrating your birthday till, say, May 9th – would that be cheating? But it would mean we could be together for it and you'd have to take me out! (very subtle that!)

My Darling, what a miserable week you have had, that strike[34] prevented you from hearing that Pearse is better and he's still improving. I was in Aunt Agnes's this evening and she reported that he's much improved so don't worry! That's very important because you can't help anyone by worrying, neither about Pearse nor our future! Once we're married I'll go anywhere you find work, so you've quite a wide field to choose from. I want to be by you and no one else, and that's not even counting where I'd prefer to be!!

This evening I had tea in Aunt Agnes's, we sat in front of a roaring fire and then we went around to the Parish Church for the M.M. Devotions.[35] Aunt Agnes has given up the job,[36] as in this cold weather she was finding it a bit too much. I think she loves being back in the flat[37] and she hates leaving it all day, certainly she has got it most comfortably arranged. Mama is 'up and down' and hence is a bit 'short' of temper and breath these last few days, but please God, this will pass!

I'm glad you got college gossip first hand, so to speak, because I have no opportunity of getting any, though I did meet Tommy Owens and he complained that you never write! I said I'd pass on the word.

34 Irish postal strike.
35 Miraculous Medal Devotions.
36 Agnes was working across town in a friend's shop.
37 Brian was in the US and Neil Porter in England, so Agnes did up the flat and moved back in.

P.S. LOOK OUT FOR SNAKES

There is nothing in our papers to compare with your Dr Shephard so send me a paper cutting next time you are sending a letter. If it goes long enough I suppose they'll make a picture[38] of it!

 16

[MARIE-THÉRÈSE TO BRIAN]
Wednesday, 10 November

I'm very sorry to see, by letter of Saturday, that the air-mail hold-up was so bad! Are you receiving post now?

Darling, I'm delighted with the Exam results – with a good thesis that means First Class Honours and I'm sure that O'Meara's disparaging remarks about college were in the light of Harvard – it must be depressing to even think of UCD[39] when in a real University!

Not knowing whether you are staying at George's, I'm still writing to Cambridge but I do hope you'll go to Bard for Xmas, it should be pleasant there. I'm going to see Fr Dargen tonight about my Baptism Cert. and Letters of Freedom, but would like your advice about something before I approach the American Embassy.

When asking for a Visa, do I ask for one for a few months, or do I mention that I might be staying in America for over a year? This might be important, as they will extend yours without difficulty, but it might be different in my case. Taft[40] seems to be keen that you should return after a year. Give me a line on this!

---

38   MT was right, as usual! *The Fugitive series and then film (with Harrison Ford) was based on* the true story of Dr Sam Sheppard. Mistakenly convicted in Ohio of murdering his wife Marilyn, he spent a number of years in prison.

39   UCD was located at Earlsfort Terrace at the time and it had only two lecture halls and one large high-ceilinged hall that served as the library, nothing to compare to the wonderful facilities at Harvard.

40   Taft was the US ambassador to Ireland.

You old Darling, I hope you are now happily enjoying Bard and having a bit of a holiday. The McCarthy meeting sounded rather sordid, like a pale reflection of a communist rally – I knew the Jesuits would be mixed-up in it somewhere!

I see by yesterday's paper that Garland C. Routt is returning to the States prior to taking up some new diplomatic post. I'll send you the cutting at the weekend; it includes my Uncle[41] presenting Routt with some Waterford Glass.

I met Sheila Creedon[42] last night and she took me for a drive, and then we went for a walk down Dun Laoghaire pier – it was a lovely night!

Before I end this miserable news-less note, Dearest, have you had a chance to do anything about your 'papers' and Baptism Certificate? Or can I do anything from this end?

41 James Dillon, Fine Gael politician

42 Sheilah Creedon was Naomi Kidney's older sister (there were three sisters, Sheilah, Naomi and Dot Rowan). When Marie Dillon suffered a stroke a few years after Theo died, it was to be the first of many. Her doctor was head of Loughlinstown Hospital, the then county hospital of Wicklow. MT was working in the factory in Dun Laoghaire and her mother was in hospital. She wanted to take time off work so she could visit her mother. She approached Mr Rowan and asked for a loan of £10 so she could buy herself food and take time off work to visit her mother. He gladly wrote her a cheque and then he suggested that she move in with his daughter, Sheilah Creedon (married without children to Con). Sheila and Con happily took her in and spoilt her rotten. She had a cooked breakfast every morning. When Con died years later, Sheila married an elderly wealthy industrialist who spoilt and took care of her. MT never forgot their kindness to her in her time of need.

18

Dearest,

I'm very glad to hear that you are getting post at last and thank goodness you are enthusiastic about something for Christmas, if the dark grey suit is that nice, get one! But bring someone along when you are shopping to help you choose!

Yesterday evening Con, Rosalie, Eva and I went to 'Sabrina', a delightful picture, as light-hearted as 'Roman Holiday', I hope you see it. I could have shot Con! She joined us with streaming eyes and coughing like a consumptive. I hope she's very sick by now! She deserves it![43]

 19

[BRIAN TO MARIE-THÉRÈSE]
Bard College, Saturday, November 13

Sorry for the delay in writing, darling, but my travel arrangements went rather 'gang agley'.[44] By just missing a streetcar in Cambridge, I was three minutes late for my train in Boston. Hence, instead of leaving on the 10.45 train, I left by bus to make the Danbury Connecticut. After a really lovely ride, through Massachusetts and Connecticut I got to Danbury at 7.50 – and discovered, you guessed – no connection! I ended up staying the night at Danbury, described as 'the hat city' and boasting only one hotel and two cinemas, and caught the 6.15 to Poughkeepsie.

From there I went to Hyde Park library (arriving about 9.15) and saw George. I phoned Bard and someone drove out and picked me up.

43 Having grown up with a TB patient (Theo Dillon), MT was painfully aware of the spread of infection, and in later years would always isolate a sick child from the pack.
44 From a Scottish saying – 'the best laid plans gang oft agley [wrong].'

In the afternoon, I went to a seminar on Joyce and saw a really lovely poster in Irish! It was done in Celtic scroll-work. I spoke to a crowd of about 50–60 at 8.30 until about 9.50 and then answered questions for a quarter of an hour or so. Then we had a reception and more questions. The talk went over quite well, I thought, and people seemed quite pleased – lots of congratulations anyway.

About six of us went to a small '21st' party for one of the students and so to bed. I was housed in a room in one of the dormitories.

Today I took a rest until about 10.30. Then after lunch I went to see, in the following order: the Carriers, then Mrs Boyce (the nurse who had been present the night before and insisted I come over) and finally onto a cocktail party at the Hirsch's – he's the professor of painting at Bard. After dinner I went to a citizenship party, one of the girls had just become an American student, and this was given to celebrate the event.

From there I went on to a dance at Zabriski. It was really very pleasant. It was a 'semi- formal' event so the girls changed out of the usual slacks, shorts and jeans into dresses – one would scarcely recognise any real feminine touch around Bard usually! Anyway (following instructions as given by you, dear) I did have a couple of dances and plenty of talk.

 20

Rhinebeck, N.Y., Monday, 15 November

Dearest Marie-Thérèse,

Today Stan sent on a letter from home, saying Pearse was a little better, and four letters from you!! You always tend to spoil me, darling, and I sincerely hope you'll continue!

Yesterday, I went to Mass in Barrytown in the morning, so I didn't arrive here till about 4.00. George is well but both of his record players are away! Actually it's not so bad, as one of the N.Y. stations (I think WQXR) plays only classical music.

There's no real news to report. Today I slept in until 10.00 and then took a bus to Hyde Park. I came back with George and the others and now I'm writing this in the middle of a performance of Stravinsky's 'Petrouchka'.

I expect to get a lift to N.Y. from some friend of George's on Wednesday and from there to take a bus to Boston, please God.

On the visa issue you might suggest that there's a possibility of my staying more than a year. The question of what kind of visa you get may have to be discussed with them. If I were to stay another year, it's probably safer to get an 'immigrant' type visa (that's in case you have to get a job to support me!). Anyway, darling, do come as soon as possible. We'll manage somehow.

And Miss Dillon, on that crack about UCD compared to Harvard, let me say, I've just as much criticism to make of Harvard as of College (though for different reasons). But on a more serious question ... what about what is, so they tell me ... called a 'honeymoon'? I had thought it might be possible to hire a car for a week or so (but I'd have to learn how to drive, get a licence and don't know how much a car would cost here to hire). On the other hand, we might just go and stay some place, what do you think? And for God's sake don't say, 'you'll leave it to me', as you know I'm quite useless on such subjects. Well now, dear, this gives you lots of questions, if not much news, but it also sends all of me and my love, Brian.

[MARIE-THÉRÈSE TO BRIAN]
Tuesday morning, 16 November

Despite the fact that I've missed you horribly the last few days, some rather funny things happened to cheer me up. Last Friday, May[45] (in Town Factory) and Silvia[46] (in Dun Laoghaire facto-

45 May was the manager of the town factory.
46 Silvia was the secretary in Dun Laoghaire.

ry) asked each of us to design and make a house-coat for quite a large order. Needless to say, I got the order, and yesterday trotted into William Street to discuss it with the wholesale people. There I met a friendly, overweight, matron with bright blue hair who said she liked it but could I make it more easy-fitting: 'you see wives wear them to breakfast without corsets and they do not like to bulge at breakfast before their husbands!' Looking at her with an expressionless face, I almost got sick from suppressing laughter. She was the roundest little woman I'd seen in a long while!

And for the first time in months I'm invited to May's for supper tomorrow night! How is she taking, it I wonder?[47]

Last night I was down in Aunt Agnes'. She was very well and delighted with news from Manchester: Pearse is getting up a little every day and Kevin[48] and Joyce have a new-born boy, called Brendan, and Ethnea[49] is to be godmother.

 22

[BRIAN TO MARIE-THÉRÈSE]
Rhinebeck, Tuesday, 16 November

Well, pet, I spent another day at Hyde Park library. During our lunch break George and I went over to see the grave[50] and the house (one of the guides, by the way, was an Ulsterman) and Eleanor, called by my favourite (i.e. most insulting) American journalist,[51] 'The Big Mouth', was at the library.

47 The fact that MT got the order for the house-coats for the Dun Laoghaire factory rather than May for the Town factory.
48 Brian's brother.
49 Brian's sister.
50 President Franklin D. Roosevelt is buried at Springwood Estate, Hyde Park.
51 Francis James Westbrook Pegler, American journalist. After 1942 Pegler assailed Franklin and Eleanor Roosevelt regularly, calling Mrs Roosevelt 'La boca grande', or 'the big mouth'. The Roosevelts ignored his writings, at least in public.

P.S. LOOK OUT FOR SNAKES

In the afternoon I had a long talk with Kahn,[52] but I rather wonder if I'll be able to get sufficient material to work on this subject.[53] Anyway, I shall write Desmond about it, please God, and also discuss it with Langer.

This evening we were invited out to supper to the house of a German doctor (1938 refugee) in Rhinebeck. We had a lovely meal and heard half of Verdi's Requiem – very effective indeed.

Tomorrow, please God, I return to Harvard, but I may first go back to Bard (and possibly stay overnight). If I must change my subject, I have this Locke-Hooker affair to fall back on and would like to discuss it with Koblitz[54] (who spent about 5 years in the Government School of Harvard). Anyway we'll see.

 23

[MARIE-THÉRÈSE TO BRIAN]
Wednesday, 17 November

You asked me do I still want stockings and the answer is yes please! I wouldn't ask for anything more but could you manage a Christmas Vogue? It'll be full of lovely things. And in return, can I send you a book?

And Dearest, could you send me Pearse and Edith's home address? I'd like to write to Edith but can't till I have it. Actually I'm not sending any Christmas cards this year. I'm writing Christmas letters for the family and close friends. It's cheaper, but I'm not actually worrying about money. We're due some wedding presents and there's bound to be cheques among them. Mama herself

---

52 Dr Herman Kahn, director of the F.D.R. Memorial Library, Hyde Park, NY.
53 Brian is still considering 'Irish neutrality during the Second World War' as a subject for his MA thesis.
54 Robert J. Koblitz, professor of government, was a strong teacher and an able scholar with a Harvard Ph.D. Dr. Koblitz maintained a special interest in students planning to continue on to law school, and promoted a vigorous engagement of himself and his students with current political and social issues.

says Myles, Rowans,[55] Martins[56] are but a few who will not forget us, which greatly cheers me.

As we pass the ½ way mark on the calendar, I'm becoming more and more excited. Only 16 more weekends and I'll be setting out to join you.

✉ *24*   [BRIAN TO MARIE-THÉRÈSE]
Bard College, Thursday, 18 November

Back in Bard, I found in the library a book I have been searching for ages in Harvard. They have two copies in the Widener and one in Lamont but they've all been out for the last few weeks. I thought of borrowing it or possibly staying over to read it. I brought my notes on Locke and Hooker and the texts with me. While I was pondering the matter, one of the fellows (Chuck), who was at the meeting the other night, asked me if I was going to the Yale – Harvard football match on Saturday – this is really an institution rather than a match; like the Oxford-Cambridge boat race. He said he was driving up on Saturday morning and offered me a lift. Since I have enough work with me to last at least two to three days, I accepted, so, please God, I'll be here till then.

Apart from that I have little enough news. 'Buzz' Gummere[57] (I think he's 'admissions officer' or something) was at my talk on Friday and still extends his offer of hospitality – they live in Barrytown. They really are very pleasant people; Quakers, I understand.

P.S. Don't worry about driving – it's a big, broad, good road and we're leaving early enough to take our time. B.

55 Naomi (Rowan) Kidney's family.
56 Mary Martin, Medical Missionaries of Mercy, Drogheda, and godmother to MT.
57 Richard ('Buzz') Matt Gummere Jr (1912-2007), US trained teacher of the Alexander Technique. He served as Director of Admissions at Bard College and taught at Columbia University Teachers College.

P.S. LOOK OUT FOR SNAKES

25

The thing that must be said in May's favour is that she's an excellent hostess. Last night's 'shower' for Silvia (the secretary in the office, who's getting married in December) was a great success. Gerry O'Kelly[58] was asking after you and says her sister in Denver says we've bed and board with her any time we feel like going that way! Looks like if we played our cards, we could do a round trip of America for nothing; that is if you'd fill in the gaps, like California and Chicago, before I get over! Jokes apart, Americans do sound nice.

I knew you'd enjoy your trip to Bard, but I'm glad to see you're the same darling, missing trains etc., but the early rising does sound strange! And I'm delighted that you're dancing too, you'll have to teach me the way to dance when we are together again. How I'd love to have been at your lecture!

The weather here is now horribly damp. We've had fog for the last few days and the first frosts, but the garden looks wonderful and the first Christmas roses are out.

Mama's birthday is on the 24th of this month, if you'd like to send a card! I know you rather I told you because I like you to remind me of birthdays too! But she's never fussy if we forget it.

 26

At present I'm a little out-of-my-depth, I discussed the lack of materials at Hyde Park with Langer and he didn't think the State Department would let me at their stuff. So perhaps it would be better if I changed my subject. God knows what this will entail, I'll write Desmond on the subject immediately.

58   Gerry worked with MT at Larhams; originally from the US.

Yesterday at Harkness Commons, apparently, someone started collecting signatures for an anti-censure petition to be sent to the Senate in aid of Joe McCarthy. Today, beside this character, sprang up an anti-Joe petition which was doing really brisk business. Joe of course is in hospital although he's looking for 15 minutes on one of the big networks on Thanksgiving. This censure motion[59] may yet blow up into something really big. People are noting that the new pro-McCarthy campaign is headed by a group of retired army and navy people. It only needs MacArthur to put his foot in for the thing to take the form of a military-palace revolt.

I see in the paper that Perle Mesta ('the hostess with the mostess' of 'Call the Madam') caused consternation in Washington circles by breaking protocol and curtseying, when the Cabinet wives were introduced to the Queen Mother. Actually, in this respect I think U.S. protocol a little unwise; of course they're simply aiming at consistency.

 27

[MARIE-THÉRÈSE TO BRIAN]

Tuesday, 23 November

I was delighted with the magazines which arrived yesterday, the Reader's Digest was particularly good. Actually I'm still chuckling at Tommy and Ronan's visit on Sunday. At one stage Tommy tried to describe someone's girlfriend to me, a 'typical German fraulein type' was his description. He then went pink, red and crimson, spluttered and began to apologise, after a lengthy explanation, with every step his foot sank deeper! I gathered that I filled that description too! Really he's a pet.

Last night I saw 'Lost Property' – a French picture at the Astor: very enjoyable, and I was home by 9.00. Aunt Agnes is coming

---

59 On 2 December 1954, the Senate voted to censure Senator McCarthy by a vote of 67–22, making him one of the few senators ever to be disciplined in this fashion. He continued to speak against communism and socialism until his death in 1957 at the age of forty-eight.

P.S. LOOK OUT FOR SNAKES

out on Wednesday. I've an idea for her Xmas present (if you haven't one already): how about a pair of fur topped over shoes? If I find out what size shoes she wears? They are rubber outside, fur around the ankle and zip up the front. They fit over other shoes and would keep her warm and dry, how about in dark brown? I've seen a pair Gerry got from America; but if that's not suitable, then a bag to hold her knitting with about 10 ounces of some knitting wool (nylon wool) possible blue or green, in it. It has to be a really nice present, as she has been so good to us.

You will send me Kevin, Pearse and Frank's[60] addresses for Xmas cards! Mama is giving me a present of my Xmas cards! That's it! Plus all my love, Marie-Thérèse

 28   [BRIAN TO MARIE-THÉRÈSE]
Cambridge, Wednesday afternoon, 24 November

A soft day, God bless it, as they say in the West of Ireland, pet. For Thanksgiving tomorrow, Egbert[61] and I have an invitation to lunch.

Yesterday, about a dozen of us went over to a settlement home in Boston for a 'concert'. And we sang along, even 'God bless the Mark', 'Linen Hall' etc. I was delighted to see that you had a visit from Ronan and Tommy – the inseparable twins.

I've just been speaking to Kelleher about doing some work on the American Fenians, but I don't know how it will pan out. Anyway, I'll wait till I hear from Desmond. The cutting about NUI was interesting, but I notice that nothing was said about making a new Dublin University 'Catholic' – also nothing about amalgamation with Trinity. This last is obviously the most intelligent (and economical) solution, but I believe Tierney is keen on creating a Catholic University. This would be a fatal mistake – especially for

---

60   Brian's three older brothers.
61   Egbert was one of Brian's flatmates.

us in history, as the hierarchy[62] would almost certainly interfere in appointments (and probably in arrangement of courses). The same problem would also face Classics, English and Economics.

Actually, given that a new College is to be built, granting it a charter of its own wouldn't entail any considerable expense. However, we must await the event.

One thing that I have very much on my mind is whether I should try and get a second year over here in America. Please do tell me what you think about this, darling. Of course, it more than likely won't happen, but I want to keep my options open.

One thing you'll enjoy in Cambridge is the selection of films offered in the 'Brattle'[63] – at present they are offering Ulanova and the stars of the Russian ballet. They also show French and Italian films.

 29

[BRIAN TO MARIE-THÉRÈSE]
Cambridge, Thursday, 25 November, Thanksgiving

I rooted out this old paper on election results, pet, since Alistair Cooke let you down. It gives no kind of real assessment, as the writers are all anti-Ike, pro-McCarthy, Hearst Republicans, but it's rather amusing, I think.

Last night I went to see 'Julius Caesar' at the 'University' with Jerry (he's of French-Canadian stock living in Maine and doing literature here at Harvard). While it is undoubtedly a good film, I wasn't particularly impressed – the acting seemed uneven and I found Gielgud very disappointing. One of the shorts was this film on shark-fishing in the West of Ireland. The night was terrible, the rain simply bouncing off the pavements.

62   Catholic hierarchy.
63   The Brattle is a repertory movie theatre located in Brattle Hall near Harvard Square in Cambridge, which started screening in 1953. It mainly screens a mixture of foreign, independent and classic films.

P.S. LOOK OUT FOR SNAKES

Today, however, was mild, though dull, and at 1.30 promptly Egbert and I presented ourselves at the Cushmans'[64] for the traditional American turkey dinner. It was quite a 'typical' American home, two daughters and a grandmother included! Really we had a very pleasant afternoon digesting an excellent meal.

Mr Cushman works in some bank and she is the daughter of the late professor of English at Yale. She promised to invite me up to meet Fritz Robinson[65] (who is a friend of Myles[66]) sometime soon.

Tomorrow I hope to see some people in the Government Department about changing my subject back to Locke, although it strikes me that perhaps 'Molyneux and the American Revolution' might have possibilities.

 30

My Dearest, I was nearly beside myself until your letter arrived this morning! Yes, I really did worry as I couldn't help feeling something had happened on the journey back to Harvard. I'm relieved that it was only 'wiper' trouble, but I feel that Chuck must be a bit of an ass not to be able to fix it himself![67] And I'm very sorry you missed the match.

Well Mama had a really happy birthday[68] yesterday. Aunt Agnes is wonderful. She remembered it and sent Mama a big basket of

---

64 His first real meeting with the Cushmans, who were very kind to Brian and MT at that time. They became lifelong friends.

65 Fred (Fritz) Norris Robinson (1871–1966), professionally known as F.N. Robinson, eminent American Celticist and scholar of Geoffrey Chaucer. He was a friend of Myles and knew John Dillon.

66 Myles, no doubt, always looking out for MT and Brian, probably arranged for the Cushmans to reach out to Brian, through his friend Fritz Robinson.

67 Chuck had offered Brian a lift and on the way they had a little car trouble and missed the Yale-Harvard football match.

68 Marie's fifty-fourth birthday.

fruit (and came to tea later). Mrs C[69] came too and gave Mama a glamorous nightdress! I got her a new type of pillow, some bulbs for indoors and some of those 'new berry' fruits she loves. I got some meringues for dessert for her and she was well enough to eat 3 in rapid succession.

Now don't bother about that pattern I asked you to get. There are many lovely dresses in the last books you sent and I can make my own patterns of most of them.[70] So I'll settle for the Xmas Vogue.

The more I think about it I'd rather be married in a small church in Boston. We'll invite about 6 people to breakfast in a hotel afterwards and then go wherever you like. So look around Cambridge for a 'handy' chaplain and a nice sympathetic old priest. Don't make final arrangements till I get notice from the priests here! My papers are very slow; it's been 3 weeks and no news!

 31

[BRIAN TO MARIE-THÉRÈSE]
Cambridge, Friday, 26 November

So you're a kleine Fraulein, eh? Owens really is wonderful for putting his foot in things, but do you mind if I prefer you as you are without any extraneous central European glamour?

Last night for a while I watched TV and James Mason on the 'Lux-Video-Theatre', which was wonderful. He is compere and fills in between the acts to say who's in the play and what's happened so far. He doesn't do the commercial 'plugs', but with a wry smile and a suspiciously cynical quirk in his voice he says things like 'and now we pass you over for – ahem! – an important message from our sponsors.' He gives the general impression that if Lever Bros. were the only soaps left he'd give up washing.

69 Mrs Campbell, Marie's girlfriend.
70 MT designed and made clothes for herself, wedding dresses to make extra money and in later years for her growing brood.

P.S. LOOK OUT FOR SNAKES

I also saw Jack Webb's 'Dragnet', which is very popular over here. It is a semi-documentary crime story series – very easily parodied but not bad.

Today for half an hour I went into the Poetry Room in the Lamont. It is great set-up and I listened to recordings of Stevens[71] reading his own poetry: C. Day Lewis[72] reading Yeats and various others reading Herrick and Shakespeare. I think it's a fine idea and well worth a visit when you get over, darling. I'm sure they probably have LPs of plays and so on.

Two other recordings you must hear – in some strange way these are part of intellectuals' musical furniture and very entertaining; Tom Lehrer[73] and Florence Foster Jenkins.[74] In case I forget, do please make a note to remind me about these, especially Miss Jenkins. (Am I being mean by just whetting your curiosity?) Actually on LPs over here there are some interesting things – but alas and alack the Juke Box is also here, and horrible!

....

71   Wallace Stevens, American modernist poet.

72   Cecil Day-Lewis (1904–1972), an Anglo-Irish poet and Poet Laureate from 1968 until his death in 1972. He also wrote mystery stories under the pseudonym Nicholas Blake. He is the father of Sir Daniel Day-Lewis.

73   Thomas Andrew Lehrer (born 1928), retired musician, singer-songwriter, satirist and mathematician He is best known for the pithy and humorous songs that he recorded in the 1950s and 1960s. Lehrer's early musical work typically dealt with non-topical subject matter and was noted for its black humour. In the 1960s, he produced a number of songs that dealt with social and political issues of the day, particularly when he wrote for the US version of the television show *That Was the Week That Was*. The popularity of these songs has far outlasted their topical subjects and references. Lehrer quoted a friend's explanation: 'Always predict the worst and you'll be hailed as a prophet.'

74   Florence Foster Jenkins (1868–1944), American socialite and amateur soprano, became known, and mocked, for her flamboyant performance costumes and notably poor singing ability. Stephen Pile ranked her 'the world's worst opera singer … No one, before or since, has succeeded in liberating themselves quite so completely from the shackles of musical notation.' Despite – or perhaps because of – her technical incompetence she became a prominent musical cult-figure in New York City during the 1920s, 1930s and 1940s. Cole Porter, Gian Carlo Menotti, Lily Pons, Sir Thomas Beecham and other celebrities were fans. Enrico Caruso reportedly 'regarded her with affection and respect'.

32

The news about your thesis is very sad, but don't worry too much and don't kill yourself working another one up in a hurry. After all, your notes on Hocke and Locker are good and you'll have July and August in Booterstown, in perfect peace, I promise, to work away at them. If there are any books I can get you here, or even in London, please write and Mr Figgis[75] and Mr Pembrey[76] will help me find them.

I'm delighted you agree about a Boston wedding and I'll find the 'loco' for the breakfast while I'm there – after all it's partly for things like that that I'm coming earlier.

I hope you celebrated 'Thanksgiving' properly with all the trimmings. O'Rourke (the gardener) was with us on Wednesday and was asking after you in detail, he always has a little chat with Miss Bennett and gives her all our news.

 33

Dearest, still here and tying myself in knots and intricacies about Locke and Hooker. I came back from Widener about 5.00 and cooked three ears of corn for myself and had some ice-cream, then settled down to work. Actually this Locke thing is quite fascinating but I need you to do something for me. Bailyn, to whom I spoke today (he's an assistant professor at Harvard), says he heard that Peter Laslett has discovered some new material on John Locke, on which he is working in Cambridge. Could you please phone Desmond and ask if he knows anything about this (in case he's

75 Figgis of Hodges Figgis bookshop.
76 Pembrey of Greene's bookshop.

P.S. LOOK OUT FOR SNAKES

forgotten, this Peter LASLETT[77] is the editor of Filmer). If you can manage this, it might help a great deal, as I wrote to Desmond on my research at some length this week.

Having again replenished what the Jesuits love to call the inner man,[78] I'm ready to write a lot more. A note from the Éire Society says that McConnell[79] of Trinity is to be their next speaker. His subject is the Book of Kells, which is not really his field, so I don't think I'll bother going. There are a couple of interesting meetings on this week and I may go along to one or two, but I want to finish at least the first draft of the Hooker-Locke thing as soon as possible.

 34

[MARIE-THÉRÈSE TO BRIAN]
Sunday, 28 November

How I missed you on Friday night. Mary's[80] party was wonderful but you were missed. Mrs Tierney asked had you introduced yourself to her brother-in-law.[81] John and Yvonne were looking very happy. Brian O'Connor and I discussed you for much too short a time, and then John and Hugh Kearney,[82] an Englishman, good looking and also in History, joined in. I mentioned that you were writing to Desmond re. your difficulties on 'Hyde Park Papers' and then they said Desmond is laid up with his leg and a slight collapse after the worry of his 'case'.[83]

---

77 Thomas Peter Ruffell Laslett (1915–2001), English historian. After demobilisation in 1945, he returned to Cambridge, initially spending time in Peterhouse. In 1948 he was awarded a research fellowship at St John's College based on his pre-war postgraduate research into Robert Filmer. In 1953, having earlier discovered and begun research into a substantial proportion of the library of John Locke, Laslett was an appointed as university lecturer in history in Cambridge.

78 The inner man - spiritual and intellectual being.

79 Albert McConnell (1903–1993), Professor of Natural Philosophy at TCD and later Provost.

80 Mary Murphy, Gerard Murphy's wife, close family friend.

81 The chief librarian at Harvard is married to Michael Tierney's wife's sister (maiden name MacNeill).

82 Hugh Francis Kearney (1924–2017), British historian, tutor in the UCD history department and later Professor Emeritus of the University of Pittsburgh

83 See Brian's letter of 8 August.

Brian O'Connor told me to tell you that the exam for the 3rd secretary is coming up in February. It's not officially advertised yet, but a friend of his told him and he said that maybe you could drop into your embassy in Boston to enquire whether you could sit the exam in America. After all, it's worth trying for, isn't it! He says that fluency in Irish[84] is an essential requirement. You will do some enquiring, even by phone, won't you, darling! He also said he'll send me a cutting to send you, of some jobs in the BBC starting next winter at about £750. But of course, the Irish Foreign Service would be much more interesting and safer! Working in England there is always the 'draft' to worry about.[85] Having found you, it would kill me if you were taken from me again.

On Saturday, I booked my passage for the 15th March. Next week I'll start working on getting my visa organised. I believe I'll have to produce my return ticket (returnable or usable at any date) in order to apply for a visitor's visa (according to my travel agent), so if the embassy advise a visitor's visa I'll buy a £74 ticket on the 'America' if you agree.

For the last 2 nights we have been having disastrous storms. On Friday night one of Mama's windows was smashed. When I rang a window mender, I was informed that we were not the only ones and he was fully booked until Monday morning.

 35

[BRIAN TO MARIE-THÉRÈSE]
(*typed letter*) *Sunday, 28 November*

Well, darling, this is not simply to show off either my typing (God bless the mark) or Gummere's new portable, but is a useful kind of test to see how long typing, as against long-hand takes me.

84   Brian studied in Coláiste Mhuire and spoke fluent Irish.
85   National Service, 'the draft', was introduced in Britain in 1947 – the last National Serviceman was demobilised in 1967. Brian being drafted was a constant and very real fear of MT's, a lingering trauma after the Second World War.

Today, I went to 10.30 Mass, had breakfast and started typing my first draft of the Locke-Hooker thing. In effect this is merely an extension of that very short essay I did for Kearney[86] on a lovely summer week-end a million years ago. Actually, however, I would rather like to go on from this to a proper examination of the relationship of the two men – especially since this would involve placing them in the general stream of political thought, e.g. their relation to Marsiglio and Aquinas, Filmer and Hobbes.

Anyway to get back to today: about 1.30 I walked over to Harkness to look over the book section of The Times and the magazine section. There was nothing of great interest in either, although Churchill's imminent birthday drew two ridiculously laudatory articles. I was tempted to hang around until 4.00 for a two-hour television production of 'Macbeth' with Maurice Evans, but I don't want to become a 'vidiot'[87] so returned once more to the fray. I worked fairly consistently from about 3.00 to just now (it's 11.15) with a break for tea. This slight mountain of work has produced an eight-page mouse – to which must be added about three pages of footnotes. I seem to have arrived at a somewhat new position; I argue that while Locke did in fact make use of Hooker in order to impress his readers, he also felt an affinity with the more Thomistic elements of Hooker's thought, but that this is in fact a misinterpretation of Hooker who was himself largely using Aquinas for polemical purposes. As you can gather, pet, it is a somewhat complicated and rather tiresome argument. However, I have hopes that something will come of it.

Today, besides your letter, I have been looking again over George's last letter. He suggests that just after Christmas we go to the meeting

....

86 In the 1950s Hugh Kearney was a history lecturer at UCD, a job he took after leaving Peterhouse, Cambridge. He had won a scholarship there from a grammar school in Liverpool. Those years in Dublin, working in a very lively history department, were some of the happiest in his life. Garret FitzGerald once said that no party was complete without someone falling down the steps outside his house.

87 Addicted to watching TV shows.

of the American Historical Association in NYC. He's very keen that I should meet some of his friends from Columbia, including Jacques Barzun – an extremely well-known writer and thinker over here (he's a professor of history at Columbia and has written books on Marx, the teacher in America and a two-volume definitive work on Berlioz). George is obviously keen that I should try to get a foot in, perhaps as an assistant teaching fellow, for next year. Also next week, I am to see someone from the International Institute of Education who is coming up here to Cambridge and will certainly enquire about my future plans. On this question you are in a much better position than I to make a decision. Would it be fair, or even possible, to leave your mother on her own for a whole year? Please, darling, do think this over carefully and then say what you really feel – after all, should you think it unwise to stay, we are not giving up anything definite – and I'd much prefer to hear your view before making any 'contacts'.

 36

Today the snow came and Cambridge, particularly the Yard, looks wonderful. The snow is still drifting down; we have about eight inches already. It is crisp, firm and white. Not even the footpaths have turned slushy and dirty yet. Naturally it is cold, but also brisk and really quite exciting. From now on, of course, it will get worse and worse.

I got your wonderful long letter, and Mary's party sounded fine. The Hugh you met was Hugh Kearney – he is by way of being something of a Hooker man himself.

I'm to meet a man from the Institute of International Education tomorrow and want to ask

a) if I stay another year, will I be allowed to take a job in the summer?

b) will this present scholarship prevent me getting an immigrant visa to return, should I wish it?

Really if it were possible to get into teaching (at home or here) I'd prefer it to Iveagh House.[88] In fact, one reason I'm keeping close contacts with Bard is that they are short-staffed in history this year and, you never know, I might wangle a year with them. While I would (perhaps – I don't really know) prefer a State University, Bard has the advantage of being a progressive Dewey[89] school. Anyway we'll see.

The return passage on the 'America' (provisional) would be O.K. with me.

By the way, pet – about managing on my $170. It will be a little tight but the average ex-G.I. grant is $130, so if we can get a place in which there are cooking facilities it will be all right. Of course, it will mean that either I have to do all the cooking or else you'll have to learn! (Here I duck to avoid whatever you throw back at me!)

Another forgotten note of reassurance, they can't draft me into the army.[90] And the portable I have in mind is a type-writer. Most of the small radios can pick up the couple of good stations (which concentrate on good music) and average American radio is simply awful – even worse than TV!

So now darling, I think I've covered everything in your letters – including what you called your 'serious' letter. They are all delightful to me – though I have qualms, since I seem to get two letters for every one I write.

My fit of writing continues and I intend to write to Laslett today. He wrote a book (really edited it) on Filmer,[91] which was very good. Desmond knows him quite well, that's why I've asked you to contact

----

88　The diplomatic service; MT had recommended that he apply.

89　John Dewey (1859-1952), philosopher, psychologist and educational reformer whose ideas have been influential in education and social reform. He was one of the most prominent US scholars in the first half of the twentieth century.

90　Brian was referring to the fact that Aunt Agnes had obtained Irish citizenship for him (a document signed by De Valera) but unbeknownst to him, because he was also a British citizen, he could still have been drafted if he lived in England.

91　Sir Robert Filmer (1588 – 26 May 1653) was an English political theorist who defended the divine right of kings.

him first. My last from Desmond giving me an O.K. was very short and just said that he'd been out of college for a week. That poor man will kill himself if he's not careful. Anyway, darling, I hope you find him a little less forbidding on the phone than in person.

I forgot to tell you that Boston is looking very festive already. On the Common they have lots of fairy lights and stars and a very fine Crib. The shepherds are surrounded by about twenty or thirty sheep and the kings mounted on their camels. More impressive though, I thought, is a huge tree, every line of which is glowing with small blue bulbs – it really makes the O'Connell St decorations seem pretty pitiful.

 37

[BRIAN TO MARIE-THÉRÈSE]
Cambridge, Tuesday, 30 November

Still being the busy bee, darling. At present I'm working on some of my Irish seventeenth century material, but I have hopes that Locke may become my central figure. At present it's difficult to say how it will all turn out.

I am at the moment debating whether or not to buy myself a second-hand portable (about $35) for Christmas. By the way, my enquiry about Laslett probably refers to a 'discovery' of his in the Public Record Office of what he believed to be the original version of Locke's 'Essay on Human Understanding' but this claim has already been challenged. I would only be really interested in material relating to Locke's political views.

On the remainder shelf of the bookshops, I noticed Myles's book on old Irish stories (but it still cost $2.70 or so). However, some very good material is on sale at the moment, I now have Langer's two volumes on 1937–41 for a total cost of about $4 (originally published at $17.50).

But seriously, I'm becoming more and more of a recluse (a

passing phase undoubtedly), so don't get worried if my letters are a little 'professional'. Thank God I'm feeling very well and hope that both you and your mother are looking after yourselves now that the winter has come.

 38

I'm delighted that you had a good Thanksgiving. You show it in much happier letters, my Darling.

Now at last I've started proceedings for a visitor's visa, which can be extended. I don't like applying for an emigration visa unless advised to by the USA people; then I would have to state that I would like to work in America should they give permission – now one of the things they want is proof that … in their own words: 'written evidence (in duplicate) that you will have adequate means of support in the United States'. Can you supply this? A note from your bank with a covering letter from you would do, I suppose! Not that this is urgent, as my plans are to have all my necessary papers – passport, letters, etc. – ready next week and then to apply for an interview with Taft – say the 8th or 9th. Today I've filled out a form which will give them something to start with.

Chapter 5

DECEMBER 1954

*Everyone has one day in their whole lives when they feel bet-
ter than they ever will again, a complex coming together of
youth, strength and confidence. Sometimes just the memory
of that day can help one survive difficult times.*

Marie-Thérèse (Dillon) Farrell talking about her youth

1

Well you can rise off your knees! I rang Desmond this morning, seemingly Peter Laslett[1] is a great friend of his. He advises you to write to him yourself, mentioning Desmond's name. Apparently Laslett, who is a fellow of Trinity College Cambridge, has written a book on Locke and is lecturing on him at present. Desmond sounds rather tired but isn't in the least upset about you changing your subject, he says 'Record Students' often have trouble finding their subject – if that's any consolation Darling!

Now I'm really tackling the visa problem and Mama and I discussed the money angle. I'll probably sell 100 shares so as not to have money worries. That will leave us at least £700 for a nest egg and £100 will leave us £50 to play with when we return, or if we find we're running out in America, we can send for it.

 2

Do you remember when I was looking for Molyneux[2] material, pet? I kept crossing the wake of some American woman historian? Well, I discover that she has published an article in the William and Mary Quarterly[3] on the subject of her research. Unfortunately

---

1 Laslett is an English historian, also interested in John Locke

2 William Molyneux (1656–1698), Anglo-Irish writer on science, politics and natural philosophy. He was a close friend of John Locke. Molyneux proposed the philosophical question known as Molyneux's Problem: 'the problem of the blind man who gains sight' is a topic that has been discussed extensively since its publication, up to the present day.

3 The *William and Mary Quarterly*, founded 1892, is the leading journal of early American history and culture. Today, the *Quarterly* ranks among the most-cited journals covering a specific time and place and is one of the most-respected and most-acclaimed historical journals in the world.

P.S. LOOK OUT FOR SNAKES

Widener's copy is at present out. I hope to see this thing soon. It may give me some ideas.

As for your visa, I'll write something like, 'I hereby guarantee that M.T. Dillon ... sufficient to support her for the duration of her stay in the U.S.' Will that do? Should you see Taft, do ask him about this and send him my regards etc.

✉ *3*
          [**MARIE-THÉRÈSE TO BRIAN**]
          Thursday morning, 2 December

Well it was fun to get your typed letter and at the same time a letter, also typed, from Fr Mathew – he's been one of the '2 finger typers' for as long as I can remember and you beat him hollow! By the way, he asked to be remembered to you and so did Mother Hogan, who has obliged me by having a German letter (to do with my Baptism Certificate) translated.

Your letter reminded me of the day you asked me to decide whether or not you were to go to America and, after fighting myself for weeks, I finally saw that you had to go. Well, it doesn't take me weeks to see that you must stay if you get the chance. But please make sure that by staying you won't end up in the army. I'll still apply for a visitor's visa and ask them please to extend it in the event of our staying over. If they say that's not possible then I'll apply for an emigration visa (using Mary Seidensticker[4] as a guarantor). So when you see your 'contacts',[5] fire ahead and fate will decide whether we stay or return to Ireland. I will of course not trouble Mama with these things for the present.

---

4   MT's cousin in America, Mary Seidensticker's mother was a Dillon (the American Dillons were descended from John Dillon's brother William Blake Dillon).
5   People whom George Roach wanted Brian to meet with the intention of staying on to work and do a PhD.

Last night I called in to see Pat Glaser,[6] her son is called Peter Nicolas. She looked quite forlorn, it was already 8 pm and no sign of Otto. Anyway the baby is fine.[7] Afterwards, I went to Joan O'Grady's[8] for a 'hen-party'. Naomi Kidney asked to be remembered to you.

 4

Locke and Hooker you always liked! And I'm sure the 'mood to work' will stay. On that subject, do write to Laslett anyway. By the way, Desmond didn't volunteer any information about a discovery.[9]

You will send me a Bank Statement, won't you? The embassy wrote me a note this morning to say they'd like to see me soon, and I want to have all my 'papers' ready by next Wednesday or Thursday.

We are threatened with another Bank strike here so I have notified my solicitor that I want to sell some shares quickly and will tell you as soon as I have the money. If Jean will put some more to your account and then you can write direct to your bank here asking them to transfer it to America. If I go in I feel they will suspect I'm pulling a 'fast-one'.

Your story about Groucho Marx is delightful. I've been reading the story of his life, written by his son, in the S.E.P.

Doc Roche called in on Wednesday – he's very pleased with Mama and gave me my vaccination cert.

---

6   Pat Delamer, wife of Otto Glaser.
7   Sadly, the baby died before his first birthday, a cot death, and the Glasers had no
     more children.
8   Joan (O'Grady) Murray-Hayden, a school friend, remained a lifelong friend of MT
     and was godmother to her daughter Miriam.
9   What Laslett gleaned from Locke's papers.

These people from 'The International Institute of Education'[10] are they the people in charge of your grant? Earlier letters from me suggested we couldn't stay on – the reasons worrying me were: in the event of my not working would we have enough to live off next year if you got a fellowship? That is the only condition you must consider ... very serious letter darling – I'm sorry but it still brings you all my love, Marie-Thérèse

 5

[BRIAN TO MARIE-THÉRÈSE]
Cambridge, Sunday, 5 December

Actually I have little news to relate. Although, the article by the Bryn Mawr[11] woman in the 'William and Mary', which I mentioned, remains unobtainable, I've still managed to type out about six pages on the 1689 parliament. Since Desmond agreed that I should concentrate on American History, I feel that things will turn out all right.

One thing I meant to tell you, pet, but I consistently forget, was that before I went to Bard I had a physical check-up (required of all Harvard students) and came out with nothing more to report, then that I'm more-or-less colour blind.[12]

Dr Sheppard's murder trial is still going on. The defence has called its first witness, but the court earlier rejected a defence plea that the case be dropped. That and the McCarthy censure is all that's in the news.

---

10 The answer is 'yes', the International Institute of Education provided funding for scholarships like the Fulbright, which Brian had been awarded.

11 Bryn Mayr College, Pennsylvania, is a private women's liberal arts college founded in 1885.

12 Brian had trouble distinguishing between red and green and would frequently ask one of his children to tell him when the traffic light turned 'green'. How he coped when driving alone defies all understanding.

6

On Saturday night Noeleen and I went to a German production of 'Fidelio' and it was a deeply stirring production and very memorable evening. Noeleen and I plan to go to the races on Boxing Day and that's something to look forward to. By the by, her father's will was in the papers: £37,000, not bad! Mama was very impressed. Mama is well and in very good form we had quite a gay weekend!

My new hairstyle is quite a success. According to the 'girls' I look like Audrey Hepburn! So now if you describe me, I'm a cross between 'Lilly' and Audrey, the worst features of both! I'm off to visit the Embassy this afternoon. I told Mr Needham firmly that I couldn't be back in time to close the place and he took it like a lamb!

 7

[MARIE-THÉRÈSE TO BRIAN]
Monday morning, 6 December

Yesterday was a day I never want to see again – terrible! First, being late for 10 o'clock Mass, I went to 11.30 as well! I then came home to find Mama cooking a chicken (from the sale). It was undercooked, when I came to carve it, and poor Mama spent the afternoon crying into her pillow that her 'cooking days were over', that she'd never look a gas-stove in the face again! Depressing!!

We then ran out of fuel and I had to let a gorgeous fire go out as there was nothing to burn on it. I was just getting tea when who should ring me (also in floods of tears, not exaggerating!!!) but Rosalie's mother, who started saying how Rosalie had come under bad influence and was a changed girl, that she had so much money and was so easily deceived! Well I really enjoyed that conversation because I really let myself go in my answer!

P.S. LOOK OUT FOR SNAKES

Five minutes later, just as I started cooking, another phone call, this time Roma[13] complaining, 'I was waiting for you to call me ... didn't know if you were in the land of the living ... tried to call you last week but I guess your phone was out of order ... ' So I asked her to call me again after Christmas and we must do something together! She's got a terrible American accent! Oh do watch that accent there is something so sloppy and casual about it that I can't stand! She used to have such a clipped, smooth voice and it's all gone!

Your letter to Mama came this morning and she loved it, we are both intrigued about this Jesuit who left the church – Father Feeney:[14] what is the story? And what does he do now? Mama and I are dying to know.

[MARIE-THÉRÈSE TO BRIAN]
Tuesday morning, 7 December

Yesterday was a pleasant yet wet day. I collected my new coat and the passport photos (I enclose one for you and I'm rather pleased with it, I hope you like it too!). I had a long wait in the Embassy waiting room and then a secretary in the Visa department looked after me. Apparently my Visa is a 'walkover', if you would send the following: a sworn affidavit made out before an attorney (justice of the peace, as they are called here) that you are responsible for me in America – the University will give you the necessary form to fill out – apparently my visa is for 'foreign students' wives' and very easy to get – it is valid for 2 years and has to be renewed every 6 months.

---

13   Roma Beauregard (née Smyth) MT's first cousin.
14   Father Leonard Feeney was a Jesuit priest (Harvard) who was excommunicated for preaching that there is no salvation outside the Roman Catholic Faith. He was reinstated to the priesthood in Nov 22 1972.

9

What on earth's the matter? Are you losing weight or taking up the H-line (or whatever it's called). Looking like Audrey Hepburn – nothing! Isn't she that flat little creature? Really, darling, I must speak to you severely or you may become Bette Davis or something! In fact I suppose you've had one of these close 'gamine'[15] hair-does (isn't that what they call them?) and I'm sure you really look your own sweet self.

On Monday, as I told you, I'm to meet this Fritz Robinson[16] and on Wednesday, I'm to have lunch with some Dublin man who wants me to speak to some Holy Name Sodality next year about Ireland – I wonder if I dare be anti-clerical![17]

I had a nice wee letter from Taft the other day and a note from Desmond just to give me Laslett's address: I've written to him. At present my draft work on the Hooker quotations will take about 12 pages of typing – including the footnotes. I got the magazine on Horace Plunkett[18] but am not clear on what kind of orders Miss Bennet wants to get from over here – is it for the book or for the I.A.W.S.[19] or what? I have also received my first Christmas card – from a fellow here studying Irish history.

---

15 A gamine is a slim, elegant young woman who is, or is perceived to be, mischievous, teasing or sexually appealing. Audrey Hepburn in *Roman Holiday* was an example of an elfish, adorable gamine.
16 Fred (Fritz) Norris Robinson, friend of Myles Dillon.
17 Considering that Brian studied for the priesthood and remained a devout Catholic.
18 Sir Horace Curzon Plunkett (1854–1932), Anglo-Irish agricultural reformer, pioneer of agricultural cooperatives, Unionist MP, supporter of Home Rule, Irish senator and author.
19 Irish Agricultural Wholesale Society.

10

Yesterday Ireland was swept by a freak storm. There was lashing wind and rain from the south and east which brought the waves over Booterstown Station – the gardener was soaked by a wave as he got off the train! Phones were disconnected when 'white' lightning struck transformers. High winds knocked down trees on the Stillorgan road and a river, a foot deep, rushed down Mt Merrion Ave and poured into Blackrock. St. Michael's, Dun Laoghaire, was completely full of water 6' deep. The river Tolka changed its course and flowed through the back doors of ten houses and out the front (according to the papers!) and it was so bad that we had a ½ day, as our lights went out at 11 a.m. and we couldn't work without them.

During the afternoon I called into Greene's Bookshop to buy a book and Mr Pembrey was asking after you. He misses you poking around and was delighted to hear that you were at Harvard.

 11

You met Eileen Walsh[20] – husband's name is Peter,[21] he's in Classics (Latin). You might give them my best wishes and congrats on the baby and say I met John O'Meara when he was lecturing here. The lecture was quite a success.

Last night I had to stop typing my new draft of Hooker as I thought I'd got something wrong, so I was up at 7.15 this morning

20 In an earlier letter MT mentioned meeting the Walshs, and not remembering the woman's name.
21 Peter Walsh held the Chair of Humanity (Latin) in the University of Glasgow from 1972 until his retirement in 1993. He obtained his PhD from University College Dublin, and remained there as a Lecturer in Ancient Classics from 1952–9. In 1953 he married Eileen Quinn and they moved to Scotland in 1959.

– and a brisk, dull morning it was – and on Widener doorstep when they opened at 8.45. Actually, I hadn't made a mistake and I'm now ready to plunge into page six.

 12

You may congratulate me, dear – I've just finished my note on 'Locke's use of Hooker' (this doesn't mean, by any means, that I've exhausted the subject). It runs to 11½ pages of in-between spacing (between double and single spacing) including 61 footnotes. Tomorrow I want to show it to a few people and discuss it with them – AFTER I'VE SENT OFF YOUR FORM. Then I want to recheck two books on Hooker and await news from Laslett. I'm hoping I may get some of the smaller journals to accept it for publication, but I have my doubts.

The Sam Sheppard murder case seems to have died out. So far the State is doing badly: the defence has shown that police pinned on Dr Sam and rather botched up their investigations; the appearance of his mistress as a State witness boomeranged – obviously from her evidence, there isn't sufficient murder motive there; he has taken the stand and is to be cross-examined tomorrow.

The Hearst papers have strangely enough not backed McCarthy in his attack on Ike. They are in fact kinder to Ike than they have ever been – possibly they fear McCarthy might draw the right-wing Republicans (or at least, some of them) off to start a new third party.

This will be a busy week for me as I have to see some people; pack up my things (I'll leave most of them here over the vacation) and see about getting to Bard by the weekend. I had a charming note from 'Buzz' Gummere, the director of Admissions at Bard, inviting me back soon and saying thanks for the talk: you'll like him and his wife, dearest, and the cute house they have in Barrytown.

By the way, will you please get something for your mother and Aunty Agnes (perhaps wool?). Also this week I'll have to write my Christmas letters. I may send you a bundle to re-post on, or I may stick Ronan[22] with the job instead.

 13

So far, darling I have a bank statement saying that I have $420, although some of it will be withdrawn by Friday! The letter from Harvard saying I'm a student will arrive tomorrow and I'm to get a statement that I'll be responsible for you – what a burden! – witnessed by a public notary. So I hope to send all these off tomorrow. (Also will send stockings and cards – to be redistributed please). I've written home for Baptism Certificates (asking for two) and asked Aunty Agnes to see about a Letter of Freedom. So there!

Well dearest I hope you kept your feet dry during the floods. It really must have been awful but I refuse to see it as an omen. The comparatively warm winter is probably melting the polar ice-cap and it's flooding the Gulf Stream.[23]

This morning I spoke to Louis Hartz[24] (assistant professor in Government) and he's reading my Locke job. I'm to discuss it with him on Friday.

Last night's visit to the Cushmans was quite fun – I met Myles's friend Fritz Robinson: he dined with your grandfather![25] (he's 82). I stayed for supper and we talked till about 10. Thursday I'm to

22   Ronan Keane.
23   Awareness of global warming even back then!
24   Louis Hartz (1919–1986), American political scientist and influential liberal proponent of the idea of American exceptionalism. Hartz used the name of John Locke to symbolise the kind of liberalism, characteristic of America. He attended Harvard as a student, graduating in 1940, and then returned to teach there in 1942, becoming professor of government in 1956. He was known for his charismatic teaching.
25   John Dillon, last leader of the Irish Parliamentary Party, MT's grandfather.

go to supper with the McNiffs.[26] He's a librarian at Lamont and she's working on the indexing of the Irish microfilm collection, which Harvard has just received. Also (tomorrow) I'm to lunch with this Dubliner who wants me to speak to some Catholic group next term – it will probably develop into a technicolour, romantic, dramatic (!), Farrellian production of Easter 1916.

I'm glad your mother's decided to watch her step over Christmas (and I'm not insulting your cooking), but if the girl's away it would be difficult. Is she going into St Vincent's Hospital? Give her my love (and don't forget some present). Are you staying home, pet, or what?

Today I got a gift parcel from home: very smart yellow woollen gloves (my other pair had just developed a hole): Irish linen hankies and braces from Mother and Dad, Aunty Peg and Ethnea respectively.

Yesterday it got very dark and last night there was a faint white ring around the moon[27] – quite circular and at a distance (like a rainbow) and I woke up to a really wet and nasty day. However I feel my visit to Hartz was a success and I am dying to hear what he'll say on Friday.

[BRIAN TO MARIE-THÉRÈSE]
Cambridge, Wednesday, 15 December

Sorry for all the rush, but I'm trying to get through a newly published book before Friday. Tomorrow I'll send you a parcel of cards – could you post or hand them out please?

26   Philip J. McNiff, superintendent of Widener and then librarian of Lamont, was a mild, soft-spoken man with a wisp of a smile poking out from beneath his usually serious manner. Mr. McNiff manifested his seldom-called-on Gaelic wrath when he saw the handiwork of the margin marker or the page puller.

27   Moon halos occur when millions of tiny ice crystals in thin clouds high up in the Earth's atmosphere split and reflect the sun's light bouncing off the Moon. The phenomenon is quite rare, as the ice crystals have to be positioned exactly right in relation to where you are looking up in order for the halo to appear.

Tonight as I left Widener it was magnificent. On the steps of the church was a crowd of about two hundred – must have been the Glee Club. They sang Christmas Carols, in wonderful harmony, as they slowly strolled around the Yard.[28] Really it was very lovely!

Today I had lunch with this fellow who wants me to speak on the 13th February. I plan to talk on the general subject of population, emigration etc. Incidentally he told me that Brian Kirby is working here in Boston.

 15   [MARIE-THÉRÈSE TO BRIAN]
Friday, 17 December

I was delighted to get your letter of Sunday, I think 'weather' is responsible for the postal holdup. The news of your medical check-up is great, but I can't believe you're colour blind! Remember how you spotted slight differences in shade between a belt and a scarf I wanted to buy once! I would suspect glasses might help your reading. How is your general eye-sight? Do tell, what colours do they say you can't see? I've sent you the Irish Times re: Wednesday storms.

Mama is keeping very well considering. She's now determined to go to hospital for Xmas (10 days) I think she can't face the thought of my cooking. She hasn't as much faith in it as you! Blind in some things but not colour blind!!

28   Harvard Yard is the oldest part of the university. It contains most of the freshman dormitories, a memorial church, classrooms, departmental buildings and offices. The Yard is a grassy area of 22.4 acres. It has a perimeter fence and twenty-seven gates.

16

Last night at the McNiff's[29] was very pleasant and out of it, I may get a couple of hours work at Widener next term (cataloguing Irish books for them) so that's just fine.

Well pet, I got my paper on Hooker Locke from Hartz today: his only criticism was that I didn't give enough space to my argumentation, which he thought was good. The new book on Locke – it came out in Aug/Sept – actually backs up the points I made, so I'm very pleased about it all.

 17

[BRIAN TO MARIE-THÉRÈSE]
Bard, Sunday, 19 December

Dearest, despite the terribly tiresome journey up, I still hope, now that I'm up here, to get some work done. I'm sure the post has gone to hell so I'm not trying to send any more cards, anyway I couldn't get any I really liked so I've written to your mother, Aunty Agnes and now you.

Of course I wish you a Happy Christmas and a wonderful New Year, but I could wish you happiness (as I do) in every letter. So just for this one letter I think I shall give you a short sermon: don't, please, my darling, don't be depressed. You and I have spun some wonderful memories out of disappointments and the smaller miseries of life and so this Christmas especially we'll be together - wondering a little why time moves so slowly but really happy and secure in our love. I'm counting on you, dearest, to be happy on the holiday – surely a couple of thousand miles of silly old sea isn't going to get us down?

---

29   Philip McNiff, librarian at Lamont library.

P.S. LOOK OUT FOR SNAKES

I'm sorry you missed the carols in the Yard the other night but I believe the Glee Club often practises on the steps of Widener in the spring, so you'll have a chance to hear them.

But I don't want to talk about things – just about us, and that means you. Being away from home for Christmas for the first time since I found my real home in you, my darling, isn't exactly an inspiring thought but I suppose it's what Toynbee[30] would call a 'challenge', and my 'response' is to write a pitifully inadequate letter to say I love you with a love that no ocean, or distance can affect and so I want you to be happy: have a good Christmas, my dearest, and (my traditional Christmas joke) when you go to the crib look at the ass and remember me. With all my dearest, gentlest love, Brian.

 18

The weekend was quite good fun, remember last year the History Department had their 'do' on Bill Kidney's birthday? Well, Bill's party was last Saturday night and I wasn't looking forward to it but, in the end, it was great fun! Then Sunday afternoon Ronan and Tommy called for tea. They were in great form and argued about politics and 'life' for a most amusing hour and promised to call again after Xmas. Tommy said he wrote you last week, so I hope you got the letter. They were asking news of you.

Aunt Agnes is coming to see us tonight as she's off to Manchester for Christmas. Your cards didn't arrive yet for 'reposting', but I'm poised in readiness to tackle them. How I long to see another Monday pass, in another week we'll be 2/3rd the way through this separation and that makes it very pleasant! 12 weeks before I sail sounds quite short. I'm delighted that you have started arranging about 'letters etc', and when you return to Harvard you should start looking around for a church where we could be married.

30   Arnold Joseph Toynbee, British historian of International affairs.

19

Bard, Tuesday, 21 December

Since arriving here I've been going round saying hello to people, but I have also spent yesterday afternoon and this afternoon in the library. Strangely enough, working over back numbers of periodicals is easier here than in Widener, as too many interested people there are likely to be using them.

I notice also that Bard library is quite strong on its Anglican writers (it was an episcopal seminary originally) and I've been using some things.

About my paper – I can't decide whether to shorten it by leaving out two sections or lengthen it by adding a new one. However, I'll continue to work over it for the time being. Apart from a futile effort to snow last night, the weather has been cold and brisk. I phoned George on Sunday (he was busy painting[31]) and he may come up for some music recital this evening. I'll probably go to Rhinebeck tomorrow. Everybody here is feverishly finishing off the tail-end of the term's work (it doesn't end until tomorrow) but fighting the holiday feeling to do it.

 20

[BRIAN TO MARIE-THÉRÈSE]
Rhinebeck, Wednesday, December 22

Rather cold again, darling, but I'm safely here with George who is well and has been very busy working on the house – painting, putting up curtains and having some insulation done.

This evening we plan to go to Hyde Park to see an Alec Guinness movie (never called 'films' here) and on Friday we're to eat out for supper. I'm hoping there'll be midnight Mass here in Rhinebeck – the church is only a block away.

---

31   House painting, not portrait painting.

Waiting for me on arrival was a Christmas card from a friend of George's I met here. I presume your mail has been caught up in the Christmas rush – hence my Christmas letter at the weekend.

I'm still thinking about my revision of the Locke thing (though, as I believe I mentioned, the new book by von Leyden[32] in fact backs up my point of view). As a more long-term project I might examine Hooker's 'influence' on other post-Restoration writers. Thank God for Widener – you know in College[33] I'd still be waiting to get this new book – and certainly wouldn't buy it at about $35 – but Widener gets stuff in very quickly.

At Bard I saw almost everyone as I had planned and Buzz Gummere in particular asked after you.

So far I haven't made any plans but I may return to Cambridge very early – perhaps by the 1st – as I have quite a lot to do. Also, it's a better base of operations for any further papers the visa people may ask for.

For relaxation yesterday, I read 'Teacher in America' by Jacques Barzun (a friend of George's). It's a criticism of American college education – very brilliant, since I agree with so much of it, I suppose. One thing is fairly certain, should we plan to settle here, it would be important that I get a PhD started – the 'Ph.D Octopus'[34] is one of the great criticisms of the present system, but the degree

....

32   Wolfgang Marius von Leyden (1911–2004) was a German political philosopher who edited the letters of seventeenth-century philosopher John Locke.

33   UCD.

34   An article written by US philosopher, psychologist and physician William James (1848–1910). The essay was about a rule that makes doctorate degrees mandatory for college teachers in the US. James argued; 'Will anyone pretend for a moment that the doctor's degree is a guarantee that its possessor will be successful as a teacher? Notoriously his moral, social, and personal characteristics may utterly disqualify him for success in the class-room; and of these characteristics his doctor's examination is unable to take any account whatever.' He states that, though the rule will increase the 'class of highly educated men in our country', such a rule will 'interfere with the free development of talent' and more importantly 'obstruct the natural play of supply and demand in the teaching profession'.

is a 'must' if one is to succeed. Fortunately my European degree is held in high repute over here. By the way, darling, would you ask Ronan how long a minor thesis in History is supposed to be? I've an idea it's about 10,000 words, but would like to be sure.

 21

Your wonderful 'heap' of nylons, 'papers' and the cards – all arrived at lunch time yesterday, result: I got so excited that I've eaten a small bottle of milk of magnesia since and practically nothing else!

Aunt Agnes came last night, bringing the most beautiful gifts: I got a really exquisite crystal vase, hand cut almost 10″ high and shaped like a chalice, and also she gave me her Bog oak hand glass – I felt very small with my tiny brooch. I do hope she likes it.

All your cards I sent off, except for Ronan's, Tommy's, Brian P. and Brian O'C and Dermot which I dropped in to Ronan and he promised to look after them. I hope you don't mind – I put my name under yours in a few cases where you hadn't put a P.S., feeling that those cards weren't so personal and you wouldn't mind.

Thank goodness I've sold my old sewing machine – for £15 – I only had two replies to the ad, but a girl in my factory bought it in the end and will pay me after Christmas.

Aunt Agnes was delighted with your letter and I now have your Letter of Freedom (a small certificate), and will send it to you when you are back at Harvard, as the Christmas post isn't very safe.

Isn't it great that Pearse is home for Christmas! Thank God, and I do hope all in Manchester will now have a very happy one!

22

Lord knows when I'll post this but I'll start, before I forget some 'details' – you know almost the worst part of being apart is not having you to share fun with – without you there's that something missing which would make pleasant days perfect.

On Wednesday night the 'girls' in Dun Laoghaire factory presented me with a huge box of chocolates and on Thursday they held their Xmas party – long looked forward to! They planned their menu to the last 'blob of cream' and when we all sat down they were almost too excited to eat – Betty (the best machinist) and Tommy (the messenger boy) sat at each side of me – he insisted on keeping his dessert spoon in his dungaree pocket for fear it would be 'pinched'. After sandwiches, Fullers cakes, cream flans, trifles, fruit and cream, tea and cider they were all sick and giggly, their thin little bodies were distended (their skirts were unzipped ½ way through the 'lunch') and one girl looked down at herself and was heard to remark: 'Oh, I'm not walking up for my wages, if Mr Lamar sees me he'll ask me to leave!' Then Tommy dragged a rather grubby brooch (a large green cat) out of his pocket saying: 'I found that last night, it's for you!' – a party I hope I never forget, a good start to Christmas.

Other news: Mama's in Vincents[35] – grumbling but obviously very comfortable – everyone is visiting her and their 'offerings' are very impressive. I gave her a box of note paper from you (which she started to use immediately) and a ½ bottle of sherry.

I am now settled in Mary and Gerard's[36] and looking forward to a very pleasant Christmas.

---

35 St Vincent's Hospital, Dublin.
36 Murphy.

Dearest: it was a very full and pleasant time – I do hope yours was even better – Christmas Day passed with too much eating and pleasant chatter. Mary and I went in on a bus (12) to Mass in White Friar St.[37] Then after an excellent lunch I subsided before a super fire and Ann-Barbara[38] played all her new records!

Yesterday evening there were a few guests in, including Billy Kingston and Hugh Morris, later they took me to a supper party Miriam Ann threw in Ina Ryan's flat – a very select party of old timers – excellent conversation, good food and some dancing. I chatted mostly (helped by a little wine!) and danced only 3 times – with different people each time – Lilia was there, Maureen, Nuala, Val and Charlie, Brian Quinn[39], Ronan, Carol; everyone (including people who never met you) were asking about and after you and I'm ashamed to say it, I left at 4.15 and came to my house, but Mama isn't away every night of the week and it's not an opportunity I'd let slip!

Today I went to the Races, losing 7/- (on a day's betting isn't bad!). It was a beautiful spring day, Noeleen was in great form and we met loads of old friends. I bumped into Roma and Hank and I'm to go in to Fitzwilliam Square for afternoon tea next Saturday!

....

37 Whitefriar Street Carmelite Church, off Aungier Street. It is maintained by the Carmelite order. The church is notable for housing the relics of Saint Valentine, which were donated to the church in the nineteenth century by Pope Gregory XVI. They were brought to Dublin from the cemetery of St Hippolytus in Rome. Years later Brian would take his children to visit 'the relic' on one of their Saturday jaunts.

38 The Murphy's daughter, younger than MT.

39 Brian Quinn (1926 – 2015) was the editor of the Herald between 1969 and 1976 and subsequently held a number of roles, including chief sub-editor at the Irish Independent. He retired in 1988 at the age of 62. He was the UCD history graduate who was pipped at the post for a scholarship in Oxford by his contemporary FX Martin, the celebrated historian. Every Xmas Eve Brian would drop into Brian and MT's for some Xmas cheer and chat.

23

My Own Darling, Thank you for your lovely letter, the perfect Christmas present. Really, dearest, you pamper me so, and I love it. I'm sitting listening to the Halle recording of Mendelsohn's 'Italian'. Last night George and I swapped presents. He gave me a lovely rayon travelling robe in dark blue, nicely packed in its own bag. Just before I left Boston I had managed to get an excellent recording of Strauss's 'Four Last Songs'[40] (John played it for me in Virginia, but I couldn't get it in Cambridge).

This morning a fine, cool day, we rose about 10 and had breakfast while listening to another Christmas gift record sent to George, the Christmas Eve Festival of King's College, Cambridge.

By the time this reaches you, Christmas will be over and soon it will be into our New Year. I do wish all these weeks would hurry by and bring us together again, but until then, my darling, I send you all my love – and my loneliness – having survived this Christmas away from each other the rest of the time won't feel too bad, please God.

So, pet, I hope you've no indigestion (or debts after the races) and for now – do look after yourself, my dear, and remember me, Brian.

 24

[BRIAN TO MARIE-THÉRÈSE]
St Stephen's Day, 1954

My Darling, How was your Christmas? I didn't go to Midnight Mass after all. Most of Christmas Eve we spent decorating the Christmas Tree. Then at 7.00 we were picked up and driven out to

----

40 Brian loved classical music and opera and many years later, when he was on *Calling the Tune*, Evelyn Cockburn's show, one of his choices was Strauss's 'Four Last Songs'. There he spoke about his great friend George Roach, and his wonderful music collection.

friends of George's for dinner. We had a pleasant evening there. George brought his new record of the King's College Cambridge Festival of Carols, which is wonderful.

I went to 10.30 Mass yesterday and we had a light breakfast. About 4.00 we had dinner – ham etc. ... It was very pleasant to spend a lazy Christmas listening to music (last night we got the full service from King's College). Still I was very lonely for you, dearest, and kept imagining what you might be doing at the Murphy's and so on.

We stayed up late talking, but I got up for 9.00 Mass this morning and I've been going over my Locke paper again – also getting through the Sunday 'N.Y. Times'.

About 4.00 we went over to visit the Cohns (people I had supper with on my last visit to Rhinebeck). It was quite pleasant and more music.

But frankly I can't take this much recorded music, though it is very lovely, and I may well go back to Cambridge next week-end (depending on how quickly I can make arrangements in N.Y.C. – I will see the Institute about travel).

This isn't terribly 'newsy' is it, darling? But life here is quiet and peaceful and I'm too full of Locke to concentrate on anything else and miss you so much, too much to be all that happy.

 25

[BRIAN TO MARIE-THÉRÈSE]
Rhinebeck, Monday, 27 December

I'm working again on Locke – I'm now double-spacing it and I'm on the 18th page (about a fifth of the space is taken up by 60-odd footnotes). I expect to finish it within one or two more pages. Actually, pet, I wanted to know about the length of the M.A. thesis from Ronan, as I thought I might submit this (in an extended form). However, I'll send a carbon copy to Desmond first and see what he says.

Apart from that, my only news is musical. Today I played 'Paint your Wagon', 'Trovatore' (a lovely recording with Jussi Björling[41]), some Schubert songs, an L.P. of the Coronation, Mendelssohn's 'Italian' (again) and a couple of single sides. It's very handy having so much music around – though more musical shows might be desirable.

The news about the baby being returned from Belfast[42] made a paragraph in the New York Times, rather surprisingly. By the by, I've just read 'The Vanishing Irish'[43] – I only took an hour over it though – I was amazed to see that Fr Murray[44] had an article in it.

 26

Your letters of Wednesday and Thursday arrived last night and saved me from feeling utterly deserted! You see in the same post was a telegram from the maid saying: 'can't come back at present father very ill' – and she was already a day late, I had fully expected her back last night. Sheila Coakley and I had just been to see a magnificently funny picture 'Mons. Hulot's Holiday' at the Astor, and I only came home after 11.00, so I'm still rather dazed as to what to do next.

---

41   Another choice of Brian's on *Calling the Tune with Evelyn Cockburn in 1999*. A school friend from Colaiste Mhuire played it for him one afternoon and he was awestruck by the beauty of the piece.

42   Patrick Berrigan was snatched from his pram on Henry Street, Dublin and found within days (thanks to an observant young woman on the train to Belfast) in a woman's home in Belfast, where the police discovered another kidnapped child, a four-year-old girl, in the same house.

43   The Vanishing Irish; The Enigma of the Modern World (1953), edited by John O'Brien, was a book of essays that caused a lot of controversy in America when it first came out. (catholicherald.co.uk/article/19th-november-1954/4/dont-blame-clerical-interference).

44   An American priest, Fr Murray, who had been studying conditions closely in Ireland, contributed an essay insisting upon the need for capital – and confidence –to develop Irish land, especially the neglected and unprofitable areas.

Mama was due home today and I only hope Vincent's will keep her till the weekend. Anyway, I don't really care! I'm too happy about the future to care much about anything else! Actually Betty (my pet machinist) has offered to come down in the evenings and do the housework which, I think, was very sweet of her.

By the way there's an intriguing rumour sweeping England at present – Princess Margaret, having read his book, has expressed a wish to meet Fr Eugene Boylan[45] and that the meeting is arranged for the 27th Jan. Needless to say everyone is intrigued!

[BRIAN TO MARIE-THÉRÈSE]
New York City, Wednesday, 29 December

My Dearest – We got here at last; the Cohns drove us up from Rhinebeck in a little under two hours – but it took us 45 minutes to get through twenty or so blocks of the city. We went to the Commodore and into one of the A.H.A.[46] meetings – very late. It was pleasant, but not brilliant or impressive. After some chatting with various people we had a snack and came to the Scholfields with whom we are staying. They have a two-room apartment – the living room is quite large and painted in dramatic deep blue. The rest of the family consists of SEVEN CATS!! Tomorrow we'll go over to A.H.A. again for some time. George plans to leave Friday morning but I may stay on for another couple of days. Then I'll go back to Rhinebeck to pick up my luggage and so return to Cambridge.

45 Dom Eugene Boylan was a prize-winning student, music-lover, ladies' man and physicist who won a scholarship to the University of Vienna, lectured at UCD and to everyone's surprise became a monk at Mount Saint Joseph Abbey, Roscrea. He became a famous writer of spiritual books, including *This Tremendous Lover,* which became a best-seller. He was in great demand as a lecturer and writer and he had the ability to adapt his message to his audience and to render 'the supernatural almost natural'.

46 The American Historical Association is the largest professional organisation serving historians in all fields and all professions. Every year a meeting is held in a different part of the country. In 1954 the annual meeting was held in NYC.

P.S. LOOK OUT FOR SNAKES

Well, darling, I was very surprised – but delighted – to hear that everything arrived on time and I do hope the Christmas passed off pleasantly. Frankly, as you may have noticed from my letters, I was rather depressed, but now I'm back on an even keel, thank God. By the by, I finished the 'Rhinebeck Draft' of my Locke paper (this damn thing must be boring you by now) and it runs to about 5,000 words and footnotes. Really I'm reasonably satisfied with it – in its present limited scope.

 28   [**MARIE-THÉRÈSE TO BRIAN**]
Wednesday night, 29 December

Sitting in a rather squalid untidy bedroom[47] `I naturally think of you! No, that's unfair, because I think of you all the time! But, Darling, you know we must have been very close on Xmas Eve, as George's record of the Christmas Eve Festival was the one Ann-Barbara and I were playing all during Christmas!

Mama's coming home tomorrow, Betty Rogers' mother is coming in as a 'daily', to stop-gap till 'our' Betty condescends to return! Shows you they really love me at work. As soon as they saw my long face this morning, two girls thought out a way to solve my problem and this girl's mother was a cook in Rosses Hotel[48] for 7 years and a nurse attendant on and off since.

 29   [**BRIAN TO MARIE-THÉRÈSE**]
N.Y.C., Friday, 31 December

My Dearest, New York is more liveable with than I had thought earlier. George and I have been unlucky in trying to buttonhole people at the A.H.A., though I met all the Harvard people that

47 A 'dig' at the 'squalid' conditions of 13, Little Mary Street, 'the Garret', Brian's old home.
48 Hotel in Dun Laoghaire.

are up, and Owen (chairman for September) invited me to lunch when I get back to Harvard.

This morning I went to see Rockefeller Centre, which is beautifully decorated for the Christmas season. I've been trying (quite unsuccessfully) to make a date to meet Alice Hermes and Mike Rado (the speech people at Bard) and hope to make it sometime before I leave.

This being New Year's Eve, my darling, I do feel rather depressed that I'm not in No. 13 with you celebrating with a few people, but you know I send you my love, my wishes for this year which has begun (by the time this reaches you) and the hope that this is a very RAPID spring so we can be together soon.

 30

[MARIE-THÉRÈSE TO BRIAN]
Friday, New Year's Eve, 1954

Your letters of 27th and 28th arrived today – and the house is back to normal thanks to this 'wonder girl's' mother. Betty Rogers has helped me out twice now: she persuaded one of the office girls to buy my machine and now her mother is running no.5 and looking after Mama till our Betty comes back.

I'll ring Ronan over the week-end about the length of the thesis.

You, Darling, sounded quite sad over Christmas – how I wish you'd been in Murphy's with me – they did everything to make mine a happy one.

Did I tell you that Myles says we are having that reception when we come back? And people are beginning to ask what we want for presents! Mrs Duff told Mama, last week, that there is a lady (who I've never met) who has some of the 'Mathew' Silver (My grandmother's family) and that she intends giving me a piece of it. Anyway, I'll put the announcement of the wedding in the papers about mid-Feb. As soon as you've settled back in Cambridge, look around for the church and priest and send me details.

31

My Own Darling,

This, to me, is such a waste, this time spent apart, and I look back to those 2 deliriously happy New Year's Eves spent in the Garret and then wishing in the New Year to the Bells – one can't see far ahead, but I'd like to see us with a few close friends by our own fireside in exactly a year from now!

Coming back from work I decided to be very naughty – I bought a large bottle of the best Champagne I could get, some paté de foi gras and some shrimps – Con, Eva and I ate and drank for 2 hours – then the girls crawled home – and here I am feeling: what a waste of time if you were only here, this will be our year and as I doze off all I can say is: Happy New Year, Darling, as happy as I can make it for you and much, much better than that! Success with the work, good health, and if this letter is slightly vague it's 3 glasses of the best which stops me saying sensible things.

The hooters and horns have started so, with a prayer for us both, All my love, Marie-Thérèse.

Chapter 6

JANUARY 1955

Overall, there have been no regrets. I think regret is a very wasteful emotion; life is a learning curve and all that and one has to always try new things.

⁊⁊⁊

Brian Farrell, talking to *Senior Magazine*, Bray, in 2005

1

Dearest Brian,

Yesterday I had tea in Smyths[1] and met my cousins again and the baby (Roma's) a sweet, dark- haired child. I've asked them to come up for the wedding, and hopefully they will. But much more important I think I've got someone to marry us: Fr Bernard O'Dea[2] O.S.B. (a monk from Glenstal) who is, at present, in Connecticut and is 'touring'[3] America all this year. So Darling, all I want, as soon as possible, is the address of a small church in Cambridge and the name of the PP so that I can send my marriage papers out and can tell Fr Bernard where and when we expect him. The guests, so far: Mary[4] and Ed Seidensticker (he's a Protestant), Roma and Henry Beauregard. Billy and Avril (they haven't answered my invitation yet), George Roche and Fr Bernard O'Dea.

Would you enquire the price of that flat upstairs from you – if it's still free – or do you think we could stay in George's for a week

---

1   Nano (older sister of Theo Dillon) married a surgeon, Patrick Smyth. Roma is one of their four children and she was married and living in America but visiting her parents in Fitzwilliam Square at the time.

2   Dom Bernard O'Dea (1909–2000) was the first Benedictine monk to be professed in Ireland since the Reformation. He served as prior of Glenstal from 1945–52. He was pre-eminently a man of God, a quality which found expression in his warm humanity and joyful, welcoming spirit. Dom Bernard was an anam chara (Irish for 'soul friend') in the monastic tradition of St Benedict, an apostolate facilitated by his prodigious memory and breadth of friendship. People flocked to Glenstal for his advice and his letters also enriched the lives of many. He was a lovable if slightly disorganised confrère. He supported Mother Mary Martin (MT's godmother) at a critical juncture in her founding of the Medical Missionaries of Mary. He believed in the dignity of work, which he wrote (in one of his articles for the Muintir na Tíre handbook) 'is intended by God to develop our potentialities'. 'Everything is working out just grand,' was his repeated comment.

3   Bernard O'Dea visited the US on several occasions, to conduct retreats and raise funds, and for health reasons.

4   Mary Dillon, a cousin of MT's from the branch of William Blake Dillon, John Dillon's brother, who had settled in Colorado.

       P.S. LOOK OUT FOR SNAKES

after I arrive and return to Boston together about the 1st April? Otherwise I'll be looking for a room, or something, in Boston.

Have you any suggestion for who is to give me away? Ed or George are both Protestants and I don't know how they would do in America (it wouldn't do here).

Dearest, this has been a poor letter, but this is part of the fun of planning and only 11 weeks to go! It's getting quite near, Thank God. I enclose your Letter of Freedom, the post should be safer now and your Baptism certificate is coming from Manchester.

All my love, Marie-Thérèse

(Later) Shawn, Ronan and Tommy called in and spent an hour here – they brightened an otherwise dismal Sunday. Ronan thinks 20,000 words, Shawn: 10,000 (for Thesis). And I'll ring Desmond during the week and let you know!

 2

[MARIE-THÉRÈSE TO BRIAN]
Monday night, 3 January

Firstly, I must explain that this notepaper is your Christmas present to Mama and she lets me use it for 'special' letters. It has also been used for notes to: James, Nano, Myles[5] and other such 'important' people. Strange I can't think or talk about anything lately without getting back to March, people are finding me rather a bore, I fear. The boys (Ronan, Tommy and Shawn) pleased me greatly by dropping in, Mama likes it too because I usually have some funny stories to tell her later; otherwise our Sundays are deadly!

---

5   MT's two uncles and aunt.

3

My Darling,

I got back 'home' on Tuesday, having missed my 10.00 train from NYC as I couldn't get a porter to manage my baggage. In the end, it was just as well, as I had a leisurely breakfast and stroll around Central Station, taking in the Kodak high-school snaps exhibition. Some of the photos were really wonderful. At 12.00 I was in a huge jam waiting to get on to platform 20 (over here you're only told the platform about ½ hour before the train time). The train was apparently late but about 12.10 they let us on to the ramp leading to the platform proper and finally I got a seat and left N.Y. Central at 12.25 (half-an-hour late). 'The Bostonian' should have arrived in Boston at 4.10 – we got in at 5.05! I brought my stuff over to 146 Upland and stayed there last night.

Today – the house hunt or Farrell the flat-catcher. Well, darling, it was tough going but I covered about 15 apartments (picking only those 'within reason') and 8 rooms – all from the housing list. Finally I took another look upstairs in 146 and once again found myself taken by the kitchen, so I took it.

I'm still arranging things in my garret (a real one this one with tall ceilings) but I believe I'll be very comfortable here. Anyway I'll soon let you know. Meantime, my darling, I feel tremendously excited and really do find time passing, so for now I send you all my love, Brian.

 4

My Dearest,

Last night, I had rather an upsetting dream about you on a bus - that combined with the fact that it's been 3 days since I've had

P.S. LOOK OUT FOR SNAKES

a letter – I can't help imagining all sorts of things! Please God, you're all right and the Postal System is to blame.

This morning I got a letter from our maid to say she'll return to us next Saturday. Also arrived, a yet un-translated letter from the Austrian Legation in London! I left Mama battling with it. Otherwise, life is deadly as I can't leave the house at night and must rise (long before any self-respecting cock!) at 7.00, to get Mama's breakfast etc., before getting to work at 8.30!

Aunt Agnes is still in Manchester, I got a letter from her yesterday saying Pearse is still improving and that everyone is well. I rang John O'Donoghue yesterday – he says he'll write to you soon but I enquired of him the required length of a thesis and his answer, 10,000 words was a minimum but he felt that anything between that and 15,000 would do – anyway, he'll write you on the subject.

 5

[**MARIE-THÉRÈSE TO BRIAN**]
Friday morning, 7 January

This is a much cheered me! Your 2 letters (of the New Year) were the best reading – and Betty is returning tomorrow. All this week I've been getting up at about 7.00 to get breakfast before going to work at 8.15, and we've been working till 6 pm these last few days, but next week we'll be back to normal.

Now that Betty's coming back, Mama's talking about staying on in the house after I go, and I think it's rather a good idea. Did I write you that I rang the American Embassy? They said that the papers will be in time (in a week or so) and that I won't be prevented from going in March, apparently there have to be 2 copies, as I have to carry one copy with me to show on arrival.

I don't think I'll stop long in New York, as the shops are probably as good in Boston, and we'll get a taxi straight from the ship to the station for Boston. For a first impression I imagine N.Y. City will be a bit terrifying! I had thought we might go to George's, but have changed my mind, as the River Hudson would be far more tempting when the weather gets really hot. The thought of only 10 weeks to go is very exciting! Mama sends warmest love. All my love, Marie-Thérèse

 6

I got five letters from you today, including one forwarded from Rhinebeck, and the Embassy note. About this last, I'll draw up the affidavit and have it witnessed Monday, and get the letter from Harvard and the bank duplicate, and I will write Taft. At the same time I shall write to George and ask him to prepare a guarantee to have ready to send on directly, in case of need, so that should be okay. So now, my dearest one, don't worry, everything is under control!

I was delighted to hear your Christmas was so happy and that you got out, but you shouldn't worry about bad dreams. Also I'm looking forward to your THREAT, to make me fall for you again! This Embassy fly in the ointment is not going to mess things; we put up with a great deal and I'll be damned if the bureaucrats are going to beat us now.

By the way, dearest, guess what? I've had an invitation to give a talk on 17th March. Should I?

 7

My Dearest, Your papers[7] go off tomorrow – I was held up getting the Harvard letter. I also wrote to Taft. In your latest letter, you

6   Brian's birthday (9 January 1929).
7   The documents MT needs in order to obtain a visa.

                         P.S. LOOK OUT FOR SNAKES

sounded more cheerful and, please God, this little tangle with red tape won't be more than a contingent problem. About my birthday, you were quite right not to waste money on unnecessary gifts – I just want you beside me, darling, and the sooner the better.

Actually, I had a very pleasant birthday. After 9.30 Mass I went into the Square to meet these people who want me to speak on the 17th March. In the evening I had some friends over, the three boys – Stan, Egbert and Paul and also Leighton Shiels, Ruth Jacobson (a friend of Egbert's) and Rose Bakst, who is working in Cambridge on some newspapers or something, and a friend of hers from the Law School. The two knocked me flat by presenting me with a cigarette lighter! Stan gave me a book and Egbert brought some cookies. We just sat around talking and had a pleasant time.

Today, apart from getting the affidavit witnessed and seeing about the letter from Harvard, I've been continuing my reading on Locke.

With all my love and a special kiss now that I'm an old man of 26.
Brian

My Dearest Brian,

Yesterday was your Birthday and I thought of you all day. I hope you celebrated somehow and well – I did too! I had Eva, Sheila and Noeleen to tea and made some of the things I'd have loved to make for you: coffee cake[8] and cream flan – but it was flat (the day not the cake) without you, and only the fact that it's now 10 weeks to go kept me cheerful. On Saturday I went and looked for luggage. I'm getting all white! And it's very cheap. It will all come to £7.6/= and it's very pretty. There is no news, except that Betty is back and will be delighted to stay at the house with

---

8   Brian's favourite cake.

Mama, a great load off my mind. On Saturday I went to a sherry party (and enjoyed it) in Gerry O'Kelly's.[9] I haven't heard from you since Thursday, so I'm looking forward to news. For tonight, then, all my love.

Tuesday (same letter) – your letters of Wed and Sat arrived this morning – wonderful news: you've moved into 'our' place already! Are Stan and Bert still in the lower flat? And are they getting another room-mate? You must talk on the 17th! You'll probably have a much more 'Irish' St Patrick's Day in America than ever in Ireland. Staying in '146' has a great advantage – everyone knows that address now, and otherwise I'd have to contact people here and give them our new address.

This morning Needham told me that Mr Lamar, who was at the same sherry party (on Sat) said I was one of the smartest people there! So now!!

Mama is delighted to be home and sends love.

Dearest, now that I see by your letters that you are well, all bad dreams are dispelled. All my love, Marie-Thérèse

 9

My Dearest Marie-Thérèse ,

I haven't heard from you since your more cheerful letter. I've sent all the necessary papers. I wrote George about whether Easter Monday would be more convenient for him and he replied not to worry on his account; that he will 'be there if you have it at 1 am on St Swithin's Day!' Also, Mrs Cushman wants to talk to me: I think she may suggest either a) that she throw a reception for our wedding guests or b) that you stay with them (in Cambridge) until you are ready to take full-time charge of me. What do you think of that idea?

9   Gerry was American originally, worked at Larham's with MT.

How can I get in touch with your Benedictine?[10] There is one local church in Cambridge, so I presume this will be the location, and what date would you like for sure? When I get FULL information on all these points I'll line everything up! As for someone to give you away, how about Jim Barry,[11] the man I met in Boston?

Now all of this is very sort of formal, pet, so I shall try and make it up in this letter by passing on a quote from the E.E. Cummings[12] book Stan gave me for my birthday:

While you and I have lips and voices which
Are for kissing and to sing with
Who cares if some one-eyed son of a bitch
Invents an instrument to measure Spring with?

 10

My Dearest,

I received quite a boost in morale today, when Needham informed me that I was to train-in the new manageress for here and that she was starting Monday! I pleaded inability (fearing that if I was a bit slack towards the end I'd spoil her chances of doing her work properly) and he said nonsense, I was the best possible person to train her! So there! Her name is Pat Plunkett, I was at school with her in Leeson Street and subsequently Caroll O'Connor[13] brought her into DramSoc years ago – she's a tall blond who was stage struck years ago. Her mother runs a small hotel on Earlsfort Terrace.

10   Dom Bernard O'Dea.
11   Boston Irish, elderly man who took Brian under his wing.
12   One of Brian's favorite poets. Brian loved poetry and had a phenomenal memory for verse, which he could quote on any suitable occasion.
13   Carroll O'Connor, American actor and director of Archie Bunker fame. He was the second cousin of the Dublin playwright Ulick O'Connor. In the early 1950s, Carroll studied English literature at University College Dublin while his wife, Nancy, was a student at Trinity College Dublin.

Last night I finished another summer frock and cut out a 3rd. Tonight Noeleen and I are going to see 'Rear Window' the picture you saw last fall.

Darling, I'm getting so excited now! I count the days: 69 till we meet and I'm deliriously happy at the thought! There is no news otherwise.

 11

I was delighted to see you approve, at least in the abstract, of the 'apartment', darling. Actually the kitchen is really good, with an excellent refrigerator and gas stove (a self-lighter) which has four jets, a large oven and a broiler. The bed/sitting-room isn't big but isn't cramped; about the size of the bedroom in no.13. It's not heaven (though close to it because of the height!) but quite compact, and after all it'll only be for about six weeks.

The attempted snow yesterday didn't amount to more than a few spots of frost and it is somewhat milder, though the wind is bitter. Yesterday afternoon the Graduate History Club had a sherry party and I went in for an hour to say 'hello' to a few people.

Apart from that I'm leading a very quiet life, but liking it. Have I told you, dear, about the movies I saw over the vacation: in NYC 'Mr Hulot's Holiday' was uproariously funny – practically no dialogue but really brilliant comedy, and the 'Belles of St Trinian's' was a good evening's entertainment. Here in Boston I saw 'Romeo and Juliet' – undoubtedly one of the most beautiful films ever made. The play is cut down, the acting not outstanding but good in an unobtrusive way – the scenery, sets, life and bustle absolutely magnificent. Don't miss it! (as a footnote to my film news, 'Lili'[14] is still running in N.Y.C.! You're doing well, darling).

14 Brian is referring indirectly to MT's new hairstyle, similar to that of Leslie Caron in the movie Lili (1953).

P.S. LOOK OUT FOR SNAKES

It struck me the other day looking through the catalogue that your mother would enjoy one aspect of academic life over here, the great interest taken in Thomas Mann.[15] All literature courses offer at least selections, and his Buddenbrooks[16] has been published as a paper, usually linked with Mann or Joyce and Kafka (or Proust). Still, I think the courses are much less stuffy and academic (though not necessarily better) than ours. By the by, pet, did I tell you I picked up *Ulysses* new for $1.45 or so?

 12

[MARIE-THÉRÈSE TO BRIAN]
Friday morning, 14 January

Your letter and photo arrived yesterday evening – the photo is very good and I love it! The news that you are cooking even better! I've not done any for 2 years and feel rather worried, but you are so sweet that you'll bear with my bad cooking, at first anyway. The thought of having a fridge excites me greatly.

On the same post came a note from the Visa people to say that my application could now be considered as they had received a satisfactory guarantee of support from you! I'm going to see them next Thursday, but I'm sure there'll be very little further trouble. Afterwards, I'm having tea in Joan Costello's, so hopefully it will be a very pleasant afternoon off! My Baptism Cert has also arrived and I'm holding it till you send the address of the church and name of the parish priest. Don't forget the date we want the church is on April 11th at 10 or 11 o'clock, whatever time suits the PP, although I'd rather like to receive

15 Thomas Mann's Magic Mountain is a novel about life in a Swiss sanatorium, Marie, MT's mother was Theo's nurse in a Swiss sanatorium, before they fell in love and married.

16 Buddenbrooks (1901) , by Thomas Mann, chronicles the decline of a wealthy north German merchant family over the course of four generations, incidentally portraying the lifestyle and mores of the Hanseatic bourgeoisie from 1835–77.

Holy Communion not too late. Do ask him can a Prod give me away? And let me know.

By the way, we're parting with the gardener as of the 1st March – a wise economy, I think, as we certainly couldn't afford £1 1/- every 2 weeks – I told Mama I'd do the garden when we come back and she could give the money to us! Jokes apart, we were thinking of doing it for some time, and he took it very well.

 13

[MARIE-THÉRÈSE TO BRIAN]
Saturday night, 15 January

Today something happened to show me how very lucky I am! I had a girl to tea whom I haven't seen for 4 years – we talked and chattered – eventually I discovered that she is still going around with the same boy she was madly in love with when I knew her before – apparently he's been failing his exams for the last 6 years and is still doing 2nd Engineering. This set me a very pretty problem – I pictured myself in the same position – but then I realised that in loving you – I love everything about you – your love of your subject, your ambition is my ambition – then I suddenly realised that some silly fortune-teller who told me I would marry for ambition wasn't far wrong! Because in those days 'getting on' meant big cars, big houses and money – whereas to me, it means a contented mind, for both of us – it means you gaining the respect and admiration of all you meet and know of you and a future to which God only will set the bounds of success – I can hear you say: 'she doesn't want much!' but you wait and see – it will all happen.[17]

Next Wednesday our bed is being delivered – it's a 'C' grade 'Odearest' divan and spring mattress 4' which cost £17 2/6-. There are 7 grades and 'C' grade should last perfectly for 20 years. Mr Ward who brought me to the 'wholesale house' has measured

17   A perfect example of a self-fulfilling prophecy.

out our room and I'll be able to fit your wardrobe (Papa's old one) into our room too – so we should be quite comfortable. I should have consulted you on the subject of 'bed'! But when I got the offer of one wholesale I jumped at it, and it would be hard to do better, I felt!

Having it here, before I leave, means we can move in immediately, when we come back to Dublin. Much as I love you, I feel my feelings would be too strong for words sharing a single bed for the first night after a sea voyage!

At last I'm mistress of my small 'Fortune' – £160 shares of Imperial Tobacco – (worth about £550 at present!). Tomorrow I go to see Mother Hogan in the morning, re my Confirmation Certificate, and in the afternoon, I call on an old lady to relieve her of her 'silver' so am leaving this letter to add the next instalment.

Sunday – a very busy day over! Mother Hogan hadn't my Confirmation Cert., but gave me details how and where to obtain it, which I've already followed up – the old dear is now a mild, small person, not as fiery and temperamental as years ago! She prays for us daily, and I've promised to call again before leaving.

In the afternoon I had tea in Mrs Duff's[18] and then Sheila Duff[19] and I went to see Miss Kelly who gave me some hideous silver! Maybe I just hate silver but I'll pack it away and try to forget its existence. There is an ashtray dish (much too heavy) and some forks and spoons but the thought behind them is very sweet. So, Darling, with only 6 weeks to go, look after yourself most carefully in all this cold and snow. The spring is coming to Ireland, our crocuses and snowdrops are out. All my love, Marie-Thérèse

....

18   Mother of Francis Arthur Duff, Irish urologist and surgeon. The Duffs were distant relatives of the Dillons. Back then it was customary to give silver for wedding presents. Needless to say this was wasted on MT, who always despised old silver, along with 'cut' flowers.

19   Sheila Duff was one of the few close friends of Marie Dillon.

14

I've just written to Father Bernard O'Dea to ask him to marry us and I've given him your address (in case he wants to know 'things') and his address is: *Father Bernard O'Dea O.S.B., St. Mary's Abbey, 528, High str. Newark 2, New Jersey.*

How far is New Jersey from you? Do you think we can go over to see him before Easter or is it too far? Dearest, I'm so excited!! The weeks pass, with 9 weeks to go! The news that you are in our flat seems to bring everything nearer. You are looking after yourself and eating properly, I hope. It must be terribly cold now, so don't neglect things – 10,000 words or no 10,000 words!

Mama isn't looking terribly well, but she's in quite good form.

Have you any idea of what church in Cambridge we'll be married in? How about the one you go to? Send me the address of the one you've chosen as soon as possible, so I can tell Fr O'Dea. I'll also tell the priests here where to send my papers. And also the name of the parish priest, as soon as you've seen him. I feel horrible giving you this job, when all you want to do is study, but the sooner the better, in case of a holdup.

 15

My Dearest, I'm once more doing a draft of my paper; this time cutting out and abbreviating a great deal and merely adding a few extra paragraphs. I hope this will be about half the length of my last draft and, please God, will send the carbon copy to Desmond so he can see that I'm working.

The material I'm leaving out would probably make a small paper under the heading: *Some New Interpretations of Richard Hooker*. However, I think instead of doing that I shall study either Hooker's influence in the early seventeenth century, or the study of Ecclesiastical Policy later. In many ways I'm drawn to the topic of Locke's reading between 1660–1680, but this is such a large field. Either way, it's pleasant to work on a 'developing' theme.

The news of Aunty Agnes's return was good to hear. She must have been tired after her journey and, of course, the Manchester air does not agree with her. Please God I'll write her tonight.

 16

[MARIE-THÉRÈSE TO BRIAN]
Tuesday, 18 January

The Book[20] arrived! I'm so delighted and immediately reread the 'The Waltz', with great pleasure. I look forward to enjoying the rest at my leisure. I was just posting off my letter of Sunday when I got yours, and I don't know whether I said: definitely April 11th (Easter Monday), so when all this information is confirmed, I'm all set to send my papers on.

Snow and ice have reached Dublin – there are no cars on the roads and the bikes are on the footpaths so one goes at risk of life and limb. I went to see Aunt Agnes last night, despite the terrible cold, she's in great form.

As you can see, I'm struggling with this dreadful pen of Mama's. She was sweet enough to give me hers when I lost my own, but it's hell to write with!! And hell to read, I bet!!

---

20   A collection of Dorothy Parker's short stories.

[MARIE-THÉRÈSE TO BRIAN]
Wednesday night, 19 January

My Dearest,

From now on I feel I should date my letters with a 'day count' – 55 to go! Today is very special, as it's exactly 6 months since one Monday evening when you flew off at 7.30, leaving me very empty and a little tearful. But that's a long ... long ... time ago and please God we'll be together for a long life-time[21] to make up for 8 lonely months.

Had yesterday been Friday 13th, I wouldn't have been the least surprised! We had a very bad day at work; during the morning tea break, one of the girls managed to burn her face, neck and chest with boiling tea. I rushed her to the hospital (took her there myself) and then sent her home. Barely an hour later, another girl got a machine needle through a finger, I sent her to another hospital (fearing that if I sent them both to the same hospital they'd think I was torturing my girls). By the time I arrived home, Mama was in a state. She'd phoned Dr Roche to come and he'd not turned up. So I rang him and arranged to send Tommy (my handyman from work) to the hospital for a prescription that the doctor would leave out. Tommy was gone 3 hours and returned boiling with rage. Apparently he was left sitting in the hall of the hospital for over an hour. But by keeping his ears open, he discovered which room the Doctor was in. He knocked and entered without waiting, saying he'd a job of work to do and that he was sick waiting for a note Miss Dillon said would be ready! All of which he is quite capable of saying, as he says the most startling things whenever he feels like it! Mama was so pleased to hear the story she sent him a packet of 30 Players.[22]

---

21   Brian and MT were married for nearly sixty years. Brian passed away after a long illness, on 10th November, 2014.

22   Popular cigarette brand at the time.

P.S. LOOK OUT FOR SNAKES

I am sending on your confirmation certificate, but I won't bother to get mine. After all, I'm sure they're not really necessary. Tomorrow I go, once again, to face the 'Visa Section' in the American Embassy! God willing, the next time I write it will be to say 'I've got a visa'!

My Darling, the days drag on so, as the time comes nearer it seems to never pass. I unpacked my wedding dress material yesterday and it's lovelier than I remembered.

So from our 'Irish' Indian summer (the snowdrops are out) All my love and a warm kiss, Marie-Thérèse

[BRIAN TO MARIE-THÉRÈSE]
Cambridge, Thursday, 20 January

Yesterday evening I went over to a party in Boston (a quiet one) but heard the most wonderful 'take-off' on McCarthy. It's a Canadian record called 'The Investigator'[23] and it does a really brilliant job.

My paper looks longer than I had envisaged and at present I'm holding up covering some new material. Still, please God, it will be a passable piece of work.

In the library today I came across two new books on Irish history; one on Catholic Emancipation, which I had seen in NYC at the American Historical Association. The other deals with 'Swift and the Irish Church', a topic, which you may recall dear, I have often said should be done. I don't know how good it is, but I'll look through it anyway.

Did I tell you that I've been invited to speak to some Baptist

---

23 The Investigator was a radio play, written by Reuben Ship and produced in 1954. It was first broadcast on CBC (Canadian Broadcasting Corporation). The play was a satire on the work of the US House Committee on Un-American Activities (HUAC) and the Senate Permanent Subcommittee on Investigations, and its chairman, Joseph McCarthy. About 100,000 copies of a long-playing record made from the CBC production of The Investigator were sold during 1954 and 1955 in the US.

church social group? When I was at that Boston High School in the autumn, a young fellow approached me and asked if I'd do it.

I'm waiting to hear from you about that Fr O'Dea[24] and so on. I hope he's not too far away, as travelling expenses could be quite high. Anyway, we'll see. I expect to hear tomorrow and will then get hustling.

✉ *19* ....

[MARIE-THÉRÈSE TO BRIAN]
Friday morning, 21 January

I never knew you were psychic! 2 letters on Tuesday, you must have felt things were not going well, but everything is going better now. Mama is back on her injection, and my 2 injured girls are improving. Yesterday was a terrific success; I sauntered into the American Embassy, to find 10 people before me in the visa office. I was taken first! And half an hour later emerged rather dazed, but holding my visa – leaving 10 people still waiting in the queue!

Dearest, you never warned me about the ridiculous little ceremony in Miss Mahoney's office! There we both stood, our right hands raised and I swore that my application for a visa was a true statement, no one can tell me that these 'Americans ain't children at heart'! Thank goodness they are big-hearted children!

Tea in Joan's[25] was very pleasant. Her sister Mary was there, and after tea the baby was brought in – a very handsome child – very quiet and contented with big blue eyes (one slightly larger than the other) a strong nose and mouth, and lovely rosy cheeks, blond of course.

Dearest, your two letters were a wonderful surprise! Are you not afraid I'll get rather fat in America! You can afford to, but I can't!

You can go back to Fr Collins and say I definitely want to be

....

24 Fr O'Dea was an ex-prior of Glenstal and a friend of Fr Mathew, and according to MT, O'Dea was a healer because he'd healed the leg of a limping dog just by touching him. MT says he was a very 'charismatic' character.
25 Joan, wife of Declan Costello.

married in Cambridge whether or not Fr O'Dea comes. I may not hear from the monk for weeks, as New Jersey is only a postal address and he could be anywhere – if he doesn't turn up, would Fr Collins consider marrying us at short notice? If Jim Barry is so hot on clerics, any chance he'd offer Fr O'Dea a bed for the night – that is, if he comes too? Just an idea! Look after yourself, all my love, Marie-Thérèse

 20

My Dearest Marie-Thérèse ,

About Fr O'Dea's location, Newark, New Jersey is just across the river from New York. Now about the church, I went down to the Square and saw Fr Collins. He says that we have to find out where you will be staying before the wedding, so as to locate the parish from which we can be married. Mrs Cushman said something about putting you up, alternately you could stay either at 146 (in which event I'd find some place elsewhere) or else you could find a suitable hotel.

Anyway I shall address myself to Mrs Cushman on the subject (I have phoned already and they are away over the weekend), and you might write and say what you think of the New Jersey arrangement. The Cambridge location would probably be better but fare (round trip) for Fr O'Dea and a room overnight will probably set us back about $25. But I think Cambridge will be a good spot.

About Jim Barry giving you away, I haven't seen him lately, but on the religious score, don't worry – he's a rabid clerical (practically runs the Oblates) and hails from West Cork. One way or another I'll find a Catholic for the job – don't worry!

So now, pet, I've said my say and, as for distracting me from my study, I can't think of a more wonderful distraction. And now, with all my love, goodnight, God bless, and do take care of yourself, Brian.

21

Yesterday evening we had a very pleasant visit from James[26] and Maura. He rang before and I mistook him for Myles, their voices are amazingly alike! They couldn't have been sweeter, asked all about our plans. He is going to send me the addresses of some friends in Cambridge that I'm to call on, and Maura was asking all about my clothes. James said should I have any more trouble with the Americans I was to call on him. He says that my experiences with them were like those of Margaret Burke Sheridan,[27] who was the last person he intervened for. So I'm in good company! Maura has promised to bring John Blake[28] out to see Mama sometime soon.

Darling, I'm starting to make my wedding dress quite soon and I've still not decided on what style. So could you send me a copy of Harper's Bazaar, the fashion book? It should arrive in a month's time if you get it soon. It would give me an idea of spring fashions 'Stateside'.

Also, do give me an idea for a present to bring George? Here are my ideas; an old silver ashtray with the Roach crest, or Irish linen hankies with G.R. on them. What do you think?

I hope to hear from Dom Bernard next week, and as soon as you give me the OK about the church I'll write an invite to Mary and Ed[29] (from Denver) and Roma and Henry[30] (from Washington) – but I want to have all my facts before issuing the invitations! 57 days before I see you, Darling! Seems quite short compared to the 182 days I've endured! – more than ¾ of the vigil gone – please God all will go well, and reasonably according to plan from now on.

26   James Dillon, Fine Gael TD, and currently Minister for Agriculture.

27   Margaret Burke Sheridan (1889–1958), Irish opera singer. Born in Castlebar, County Mayo, Ireland, she was known as Maggie from Mayo and is regarded as Ireland's second prima donna, after Catherine Hayes (1818–1861).

28   John Blake Dillon (1945 – 2021) was James and Maura's only child and MT's first cousin.

29   Seidensticker (Mary was a Dillon).

30   Beauregard (Roma was Nano Dillon's daughter).

22

On this mail, I'm sending Desmond my paper, 18 pages in all. I suggested to him that I might submit an extended version as a minor thesis and hope he'll write me soon on the subject. Actually I'm not convinced that it's all that appropriate for a thesis, but we'll see what he says anyway.

Tomorrow, please God, I'll go over to Boston and ask Jim Barry to officiate in giving you away. Have you heard anything further from Father O'Dea?

I had a letter today from Taft saying he looked into the matter of your visa and believed there would be no trouble about it, so that should be all right now.

Just for a change I went to the Brattle last night and saw an excellent French movie called 'Carnival in Florence' with Louis Jouvet. It's fairly old, I think, but very good. The Brattle really does show some excellent films – mostly old-timers or foreign.

My paper still proceeds, but I'm going into some other aspects just now. For relaxation, this evening, I sat watching the ice-skaters in the Graduate Common.

 23

Still no news from Dom Bernard, which I fear means he's away from New Jersey at present, but couldn't you call the parish priest despite this drawback, and when you've started negotiations with him I can send my papers to him?

Aunt Agnes was quite a changed person last night – bright, cheery and looking very well – she put her knitting away and we had a very pleasant evening by the fire. She gave me your

Confirmation Cert which I'll post to you during the week – did you get your Baptism Cert?

The Baptist Social doesn't sound very exciting. What are you to speak about? Unless you stick to purely polite reflections on the 'this and that', won't your news be too Catholic for them? Now St Patrick's Day sounds much better fun and I'm looking forward to celebrating it on 'The America.'[31]

 24

Wednesday night, 26 January

Got your letter of Friday this morning and I am delighted to see that you too saw: 'Mr Hulot's Holiday'! I saw it the Tuesday after Christmas with a French sound track at the Astor and loved every moment of it! Sheila Coakley and I behaved rather badly at it, got rather hysterical when the 'fox' got his spree ...

I'm dying to see no. 146 but, and it's rather indelicate of me to mention it, is the bed-sitter ... well has the bed-sitter room? I mean is there a bedroom for 2?! You didn't mention. I am excited to see we'll have a fridge. I'm looking forward to making ice-cream and a particularly good lemonade I learned to make in Switzerland.

25

[BRIAN TO MARIE-THÉRÈSE]
Cambridge, 30 January

My Dearest, Well I saw the priest in St Paul's and he says to be sure and have three documents each: a Birth Certificate, Confirmation Cert and a paper from your mother (and from my folks) signed in the presence of the P.P. of your parish to say you're free to marry – this latter would save us having to get Letters of Freedom from

31   The liner that she is taking to join Brian in America.

each parish in which we have lived. Anyway, that simplifies the issue somewhat.

My visit to the Baptist Church Youth Fellowship tonight was rather fun. George Wilkins picked me up and we drove to his house in Quincy. There were about 25 young people, the minister (an ex-navy chaplain), and his wife. First they sang a hymn, then one of the young men read a prayer and a short 'moral' type story and another hymn. Then I was 'on'. I spoke for about half-an-hour, mainly on the emigration-economic-birth-rate and historical 'tradition' problem: why can't we do better and keep more people at home. They asked questions for about 45 minutes.

After a break for coffee, cakes and cookies (all biscuits are called cookies over here), we sat around. The majority of them sang 'jazzed up' hymns around the piano and talked to the minister and a couple of others. It was really quite interesting, as he comes originally from the more rabid part of the 'bible-belt' – western Texas: he, however, rejects the background. But he could remember the covered wagons going out West when he was a boy. All-in-all it was very pleasant, and a new facet of American life. George drove me back here at about 12.00, and here I am to ask – did you have a good weekend?

I'll talk to you for many hours about the Americans being children, when you get over. But it's a good thing to remember, that the most important factor to be considered about getting-on with Americans, is that they are DIFFERENT. Don't judge them by your own standards and don't look for too much subtlety, nor mistake their very real generosity and hospitality for hypocrisy. I think Jim Barry would almost surely put up your Fr O'Dea.

All my love, Brian.

Chapter 7

FEBRUARY–MARCH 1955

*Father's funeral[1] was awful. Later that day Mary Murphy
took me for a walk across St. Stephen's Green and we stopped
on the bridge to admire a Japanese Cherry tree that had just
been planted. Its pale pink petals promised so much. It promised to be there forever, and it has kept its promise, as each
year I seek it out in March.*

Marie-Thérèse (Dillon) Farrell

---

1   Theo Dillon died on 27 March 1946, at the age of forty-eight.

Cambridge, Thursday, 3 February

My Dearest,

One thing you are going to miss, and it's a pity, is the Yard under snow. It is really beautiful, even now. The weather is cold but dry, with sunshine until about four in the afternoon. All the buildings seem to be underlined by the white ridges of snow. People hurry through the cross paths from one lecture to another, or else stroll more leisurely along the broader walks to the coffee-shops on the Square. On the roof-tops, workmen shovel down snow from the gutters, and the steps of Widener are a blanket of ridged, pure-white snow, except for the wooden laid centre part.

Yesterday, the term opened and I arose, I might say gallantly, to the occasion. By mistake, at 9.00 I went to a lecture in Roman History (I meant to go to one on U.S. Foreign Policy) which was very unfortunate. Anyway afterwards I spoke to May[2] – the young academic giving the diplomatic course. From the comments I heard on his course, I think he'll be a hit! At 10.00 I heard Samuel Eliot Morrison[3] – one of the 'greats', now in his last year, who is giving a course on the Revolution, and after the lecture, we walked over to Widener together. At 11.10 I went to a survey course by Professor Stampf (California) on modern American history, and at 2.00 I heard Bailyn[4] on the History of American Education

---

2   Ernest Richard May (1928–2009) American historian of international relations. His fourteen published books include analyses of American involvement in the First World War and the causes of the Fall of France during the Second World War. He joined the Harvard University faculty following the completion of his military service in 1954, and remained there full-time until his death.

3   Samuel Eliot Morison (1887–1976) was an American historian noted for his works of maritime history and American history that were both authoritative and popular.

4   Bernard Bailyn (1922–2020), American historian, author and academic specialising in American Colonial and Revolutionary-era History. He was a professor at Harvard University from 1953.

P.S. LOOK OUT FOR SNAKES

and had another talk with him. Incidentally, dear, Bailyn wants to see my paper. During the 12.00 to 2.00 break, I registered, had a doughnut and coffee and made a luncheon appointment with Prof. Owen (he's chairman of the Dept.) for Friday.

In the afternoon, I met Professor Hull, who is in the Celtic Studies department, in fact, he IS the department. I had a lovely chat with him about Ireland, Gaelic and what have you. So all-in-all it was a pleasant and profitable day. I may also try out some of the courses in the history of political theory.

Morison was rather delightful in his lecture, saying at the outset that he was glad to see everyone was wearing a coat! He added that another necessity for his course was that people should wear ties![5]

All-in-all, I really have fallen for Harvard. All the time, one picks up ideas, which throw a new light on old ideas about other aspects of history. Also it seems spring has come and that means Easter is getting nearer – until then, my darling, all my love, Brian.

[BRIAN TO MARIE-THÉRÈSE]
Cambridge, Sunday afternoon, 6 February

Well, dear, I see it's happened, Mendes-France[6] is out. One rather wondered how long he would last. Apart from that and the Chinese question,[7] there are two big questions in the Times today. One is the problem of paid informers in the 'witch-hunt' trials – one of the ex-Communists has just admitted to perjury. The other is a Supreme Court decision that Theatre and Boxing monopolies come under federal anti-trust laws: the decision on

---

5   Morison was a stickler for proper dress code and would ask students who appeared without a jacket and tie to leave. On one occasion, the object of his displeasure turned out to be a disabled war veteran who hobbled painfully out of the lecture.

6   Pierre Isaac Isidore Mendes-France, known as PMF, was a French politician who served as President of the Council of Ministers for eight months from 1954 to 1955.

7   Communist China's agrarian policy.

Theatre was 8–0, on Boxing 6–2 (Frankfurter[8] was one of the dissenters).

Yesterday's mail brought yours of Tuesday morning. About the church, I'll collar the PP as soon as he returns, around the middle of this month. I'm glad Miss Kelly is holding on to the reservations, as we'll almost certainly need them. Booking in Boston is impossible, the U.S. lines tell me; but don't make it final until I hear from I.I.E.[9] and let me know exactly what class of passage is booked, please.

Also in the mail was another request to speak in Connecticut on March 13 at an Irish dinner. I'll let you have the details on that when I can.

Work proceeds apace, though with all these lectures my research has naturally slowed down. On the other hand, in terms of teaching in Ireland or England, obviously a sound knowledge of American history would be an advantage. By the way, darling, did I tell you I was doing a little on Irish neutrality? Your uncle's speeches on the 1938 agreement[10] are interesting.

Weather here continues cold, and going to Mass this morning it was very gloomy. We may have rain before evening. Hopefully, it'll clear away the remains of the dirty snow.

That's all my news, dearest, but what is happening to time? It seems to have slowed to a snail's pace. Still, it won't be long before spring, and you arrive, and then there'll be a million things to talk about and arrange. Meantime, can you keep a secret? Honest? Well, don't tell anyone or anything, but I love you very much and please look after yourself till I can look after you.

With all my love, Brian.

....

8   Felix Frankfurter (1882–1965), lawyer, professor and jurist who served as an Associate Justice of the US Supreme Court from 1939 to 1962. He was a noted advocate of judicial restraint in the court's judgments.

9   Institute of International Education (the body financing at least part of Brian's trip).

10   The Anglo-Irish Trade Agreement was signed on 25 April 1938 by Ireland and the UK. It aimed to resolve the Anglo-Irish Trade War which had been ongoing from 1933. James Dillon, who was deputy leader of Fine Gael at the time, spoke out against the agreement.

P.S. LOOK OUT FOR SNAKES

P.S. If in some way I get a chance to stay on for a year, tell me honestly, would it be possible to take it without hopelessly upsetting your mother? B.

 3

Did I tell you I had a letter from Mary Raleigh?[11] She was in college with me and is now over here in Rhode Island teaching for six months. I've just sent her a note; she may be willing to be your bridesmaid. I also got a letter from George.

About us, the more I think about our life the more delighted I am that we are both having this opportunity to see this country. I know that my own thinking on many points has changed since I came here, and I think you'll find the same thing, dear. One thought about the Irish situation which has been running through my head, is that what we need (as a nation) is a New Deal: someone who will come along and try to face all our problems simultaneously instead of dissipating energies in piece-meal reforms, which achieve nothing. Ireland's real problem is our own apathy, and frankly while I consider emigration (especially by 'intellectuals') something of an escapist nature it is difficult to see what else can be done. Perhaps after all we missed the

---

11 Mary (née Raleigh) Kotsonouris (1931–2021), was a close family friend of the Farrells and godmother to one of Brian and MT's younger sons, Brian. She was awarded an LLB in UCD – she was the only woman in her class – in 1965 and qualified as a solicitor in the same year. Between 1965 - 81, she worked in a law practice in Dublin, and was appointed a judge of the District Court in 1981.

boat by not returning Seán McBride[12] at the head of a large party in the immediate post-war years.

Another point I wanted to raise with you was picked out by yourself, dearest – though I don't remember being particularly explicit about it. That's this thing about wanting to teach. As you probably guessed, seeing the enormous material advances made in this country, the thought of life in Ireland is a little forbidding, yet basically my real objection is the long-standing grievance that there is no equality of opportunity – because there is no opportunity. At this stage, I think some teaching experience in Ireland (or England) plus a bash at a PhD might be our best plan, but somehow I feel that many of my present ideas are a little 'abstract' and your arrival will help me clarify my thoughts. I can only discuss this kind of thing with myself up to a certain point, then I need your guidance.

Our long-standing debate on education (and I mean NUNS) will, if I may hazard a guess, continue, but I'm not so keen on American-type education as I am, for instance, on the British. There, undoubtedly, the Socialists have done a fine job – though, of course, certain adjustments still remain to be made.

I haven't heard from John or Betty (Kelly)[13] so I presume they've gone to Italy. By the way, did I tell you that I gave the linen

---

12 Seán MacBride (1904–1988) was the son of Maud Gonne and John MacBride (an Irish republican and military leader executed by the British government for his participation in the 1916 Easter Rising in Dublin). In 1919, aged fifteen, he joined the Irish Volunteers, which fought as part of the Irish Republican Army, and took part in the Irish War of Independence. He opposed the 1921 Anglo-Irish Treaty and was imprisoned by the Irish Free State during the Civil War. In 1946, MacBride founded the republican/socialist party Clann na Poblachta. In the 1948 general election Clann na Poblachta won only ten seats. The party joined with Fine Gael, the Labour Party, the National Labour Party, Clann na Talmhan and several independents to form the first inter-party government, with Fine Gael TD John A. Costello as Taoiseach. In 1951, Clann na Poblachta was reduced to two seats after the general election. MacBride kept his seat and was re-elected again in 1954.

13 From Cismont, Virginia, where Brian stayed in September.

table napkins to Mrs Cushman? Really, I'm afraid I was being a little 'diplomatic' about it, but it seemed a good thing to do.

This week I had a short note from Desmond and will write soon about this Locke-Hooker affair which continues to hold my interest – so prepare to be bored when you meet me, darling. Of course, you will be busy on your promised attempt to make me fall in love with you again, so there'll be Patrick's Day walks over Killiney, Halloween parties, Conferring dances and coffee cakes to be made. All of this presents problems over here, but knowing you I'm sure you'll get round it.

But seriously, dearest, it will be wonderful just to see you once more and be treated to that most charming of all smiles that simply mesmerises. Until then, be extra careful and be good. With all my love and a tender kiss, Your own, Brian.

[MARIE-THÉRÈSE TO BRIAN]
Monday night, 7 February

Last night I amused myself by examining the map of Cambridge, which you sent me last September. It helps to make everything you write about much nearer – the names are so English and indeed some street names can be found in Dublin too.

Aunt Agnes didn't come out tonight as Annie has the 'flu' and she's helping in the shop – I do hope she'll take care not to get it herself. I spent this evening sewing and now face the job of deciding on a design for the dress! All my dresses are complete, except for the hems, which is my way of preventing myself from wearing any of the dresses before I leave. I do hope you'll like everything (and that includes me!)

The Eastern news is very disturbing.[14] What do you think of it?

----

14   Communist forces on the Chinese mainland – within firing distance of the Tachens – threatened the Nationalist strongholds for several weeks.

Myles says there won't be War, as 'Wall St.' stands so firm, but how do you think the Americans are going to handle the evacuations?[15]

 5

I do hope Fr O'Dea can come and marry us. It will mean such a lot to me. You see I always wanted to be married by Fr Mathew,[16] but really one Benedictine is almost as pleasant as another. So tell your local priest, that although we won't know about Fr O'Dea for at least a month, can he guarantee that we'll still be married at Cambridge?

The Vogue and Reader's Digest arrived just before the weekend and are very good, thank you, Darling.

Dearest, I've just realised that 10 weeks from today we'll be an old married couple, despite your fussing P.P.! Mama sends love. Aunt Agnes was in very good form and took me to the pictures in Blackrock: the 'Snows of Kilimanjaro'. There is no news from Manchester, which Aunt Agnes feels is good news.

So be firm with these priests, for my sake, with all my love, Marie-Thérèse

 6

My Darling, your happy and successful letters brighten these dreary days. I imagine that researching, with no lectures going on,

---

15 Vice-Admiral Pride of America's Seventh Fleet announced that nearly 14,000 civilians had been taken from both North and South Tachen to the port of Keelung on the Nationalist island of Formosa.

16 After Myles, Fr Mathew (Brian) was probably MT's closest uncle, and when her father was dying, her mother asked MT to tell Fr Mathew to come as she needed his support and help.

P.S. LOOK OUT FOR SNAKES

must have been terribly dull, it's a wonder you didn't get quite depressed. You'll find time flying now that the term has started!

1) Don't bother about a Harpers – the Vogue was good enough.

2) Your passage Tourist Class (June 15th: Cabin A.8. Bed:4)

3) Tackle the P.P. again, when he comes back – Easter Monday suits much better than Tuesday!

And my Darling, as we all do, you left the most important question to a PS[17]. The honest answer is YES, I do think it would upset her hopelessly! You see, with us gone, I now see, Mama would have nothing to live for, I think she's just living for our return already. I've never dared suggest to her that you might be tempted to stay on, because I felt that the sense of insecurity such a suggestion would create would be terribly bad for her. Would it help your cause that much? Please answer truthfully; this is not a rhetorical question! I thought a year or two of doing a Doctorate would be as good over here, and then back to the States or anywhere ... but don't leave it to me to decide! Consult someone in the History Faculty at Cambridge about the merits of an extra year in America v. a year at Dublin; don't forget the added advantage of needing less money coming into the home in Dublin than in America, as we have a home[18] ready for us.

I'm charmed about March 13th[19] and 39 days to go. I'm driving everyone 'batty' because there are 3 calendars at work, which are crossed off, with great ceremony, every evening.

For tonight then Darling, all my love, Marie-Thérèse

Friday Morning (same letter)

A letter arrived from Rev. Bernard O'Dea this morning – he is delighted to come and marry us, and sent us both his blessing and congratulations. He goes on to say that there are quite a few

---

17 The question was, 'would your mother mind terribly if we stayed on another year?'

18 They have a home waiting for them with Marie Dillon at 5, Trimleston Gardens, Booterstown.

19 Brian was asked to speak at an Irish dinner on March 13 in Connecticut.

formalities to be gone through with the civil authorities. He also wants to know who, in Boston, will he apply to for faculties to marry us. So would you get in touch with him and I'm so happy that he can come!!!

 7

Ronan and Tommy called over this afternoon in their usual good humour. Ronan and I are probably going to see UCD's play for the Inter-Varsity Festival next Wednesday – 'Faustus' produced by Lilia (Ronan says it's terrible, but we'll see!). They had little news except that Therese Campbell and Tony Cronin[20] were married during the week! Tony is just back from a trip to Russia and is writing a series of articles on his trip in the Irish Times, it's quite good reading.

Ronan was delighted to hear that Father O'Dea is marrying us; he thinks he's a marvellous man. By the way, do you think it's a good idea to get Carroll O'Connor's[21] address (in NY) and contact them? I'd love to see Nancy[22] again – I believe Paddy Gallaher has it.

Write and tell me as soon as you have the date of our wedding settled (Monday preferable, otherwise Tuesday) so I can write and invite my cousins, Mary and Roma.

20 Anthony Cronin (1928–2016), poet, novelist, biographer and cultural commentator.
21 Carroll O'Connor was active in Dramsoc UCD and was directing the play that Brian performed in, when MT suddenly appeared with the large scissors to adjust his tunic, and the rest is history.
22 Carroll's wife.

P.S. LOOK OUT FOR SNAKES

8 ⋯⋯⋯⋯⋯⋯⋯⋯⋯⋯⋯⋯⋯⋯⋯⋯⋯⋯⋯⋯⋯⋯⋯⋯⋯⋯⋯⋯
[MARIE-THÉRÈSE TO BRIAN]
Tuesday morning, 15 February

Con is off to London tomorrow, she's been called for an interview in connection with a job she's applied for. My going has rather un-settled the 'girls'. Sheila Coakley is coming over here next week-end. Tomorrow Eva and I hope to go and see the UCD entry for the Drama Festival (Faustus), and on Monday Eva, Con, Rosalie and I are having dinner in Jammet's[23] and then off to see the Pike review (a small celebration for my departure). As Lent starts on the 23rd, we're going 3 weeks early.

Did you see James Barry yet? If he can't put up Fr O'Dea, look around for a suitable small hotel near the church, the same hotel might give us a room for our wedding celebration, and this would give you an idea of how much it all will cost us. Poor Darling, I'm sure you're cursing me with your 4 lectures a day and other work, but I've a horrible feeling that if one doesn't do things in plenty of time the 'snags' prong all the worse! All my love, Marie-Thérèse

9 ⋯⋯⋯⋯⋯⋯⋯⋯⋯⋯⋯⋯⋯⋯⋯⋯⋯⋯⋯⋯⋯⋯⋯⋯⋯⋯⋯⋯
[MARIE-THÉRÈSE TO BRIAN]
Wednesday, 16 February

The outing last night started badly. We decided not to dine out, as money was suddenly of primary importance to us all (Con going to London on March 19th, Rosalie's income tax being long over-due, and Eva vaguely talking of going to South Africa), but the

---

23 Jammet's opened on 6 March 1901 at 26–27 St Andrew's Street. It was established by Michel Jammet (chef for nine years to George Cadogan, 5th Earl Cadogan), and his brother François. For a long time it was the only French restaurant in the city. It was mentioned in James Joyce's *Ulysses*. Jammet's moved to 46 Nassau Street in 1926. In 1928, *Vogue* described it as 'one of Europe's best restaurants ... crowded with gourmets and wits', where the sole and grouse were 'divine'. The restaurant closed in 1967.

plan was: meet in the Gresham at 9.30 and have some coffee and drinks before heading for the 'Pike theatre'[24] at 10.30.

Eva and Con didn't arrive till 9.50 and the stupid waiter forgot our order. The result was cold coffee at 10.15 and a dash to the 'Review', which made up for everything! It was terribly funny and left us weak with laughter. Milo O'Shea plays the part of an 'ugly sister' at the Gate and then drives quickly across town and clowns in Herbert Lane from 11 to 1.30 am!

I'm feeling rather deflated by an income tax demand for £9. 16/=[25] which shatters my calculations for the next few weeks, and forces me to give up smoking for Lent! This may be a blessing, when I think of all I could have saved by not smoking over the years.

Your suggestion for Mary (Raleigh) as my bridesmaid is a super one! Give me her address and I'll write and ask her, or will you?

 10

[MARIE-THÉRÈSE TO BRIAN]
Friday night, 18 February

We've had our first big wedding present: Uncle James sent us a cheque for £25![26] I'll bring it to America and we'll enjoy it! I'm applying for a permit to bring £50 to America. I'm writing a thank you letter to James tomorrow, but if you think it's a good idea – do write a note too – mentioning the fact that you've

---

24   The Pike Theatre was located in Herbert Lane. Established in 1953 by Alan Simpson and Carolyn Swift, the Pike offered Dublin audiences continental-style late-night revues and modern international playwrights such as Tennessee Williams and Eugène Ionesco. In its early days it staged two notable premieres – the first complete English-language production of *Waiting for Godot* (1955) (the London production had been censored by the Lord Chamberlain) and Brendan Behan's *The Quare Fellow* (1954). It was a favourite of critics such as Ulick O'Connor (critic for *The Times*) and Harold Hobson (critic for *The Sunday Times*).

25   Worth approximately €275 today.

26   Worth about €750 today.

P.S. LOOK OUT FOR SNAKES

been looking over his 'neutrality' speech.[27] The address is 7 St Mary's Road, Dublin.

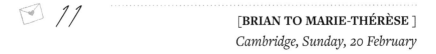

As I thought, Mrs Cushman launched immediately into a suggestion that you stay with them between your arrival and our marriage. They have a lovely house and I think you'll feel at home there. They have two children – Katherine (whom they call Kit) is a rather quiet but very bright kid and easy to get on with, she's about 13/14; Ann is about 8, I suppose, and a 'compulsive talker' and not so easy to get on with. However Mr & Mrs Cushman are really quite charming and say you'll have your own key and room and can come and go as you like. So it sounds all right to me, but this is just to check with you, so please let me know soon if you'd like to stay with them. Frankly, I think it would be easier if you did – after all, they could chaperone us.

Today was lovely, indeed I went out without a coat and had a pleasant time with them. Mrs Cushman is quite delighted with the napkins (I gave them to her for Christmas instead of to the Kellys[28] if you remember). After lunch we listened to some music, then Mr C, Kit and I went for a walk. After afternoon tea he drove me home.

By the by, in case you think I don't read your letters (which I treasure, darling), I know you already said 'yes' to the Cushman invitation, but I'm double-checking with you. And while I think of it, about the present for George (if you haven't got anything yet), over here most people use table mats rather than table cloths.

27   On 10 February 1941, James Dillon, deputy leader of Fine Gael, made a speech voicing his support for the Allies against Nazi Germany: 'It may be a policy of this government to stand neutral, but I am not neutral. The issue at stake means whether I want to live or die.'
28   The Kellys of Virginia.

Just back and got your two letters of Thursday and Friday, the Dram Soc show looks very impressive.

But I want to tell you about the Church. It will be St Peter's, Cambridge. I phoned Fr Whittier and he's checked. Since you will be living in this parish subsequent to the marriage, this is the church! I have just returned from Fr Logue in St Peter's and he suggests you send the papers to me immediately. I'm really delighted with the news – the Fr Whittier I saw in the Sacred Heart was a rather unpleasant, pompous and not too bright young man (just the type to send Martin Luther on a rampage by insisting on rules and regulations). Fr Logue on the other hand was very pleasant and helpful. I'm writing the news to Fr O'Dea this evening.

Well your Uncle James has turned up trumps, but I'd rather wait to meet him than write a 'thank-you' note in the air – by then, anyway, I'll know more about the neutrality business.

I'm delighted to hear that Aunty Agnes is well and hope your mother continues to improve. How about you, pet? Hope you're looking after yourself.

I'm sorry, I didn't tell you that it was a Communion breakfast I spoke at in Quincy – hence the early rising act. I've just turned down an invitation from the Book Club of the State Teachers College to speak on Mar 21st, but said I'd go on some other date.

 [MARIE-THÉRÈSE TO BRIAN]
Thursday morning, 24 February

Mrs Cushman is a real darling to put me up! I'm looking forward to my stay with them, because that is such a good way to get to know the American way of life (and some American cooking too!). I'll write and thank her at the weekend. So you've got us beautifully organised.

I hope you got my note saying – I think Mary's a great idea for bridesmaid, and go ahead and ask her. Now that we know the place and date (St Peter's Cambridge on Monday April 11th), I'll go ahead and get my papers. But if I send you my papers try and let as few people as possible see them – my Baptism Certificate isn't a very 'pleasant' document – being a rough 'family tree'[29]. I think it's about 6 months since I got it but I'm not getting another, it took two months to get and cost about 15/=. You can tell your Father Logue it's not every girl was baptised in a nursing home[30] in Vienna! If he's worried he can baptise me again and issue another!

Tonight we have our party at work and the girls are all excitement – 'Lent or no Lent', it's quite an ambitious meal they are planning.

You're quite right about the table cloth, I forgot! Well I might make it nice mats for Mrs Cushman and I'll think of something for George!

Poor Mama is getting quite depressed now – maybe you can write her a note every few days when I'm at sea – after the 11th March I won't get any more of your letters and she'd love some cheerful words from you then.

 13 .... **[MARIE-THÉRÈSE TO BRIAN]**
Thursday night, 24 February

This is a very tired girl who is writing you after one of the best parties ever given for her! The evening was far better than I could have hoped for – even the presence of Mr Needham couldn't damp the high, good spirits of the girls and Tommy – the same boy, barely 18

---

29 Marie Dillon was illegitimate and she in turn had an illegitimate daughter, Ruth (before she met Theo Dillon), who remained in Switzerland and was brought up by her father's family.

30 Theo Dillon had recovered from TB and stayed on in Europe to study ways to cure it. He was studying in Vienna on a post-graduate scholarship when MT was born in 1928.

years old, danced all 20 girls present off their feet and kept us all amused – in fact we decided that his future lay on stage. I'll hold this letter over till the weekend, so for tonight just a kiss ...

Saturday

Last night I supped at Murphy's where I had a very pleasant evening. They presented me with a very generous cheque – £10 – 10/- ! Also Mr Lamar gave me £8 as a wedding present, and the girls and Tommy gave us £6!! Really they were so sweet that I had to think about you very hard not to regret leaving them! Also O'Rourke (the gardener) refused £5 (of the 25 that Mama was giving him) and said to give it to us. I'm bringing most of this money on with me (£50 in all), and it can pay for our wedding!

I wrote Mrs Cushman a short note thanking her for the invitation and saying I'm looking forward to my stay. I'll go and see the priest tonight or tomorrow and will send you my papers on Monday if possible. Will end here as I've so much sewing to do.

 14 ·····································

[MARIE-THÉRÈSE TO BRIAN]
Sunday night, 27 February

Yesterday, my sewing progressed better than expected, thanks to the help of Mary McLean, a girl who used to sew for me years ago. Today I spent the day in bed, a luxury I haven't enjoyed since my vaccination in mid-October, and I had just sufficient excuse in 'inflamed tonsillitis', my tonsils being non-existent, but the roots (I think) are very tender, and that got me great sympathy!!! A most important ingredient for a 'successful' day in bed!

Tomorrow I'm to see Miss Bennett who is in Loughlinstown Hospital having had a stroke about 10 days ago – at the time we all got a terrible shock, but she's surviving and recovering well, I believe.

Mrs Cooney rang me up today to say that Shawn's[31] in bed with the flu and a temperature, but hopes to be all right by Wednesday (to give that party he's promised me before I go!). I'm almost hoping he'll call it off, as I dread the flu-germ just before sailing – re sailing ... there appears to be a very 'foxey' arrangement between C.I.E and Cobh Hotels and Taxies ... it is impossible to reach Cobh by public transport on the same day as sailing, despite the fact that I won't be sailing till 8 p.m. on the 15th! I've to check in at noon and the Cork-Cobh train doesn't get to Cobh till 4 p.m.! So I've to go down on Mon. 14th and stay in Cobh till Tuesday!

By the way, do you get the Irish Times in Cambridge? I'm planning to put in the announcement:

'B.B. Farrell – M.T. Dillon – the marriage arranged between Brian Farrell and Marie-Thérèse Dillon will take place at St Peter's, Cambridge, Mass., U.S.A. on Monday April the eleventh'.

 15

[MARIE-THÉRÈSE TO BRIAN]
Monday, 28 February

I've ordered your books – you are 'one-up' on Mr Pembrey (Greens). He had not heard of that book on John Locke. He looked up the publishers' list and there it was, just out, so he'll have it by next Wednesday, and you'll have it in 3 weeks. I'm bringing it along with more good news: I've got dollars to the value of £50 to bring out with me, so that settles it. You don't touch your money here; we'll be jolly glad of it on our return. Also I got my little pen in the lost property of C.I.E. today, and I'm so glad to have it back after 6 weeks. I've found what I think would be a lovely present for George: a pair of silver serving spoons – Irish silver Georgian design, dated 1795 – in very good condition. For Mrs Cushman some mats and

---

31   Shawn Cooney studied in UCD with Brian and took photos of Brian and MT on Brian's graduation day.

if I can afford it and some Irish whiskey for her husband (this last advise me if it would do as I won't get it till just before sailing).

N.B. I've tried very hard to get my marriage papers to send you, but the only way they can get to Boston is through the Dublin Archbishop's office straight to the pastor at St Peter's! So relax, if they get there in 2 to 3 weeks' time it's not our fault. Give your Pastor a ring and say he'll be receiving the papers from the Bishop of Dublin - that should keep him quiet! After all it was his holiday which delayed us, so if he only gets them the night before he'll have to accept it!

I'm writing to Mary in this post to ask her to be my bridesmaid and to describe it roughly! I do hope she'll agree.

Joan O'Grady has just been here this afternoon with a work proposition for me, on my return. She is thinking of getting Irish linen embroidered in the Canary Islands and I would make it up for her. She is going to try to sell hand-embroidered Irish linen blouses (of a very superior type) to the big houses in Dublin – the work is exquisite and she's given me one as a present – you'll see it soon! I'm interested, as I'll never be able to give up sewing,[32] I know, and yet I do so hate customers, this would be a pleasant way of working at home without the 'pests' coming and going.

 16 ....
[BRIAN TO MARIE-THÉRÈSE] (*Typed letter*)
Cambridge, Tuesday, 1 March

Dearest Marie-Thérèse,

I had a letter from Mary Raleigh today saying she would be up in Cambridge at the weekend, so I can ask her about the wedding then.

This is being typed on the Underwood which I'm thinking of buying. How do you like the type? Actually, I think it's rather a

....
32 MT never gave up sewing. She designed and made clothes for her seven children and herself on a Singer sewing machine at the end of the family dining table.

P.S. LOOK OUT FOR SNAKES

bargain myself at $25. Certainly at home a machine would cost me much more.

I haven't heard from you since last week and hope that everything is all right. Of course, you explained that your letters would be less frequent, but as the time for your arrival gets closer I seem to lose patience, waiting to see you again.

I'm still busily at work, as I want this thesis to be as good as possible. I remain undecided as to the form. Perhaps I shall go on to discover the influence of other writers like Locke just before the revolution of 1688. Anyway, I am back at work on the problem, which is the important thing.

More and more I'm realising how accustomed I have become to people, customs and life in general over here. I do hope you will find it as pleasant as I do. Above all else (and particularly since you are likely to meet some Americans aboard ship) try to see this country from the beginning without prejudice. This sounds rather pedantic, perhaps – or more likely, like the product of brain-washing. Actually it's neither. It's simply that, as I learn more of the historical development of this country, I understand more about certain present attitudes, which at first sight I tended to condemn.

Yesterday I arranged about my ticket in Boston and then went in to have a few words with the Consul. They have a pleasant but relatively tiny office in Hancock House. It's on the twenty-second floor, which gives them a great view, but scarcely does great honour to the country.

Just now I'm sure your mother is very lonely at the thought of your departure. Aunty Agnes in her last letters has said how much she will miss you too. But it is only for a few months and, before she knows it we'll be back home, please God. Anyway, tell your mother not to worry, I'll look after you, pet.

That's all for now, darling, but I do miss you so. Look after yourself and hurry over and look after me. Good night, dearest, and all my love, Brian.

17

Today I took myself to the pictures, as Shawn Cooney's temperature went to 100, so we called-off the party! And that's how I happened to be coming home from the pictures alone this evening, and suddenly it was mid-July – just 10 days before you were leaving – one summer evening, you were seeing me home and I was sitting beside you on the bus pretending to be interested in who was going into and leaving the toilets at College St. and crying quietly, to myself, wondering how I would endure the months to follow. And suddenly, the months have almost all passed and in 10 days' time I'm sailing after you.

About sailing, very important if you are coming to meet me in New York (on Tuesday 22nd) you should get a 'pass' from: Customs House, Bowling Green, New York City. If you want to come beyond the Customs barrier on the pier – maybe you could drop them a card about it quite soon. (I cannot yet tell you what time we are due in N.Y.!)

 18

I got your rather excited letter: Mary Murphy v. ArchBishop, and can only hope the papers arrive in time. Otherwise we have but 2 courses open to us: postpone everything till the papers arrive or live in sin! Let's just hope the papers arrive.

Today I called down to Little Mary St to collect your book and by lucky chance met Aunt Agnes, who helped me in my long search! I got your book called: 'The Second Treatise of Civil Government' by John Locke, and I've got the 2 other books on Locke from Green's – also Irish Mist for Mr Cushman and a small Belleek (white

P.S. LOOK OUT FOR SNAKES

porcelain) vase for Mrs Cushman. I decided better than linen, as we gave her that for Christmas. When I arrived home, I found 12 wonderful Waterford sherry glasses from Eve – without a doubt the loveliest wedding present we've got so far! And some very pretty butter forks (2) from the Mooney girls in modern Irish silver.

Last night I had the 'girls' from work to supper (a deadly experience) but had to be done – they all arrived with silly presents, one present is so peculiar that Mama and I have been arguing all day as to its uses – I say it's for growing cacti in and Mama says for standing pots in – Mrs Ward suggests it's for cheese – so you can imagine what it looks like!

My Darling, by the time you get this I'll be on the sea (by God's grace), and then only a few more days to our meeting –

You can't answer this, but you can decide what to do: the Sunday after I arrive will be the Anniversary of Papa's death,[33] and I very much want a Mass said for him on that day. Can you arrange it? If this is terribly difficult don't bother, but I would love to have it said where I can attend.

That's all – and don't drink too much on St Patrick's Day!

P.S. Delighted that George is bringing linen, and promise only to flirt not to run away on the journey across!!

P.P.S Details for the Mass are: Theo Dillon – died 27th March 1946

 19

[BRIAN TO MARIE-THÉRÈSE]
Cambridge Thursday, 3 March

The Larham Organisation certainly seem to have given you a royal send-off and rightly so. Also the Murphys – really it is all quite wonderful. You can help me to write thank you letters when you come over.

---

33   Nine years earlier, Theo had his gall bladder removed; he died three days later from complications.

Now that I'm sure they'll consider my work for a minor thesis, I'm doing everything I can to cram-in reading. Please God, I'll write it up at the beginning of the summer.

I now have another two speaking engagements – quite the orator, eh? The first one is on Sunday, at a Catholic Girls' Club in Boston, and the second one is on the 16th, at some Rotary club, about 50 miles south of Boston. As you can see, I'll really be getting around and about, during the Patrick's Day season.

I'm still being very good and going to lectures, which take up my mornings, and then I usually have a sandwich and go into Widener. I take a coffee break in the afternoon and usually leave for home about seven, where I eat properly and at leisure and do a bit more before bed. Some days I take all my meals around the Square so as to get as much time as possible in the library.

No dear, I don't get the Times, but please say 'marriage announced', not 'marriage arranged' (sounds too much like match-making). As for getting a suit in N.Y.C., I'd really prefer to leave N.Y. as quickly as possible, and Boston has a huge shopping area, believe me. Anyway, I may get a suit before you arrive.

You sound awfully busy with all the sewing, darling – don't overdo it. As you say, I shan't touch the lolly in the bank (that is, if there is any). Will they let you bring £50 with you? If not, deposit it to my account and I'll get it transferred.

 20　　　　[**BRIAN TO MARIE-THÉRÈSE**] (typed letter)
Cambridge, Friday, 4 March

My dearest, Writing to George yesterday, I expressed the hope that at least one day, while he's here, it might snow, because the Yard looks so wonderful under a blanket of snow (maybe because it hides the diversity of architectural styles). Anyway, after today all I can say is 'shut ma big mouth' – 'cos the snow is here.

I woke up to snow drifting by the windows. By the time I left – about 8.45 – there was a depth of about eight inches. It took me over twenty minutes to walk to Longfellow (I calculated that everyone would be trying for street-cars and so I walked in the middle of back roads). Traffic was in chaos and May[34] didn't arrive to lecture until almost 9.30. Even with what we've had – light snow on and off all day – now it's beginning to freeze. I decided that discretion was the better part of valour and left Widener at 7.30.

So now here I am ensconced among my books and passing on one piece of advice, which I had forgotten earlier. Do bring a pair of heavy shoes, or better still boots if you have them, dear; you may well need them. Also, but you've probably planned this as part of your 'sea' dress, a heavy coat.

Today after my round of lectures, I settled in Houghton, instead of Widener for a change. Here they keep their older books, manuscripts, papers, rare editions etc. I was working over a couple of early pamphlets, one of which was bound in a volume of tracts from John Donne's library and has a Latin epigram of Donne's on Hooker. It isn't particularly good, but it is rather interesting, and unpublished to my knowledge. There is a hand-written comment on the various marginalia by Charles Eliot Norton, one of the great Presidents of Harvard. Unfortunately, Houghton closes at 5.00, and, as I haven't yet finished my work over there, I'll have to turn to some other material back at Widener. One thing which I have yet to do, is to go through the introductions of the various seventeenth-century editions of Hooker (and perhaps the contents too).

Anyway, pet, the future line of research seems to be taking shape. I shall probably concentrate on the position of Hooker in the later part of the century i.e. during the time Locke's own thought was being formed, and with particular reference to certain key concepts.

34   Ernest Richard May, Harvard historian.

I received your beautifully typed letter this morning. I put our pre-wedding notice in the Irish Times and will send you a cutting on Monday. I'll also send a copy of the paper to Manchester. I wrote to Mary Raleigh asking her to be bridesmaid, and I've also asked Roma and Henry to come and Mary, Ed and Bill Seidensticker. Last night Mrs Jonas (no. 6) gave us a wonderful rug. We're expecting Miss Chenevix[35] (Miss Bennett's friend) to tea.

These two weeks will fly past, and then you'll be showing me how to eat with my fork only[36] and so many other things!

My Dearest, Yesterday, the snow ploughs were out again, but we had sleet rather than snow, and most unpleasant it is too! Anyway I called over to pick up Mary Raleigh in Huron Ave., where she was staying with some friends. We walked around the Yard for a while and through Widener and then had lunch. Of course, we had a long talk about college, the old days and friends, but I did make a point of asking if she could be here on Easter Monday. Mary isn't sure about this yet, as she may be going to N.Y.C. over Easter,

---

35   Helen Chenevix (1886–1963) was an Irish suffragist and trade unionist. In 1911, she worked with Louie Bennett to form the Irish Women's Suffrage Federation. The two later founded the Irish Women Workers' Union. Chenevix and Bennett were constant companions, leading to speculation that the pair were romantically involved. It is now assumed that they were a couple. It has been said that they were part of an influential network of lesbians living in Dublin. Bennett moved into the house beside Chenevix, and they also lived together for a period of time with Chenevix caring for Bennett during her final illness in 1956. In Pax et Libertas, Chenevix wrote that Bennett was 'the best loved woman in Dublin' and that 'Peace and Freedom were her twin ideals'.

36   American style.

so there was no point in asking her to be bridesmaid in advance. However, don't worry, dear, I'll get you a Catholic girl for the job.

I left Mary about 4.30 and it was a bit late then to start work, so I took in a movie instead. The University was showing 'Six Bridges to Cross', but I really went to see 'Tonight's the Night' again – do you remember we saw it in the Adelphi one night and had a good laugh? Despite you're not being with me, I did enjoy it – and Liam Redman's line 'Somebody ought to murder that man' – was wonderful.

When I got back I did some reading and had an early night. This morning going to Mass was an obstacle race, more like training in Antarctic Warfare. Much of the snow had frozen and it was very slippery underfoot; also, some of the slush, especially in gutters, was deceptively solid looking and a wet reception awaited the unwary foot.

I got through quite a bit of work and it's now 2.15. I'm waiting for someone to pick me up and take me over to this girls' club in Boston. In case I'm late returning, I'll post this in transit, so for now, my darling, all my love and take extra, special care of yourself. Give my love to your mother and tell her to keep bundled up if the weather over there is anything like ours. God bless, pet, Brian.

 23 [**BRIAN TO MARIE-THÉRÈSE**] (typed letter)
Cambridge, Monday, 7 March

My dearest Marie-Thérèse, I've just come back from St Peter's where I had a chat with the pastor, Mgr Murphy, and gave Fr Logue my papers. Your letter of March 1st was waiting for me. They are not pressing me too much for your papers BUT I would sooner see them over here than trust the 'efficiency' of the Chancery Office in Dublin – Archbishop or no Archbishop. I willing admit to being prejudiced, but some of the clerics in that diocese are not bright (note the masterly self-control in that understatement) and they are quite likely to send the papers by regular mail, so as to ensure they will be late. Anyway, I can't see why they can't give you the papers; they are yours, after all. Of course, in common with J.C. McQuaid, many Irish clerics suffer under the general delusion that Irish usage is the only possible test of propriety, if not orthodoxy.

Frankly, I prefer to trust people on the spot here, those whom I've met, rather than some unknown moron in Whitehall. Anyway I'm writing to Aunty Agnes to have the banns[37] called, as they have asked me. Will you check to see if you have a dispensation in your case, and if not ask Fr Very-very (it's Fr Daly isn't it?) to call them and then send notification on to Fr Logue, St. Peter's, Concord Ave., Cambridge. A final touch: I'm sure Mgr Murphy would not be particularly impressed to get papers simply because they are from an Archbishop of Dublin – Murphy has the prouder title of being a Harvard man.

The news of your presents sounds fine. Are the mats linen or lace? The drop of Irish for Mr Cushman is a good idea – I know he likes it. Since Jameson's 7-year-old can be had here, a 12-year-old, or a Liqueur whiskey, like Irish Mist, would be a real treat. Thank you, dear, for the job you did on the books for me with Mr Pembrey.

I hope your mother is keeping well and that you are really looking after yourself. All my love, dear, do take care.

(in handwriting) I do miss you, pet – even more than ever just now, but in case I forget to say it later, do have a good trip and enjoy yourself. Love Brian.

 24 ·· **[MARIE-THÉRÈSE TO BRIAN]**
Monday, 7 March

Well, the notice is in the paper today and looks quite good! I'll send you a copy today, but mainly for the front page which describes

··································
37 To have the marriage announced from the pulpit by the parish priest.

how some revolting North of Ireland policeman went 'gun-happy' on the 'border' last night and shot 3 people (in 2 cars). Really those 'northerners' can be quite unpleasant!

I'm delighted George is with you, and I hope you two are painting Boston quite red! As for the honeymooning, I really don't know where I'd like to go! I think I'd rather go to George's before our wedding, so that we'll be friends before the ceremony and not be meeting as strangers at Easter. I'd love a few days in the country on arriving in America, because I imagine even Boston will be quite overwhelming to a 'quiet Dubliner' like me. But best you decide what to do, because you know and are on the spot.

Congratulations on all the speaking engagements. I'm longing to hear one of these meetings you are speaking at.

I'm only bringing £50, and today I was into U.S. lines, there is a chance I may be getting a 2nd or 1st class accommodation if some nice man in the office can fix it! Wouldn't that be super! Anyway I'll know in a day or two.

P.S. Scribble a note to Mama if you have a moment: about your talks. Make it nice and cheerful and she'll love it. I'll love you for it! M.T.

 25   [**BRIAN TO MARIE-THÉRÈSE**] (typed letter)
Cambridge, Tuesday morning, 8 March

My Dearest, I stayed in to do some work this morning and I've just received your letter of Wednesday night. I've also written a post card as per instructions to the Customs House people in New York.

But really I do object to your 'If you are coming to meet me in NY.' You don't think I'd let you run wild around the City all on your own, do you? Nor, I'm afraid, am I likely to let you be seen by anyone over here, till I've seen you.

It has been a long, long time, my dear. And – as the newspapers say – 'Now That It Can Be Told'. But I've missed you all the time. You have me so pampered, that I really do need you to look after me. So pet, have a good, restful time on board ship and be prepared when you land to take care of me.

The news of the presents[38] is exciting (I suppose), but I won't be diverted from the real news, that we'll be together in just a fortnight, by such frippery. Oh yes, on the linen question, there's no need to load up with anything, George is bringing some stuff up this week (I expect he'll arrive on Thursday). So the answer is a definite NO.

On Monday March 28, I've been invited to give a talk to some small group in the State Teachers College. Incidentally, there's no money in it. Anyway, I've threatened to bring you along. How do you feel about that? We can see how you feel when you arrive, please God.

Today, Thank God, is a lovely, brisk day with bright sun shining over the snow. How's the weather with you all? And how is your mother feeling? She must be feeling lonely, but it won't be for very long – after all, we have managed to stick it since July, whereas you'll be leaving in March and will be back by June. Do say hello for me and say that I'll write very soon (promise).

Now, for a moment, to get back to you, YOUNG WOMAN. Behave yourself on board ship: I don't mean you mustn't flirt, but you mustn't run away. Do take good care of yourself, my own, and remember me to everyone in Dublin. Remember too, that I'm waiting for you and make sure that the ship makes good time.

(in handwriting) With all my love and a special kiss because you look so lovely today (I know you do), Brian

----

38   Wedding presents.

P.S. LOOK OUT FOR SNAKES

EPILOGUE

On 15 March 1955, Marie-Thérèse stood on the quay at Cobh[1] with her best friend, Naomi Kidney, for one last photograph[2] before setting off to join Brian in America. Anyone looking on would see two smartly dressed young women, arms linked with hope in their eyes.

Her wedding dress was packed, her papers were in order and the capable Mrs Ward had moved into their home in Trimleston to look after Marie Dillon[3].

So what happened when Marie-Thérèse landed on a rainy Tuesday, 22 March 1955, at New York Harbour?

Well, Brian was waiting, no surprises there. They went off for lunch and what was said there remains between them, but no doubt they took up where they'd left off, as if they'd never been parted. Although she did comment in a letter to her mother: 'It's funny: he had such an American accent when I arrived – now I don't notice, which means one of two things: either he's lost it talking to me, or I've got one too and don't notice his!!'

New York was exhausting, so Brian quickly whisked Marie-Thérèse off to George Roach's beautiful home in Rhinebeck, where she was to get her first taste of American hospitality; no one did it better than George. They had the run of his house, its gardens and the wonderful library of gramophone records. After a few days, George put them on the first of the four buses that

---

1   County Cork

2   Taken by Bill Kidney. Both Naomi and Bill drove MT down to Cobh and stayed overnight to see her off. MT was touched that Bill cancelled all his appointments for the two days.

3   MT wrote to Brian that her mother was being wonderful and that made the parting easier.

they had to take to get to Harvard. There Marie-Thérèse had her second encounter with the generous, open-hearted spirit of Americans when the driver of one of the buses, on overhearing that Brian wanted to buy a hat, took them, on one of their long stopovers, to a hat factory and even donated some money towards the purchase. American kindness and consideration reached its zenith on arrival at the Cushmans, where she was welcomed with open arms. This typical, loving American family provided Marie-Thérèse with a home for the two weeks leading up to her wedding. She had her own room, beside the bathroom.[4] They showed her the sights and helped her plan the wedding and reception.

Fr Bernard O'Dea married the young couple on Easter Monday, 11 April, in front of an intimate group of friends, some of whom Marie-Thérèse had only just met, but she didn't mind. Everything went as planned and that was all that mattered. Roma,[5] her American cousin, came with her husband, Henry Beauregard. James Barry gave her away, Mary Raleigh was her bridesmaid, the Cushmans and Brian's flatmates and some fellow students rejoiced with them.

After the wedding, the young couple moved into the small bed-sit at 146 Upland Road. Brian continued with his studies and Marie-Thérèse spent most days at the Cushmans, where she sewed dresses for the girls and learned new recipes from Mrs Cushman. She wrote to her mother, 'I'm shopping for Brian's meals in these "super-markets" which you saw in Bern,[6] where you get a wire "pram" when you walk in the door and then fill it with everything you want (and lots of things you don't want too) and then stagger out!'

Brian was keen to show Marie-Thérèse the sights, and wrote to Marie: 'I'm having fun watching Marie-Thérèse learn about the

---

4   Both George Roach and the Cushmans put her beside the bathroom, out of consideration, which she didn't quite understand at the time, not until she had a family of her own in a house with only one bathroom.

5   Nano's (Theo Dillon's sister) daughter.

6   Switzerland.

"American way-of-life" at first hand. She is now very competent on the street cars and subways. We disagree (as always) and I find myself being pushed into a very pro-American position and defending all sorts of things, which I don't actually approve of!'

Despite American hospitality, Marie-Thérèse wasn't impressed with America. She described the subway train as 'an invention of the Devil's to see how many people you can fit into the smallest possible space – the result is terrifying.' She was flabbergasted when a chatty shop owner told them that 'her gardener (an Italian who came over 25 years ago) has a car and has sent all his sons through college, although he can't read or write himself.' But she was very proud of her husband; 'We went into Boston to the Eire Society (which was being addressed by Michael Bowles (R.E. musical director) on Irish music – a very dull meeting, the only amusing thing being the way Brian hissed through his teeth every time someone made a historical or grammatical mistake, which was quite often!'

For the last month of their stay in America, Brian and Marie-Thérèse moved in with George Roach and spent the early summer days listening to classical music, cooking together in his well-equipped kitchen and looking after a stray rabbit that wandered in one day. Finally the time came for their departure and, thanks to family connections, they returned together: 'We have a double cabin for our return passage, courtesy of Ray Maloney (the chief bursar), to whom I was introduced by Dr O'Grady![7] Friends are great things!' It further fortified Marie-Thérèse's conviction that in America 'they were nobody but in Ireland they were somebody!'[8]

On Tuesday, 21 June 1955, Brian and Marie-Thérèse arrived at Cobh. Tired and overwhelmed with what faced them, they took the train back to Dublin. The honeymoon was over, they had enjoyed the freedom and frivolity, but now they had to face

....

7   The father of Joan (O'Grady) Murray-Hayden.
8   One of the arguments that MT made to convince Brian not to stay on in America.

harsh reality. Brian had no work, no future in Ireland, and Marie-Thérèse's mother was dying. But they weren't alone, and the family network didn't let them down. Mary Martin[9] sent her sisters to take care of Marie Dillon, and Michael Tierney[10] called Brian into his office for a meeting. Tierney said that he owed a debt to Theo Dillon, and offered Brian a job in administration.[11]

On Monday, 1 August 1955, Marie Dillon passed away, a few months short of her fifty-fifth birthday. She was buried beside her beloved Theo in the Dillon plot at Glasnevin Cemetery. Marie-Thérèse absorbed her grief and looked forward. Brian had a job, they had a home and she was pregnant.[12] Life was to be lived and she wasn't going to waste a moment.

....

9   Founder of MMM (Medical Missionaries of Mary) Drogheda, and close friend of Theo and Marie Dillon.

10 President of UCD and close friend of Theo Dillon.

11 Professor Brian Farrell joined the administrative staff of UCD in 1955 and later became Director of Extramural Studies. From 1966, he lectured in the Department of Politics, and went on to become senior lecturer, acting head of department and associate professor.

12 MT's firstborn were twin girls, Naomi and Jeanne-Marie. Sadly, Jeanne-Marie died after a few days. MT went on to have six healthy babies (Bernard, Miriam, David, Rachel, Theo and Brian), all of whom are still thriving, Deo Gratias.

Lightning Source UK Ltd.
Milton Keynes UK
UKHW020411250822
407727UK00006B/861